John Parker is the autho_____l
books (see www.john-p_____le
*Story of the Special Boa*_____ of
Britain's most elite and secretive _____nd
writer all his working life, he viewed th_____and
troubles over many years from senior editorial roles in F_____reet.

**Military and Investigative books by John Parker**

*Desert Rats: From El Alamein to Basra, the birth of a
    military legend*
*Task Force*
*Strike Command*
*Total Surveillance: The Big Brother World of E-Spies,
    Eavesdroppers and CCTV*
*Silent Service: The Inside Story of Britain's Submarine
    Heroes Commandos*
*The Killing Factory: The Secret World of Germ and Chemical Warfare*
*The Gurkhas: The World's Most Feared Soldiers*
*SBS: The Inside Story of the Special Boat Service*
*The Walking Dead: Judge Liliana Ferraro, Mafia Hunter*
*At the Heart of Darkness: The Myths and Truths of
    Satanic Ritual Abuse*
*King of Fools: Edward VIII and his Fascist Friends*

THE LIFE AND MYSTERIOUS DEATH OF
CAPTAIN ROBERT NAIRAC

# SECRET HERO

## J O H N
## P A R K E R

**metro**

Published by Metro Publishing Ltd,
3, Bramber Court, 2 Bramber Road,
London W14 9PB, England

www.blake.co.uk

This paperback edition first published in 2004

ISBN 1 84358 100 0

British Library Cataloguing-in-Publication Data:

A catalogue record for this book is available from the British Library.

Design by www.envydesign.co.uk

Printed in Great Britain by BookMarque

1 3 5 7 9 10 8 6 4 2

Papers used by Metro Publishing are natural, recyclable products made
from wood grown in sustainable forests. The manufacturing processes
conform to the environmental regulations of the country of origin.

Every attempt has been made to contact the relevant copyright-holders,
but some were unobtainable. We would be grateful if the appropriate
people could contact us.

# Contents

# ACKNOWLEDGEMENTS

It will be evident from these pages that this work relies heavily on first-hand testimony for a narrative in which the story of Captain Robert Nairac's activities in Northern Ireland unfolds largely in the words of those who were there at the time. This was only made possible by the willingness of numerous key sources to be interviewed, most of whom have never previously spoken publicly on this subject. They are drawn from a relatively small group of people who knew him well or who worked closely with him during his undercover role on secondment from the Grenadier Guards to intelligence elements of the British Army and the SAS.

Unless otherwise stated, all quoted passages contained herein are derived from original research and extensive recollections by those friends and military and intelligence personnel, taped during conversations with the author. The author has largely relied upon their own words to tell this story, since they alone were close witnesses to the events that surrounded Captain Nairac during the last four years of his life, the bulk of which was spent in Ulster. A number of those interviewed prefer to remain anonymous because of the nature of their work at the time or because they are still in sensitive occupations, some connected with international security operations.

Their conversations, however, were recorded for use. The author wishes to record his sincere thanks to all those who participated and for their invaluable contributions during numerous meetings, interviews, telephone conversations and transcript checks. The responsibility for accuracy, however, remains with the author.

# Prologue

## NAIRAC AND THE SAS

The Grenadier Guards is a proud regiment, proud of a 'glorious' past and especially proud of its heroes. Leading the roll call of honour of what Prince Philip has described as 'one of the world's most renowned military organizations' is the name of Captain Robert Nairac. His award shines out in the regiment's history, significantly above those of the clutch of generals and brigadiers who have been awarded the Most Honourable Order of the Bath, the Most Distinguished Order of St Michael and St George or the Royal Victorian Order. His entry stands alone at the top of the regiment's long and distinguished list of over 300 officers and men whose achievements have been recognized by medals, honours, mentions in dispatches, certificates of merit, gallantry, good service and other commendations since 1945.

Robert Nairac was the regiment's only post-war recipient of the George Cross, the second-highest honour attainable in Britain after the Victoria Cross. It was awarded to him posthumously, confirmed almost two years after his death at the hands of the IRA.

The medal consists of a plain silver cross with four equal limbs, and the cross has in its centre a circular medallion bearing a design showing St George and the Dragon. The inscription 'For Gallantry' is set into the medallion, along with the royal cipher 'G VI' in the angle of each limb. The cross is suspended by a ring from a bar adorned with laurel leaves on a dark blue ribbon. Awards of the George Cross – originally intended primarily for civilians – to the fighting services are confined to actions for which purely military honours are not normally granted or are considered of insufficient merit. According to its original statute, it is 'awarded for acts of the greatest heroism or the most conspicuous courage in circumstances of extreme danger'.

Yet enquiries at regimental headquarters for greater detail about the actions which were considered to have deserved this honour are simply referred to the citation that accompanied its announcement. Nairac's mother and father, Dr Maurice and Mrs Barbara Nairac, to whom the medal was presented by the Queen, were especially proud of the citation, which reads as follows:

Captain Nairac served four tours of duty in Northern Ireland, totalling twenty-seven months. During the whole of this time he made an outstanding contribution. His quick, analytical brain, resourcefulness, physical stamina and above all his courage and dedication inspired admiration in everyone who knew him.

On the night of 14–15 May (1977) he was abducted from a village in South Armagh by at least seven men. Despite his fierce resistance, he was overpowered and taken across the border into the nearby Republic [of Ireland] from Northern Ireland where he was subjected to a succession of exceptionally savage assaults in an attempt to extract information which would have put other lives and future operations at serious risk.

These efforts to break Captain Nairac's will failed entirely. Weakened as he was in strength though not in spirit by the brutality, he made repeated and spirited attempts to escape but on each occasion was eventually overpowered by the weight of the numbers against him.

After several hours in the hands of his captors Captain Nairac was callously murdered by a gunman of the Provisional IRA who had been summoned to the scene. His assassin subsequently said, 'He never told us anything.'

> Captain Nairac's exceptional courage and acts of the greatest heroism in circumstances of extreme peril showed devotion to duty and personal courage second to none.

There is a special place for Nairac's records at the regimental headquarters of the Grenadier Guards at Wellington Barracks, Birdcage Walk, London. But its archivists, bound by the Official Secrets Act and faced with the secrecy surrounding the type of work in which Nairac was engaged, have always been reluctant to reveal much detail to writers who have attempted to unravel the facts from the fiction that has grown up around Nairac's story since his death.

The quest of these writers became more pertinent as the twenty-first anniversary passed, while the people of Northern Ireland prepared to vote in the referendum that produced overwhelming support for the peace process, for his work as an undercover soldier was, as he saw it, in the cause of peace – although many in the region who recall those times vehemently disagree, and the passing of the years since his death has not resolved many of the issues that concerned him and confronted him.

Further, Nairac's memory has been considerably tarnished by allegations concerning his involvements and associations in Northern Ireland, much to the chagrin of his family. His father Dr Maurice Nairac made early statements of disgust, but otherwise his family have steadfastly refused to be drawn into the debate, which is understandable. To a family hit by earlier tragedy, with the sudden death of Robert's brother David, from illness, at the age of twenty-four, the particularly harrowing death of the second son became a burden almost too heavy to bear. This was further heightened by the fact that Robert Nairac's body has never been found. For some time his mother Barbara, now in her eighties and widowed, clung to the hope that he may still be alive, imprisoned somewhere by his captors, perhaps to re-emerge like the hostages of Beirut. There was, however, no doubt that he was dead. His killers were quickly apprehended, tried and found guilty – in spite of the absence of a body. To this day the IRA has refused to disclose the manner in which it disposed of his remains, or where. Lately, claims by former IRA men that the body met a particularly gruesome end have only added to the family's anguish.

Like countless other families on both sides of the conflict in Northern Ireland and the British mainland who have had to wrestle with the consequences of almost three decades of atrocity, murder and bloodshed committed by the sectarian extremists, the Nairac family found nothing to console them, save for the George Cross and the glowing tribute to his memory.

In deference to his family, Robert Nairac's personal and private life will not form part of this book, other than in passing references. His military work, however, is of legitimate public interest. From a military standpoint, questions remain from the twenty-seven months in total that he spent during his four tours in Northern Ireland and the Nairac incident will probably not rest until they are answered. 'Like all such situations,' one senior military intelligence figure assured me, 'conspiracy theories will continue to abound. But abound they must because as far as we are concerned, there was no conspiracy and no cover-ups of the kind that we have been accused of in the past. That is not to deny that there are matters with which Captain Nairac was concerned that by their very nature must remain beyond the public domain, certainly for the foreseeable future and some of them for ever. But then, in the circumstances, you would expect nothing less, would you?'

That is true. The restrictions of the Official Secrets Act, coupled with the ongoing need to preserve the safety of undercover soldiers, men and women, who survived those years, prevent any formal reopening of the case or a public inquiry, which has been demanded in various quarters on numerous occasions.

In any event, few in high office would care to revisit the 'circumstances' that arose between 1972 and 1977, which became known as the Dirty War: not merely a tripartite battle between the

British security forces, the IRA and the loyalists, but a time of internecine rivalries, sometimes quite vicious, between the various security agencies in the field who were supposedly on the same side.

Nairac, as will be seen, was at the very heart of that situation. His work was always classified and usually top-secret. And as the officer said, that secrecy has bred conspiracy theories, suspicion, rumour and conjecture, which have gone unanswered or uncorrected, largely because no one in authority would talk about them.

Why was he out alone and without back-up on the night he was killed, in an area so notoriously dangerous that troops patrolled it by helicopter? Was he shopped by his own side? Why did no one suspect that the IRA already had photographs of him? How was the *Irish Times* able to produce a photograph of him in uniform taken on the streets of Northern Ireland, the newspaper claimed, three months before he was killed – hardly appropriate attire for an undercover soldier normally seen in scruff order? Why was his room awash with top-secret files that as a liaison officer, he might not be expected to have? Why did he possess a collection of photographs of scene-of-the-crime events in Northern Ireland that one of his senior officers described as verging on morbidity?

Did he personally shoot senior IRA commander John Francis Green after a surveillance operation, as has been claimed repeatedly by a former intelligence officer who claims Nairac gave him a photograph of the body? And since the same gun that killed Green was used in the massacre of the Irish pop group the Miami Showband not long afterwards, did he also mastermind those killings, as suggested by MP Ken Livingstone, amid uproar in the House of Commons in 1987?

Why, when senior officers had suggested to their commanding officers that Nairac was beyond control, was he kept on in the job? Was he in fact working to a higher order?

Did the IRA turn in Nairac's killers themselves so that the arrests were made in double-quick time? And why were all the gang freed early, one of them within a month of his trial?

These are but a sample of the issues to be confronted in this book. The official line, as ever, has been to keep the lid on the vast arena of undercover work that has proceeded in the fight against the paramilitaries in Northern Ireland since 1969. That is to be expected, not least for the continued safety and well-being of its operatives, since it involved virtually every intelligence agency and Special Forces unit available to the British government. In the beginning they were a meagre bunch untrained in the special needs of the province. They eventually expanded to include Military Intelligence, the RUC Special Branch, the Special Air Service, the Special Boat Service, MI6 and MI5 and a top-secret Special Duties unit.

At various times in his brief career, Robert Nairac worked to, for or with most of those services in his roles as an undercover soldier and liaison officer in intelligence. He was one of many such operatives and not the only one to be killed by an IRA bullet – although the more straightforward killing of soldiers, undercover or not, seldom remains in the headlines for long.

Nairac's ultimate murder, and a brutal and vicious one at that, was as much to do with the demands and the diversity of those working relationships as to his own insistence on pushing himself to the limit. This will become apparent as detailed explanations emerge in these pages from the military personnel who worked with him and who have spoken for the first time about those relationships and the young captain's ambitions. Their interviews, given exclusively for this book, enable a more precise picture to be drawn of his activities, and specifically those during the last months of his life.

Most of the service personnel who have contributed their recollections and opinions are former senior officers of the Special Air Service (SAS) regiment and/or intelligence services. One is a former Guardsman, who eventually transferred to the SAS. However, contrary to unequivocal statements by countless writers and newspaper headlines to the contrary, Nairac was not a member of the SAS. To understand his work, it is important to clarify his position in regard to the SAS.

It is true that the Grenadier Guards, with whom Nairac served, had a long and successful partnership with the SAS, dating back to 1964, when a Guards Parachute Company was attached to 22 SAS as an independent squadron for service in the Borneo confrontation. The link was adjudged so successful that it became a permanent fixture. G (for Guards) Squadron was formed within 22 SAS in the late 1960s, based at Hereford, and very few Guardsmen or NCOs who passed the rigorous selection procedure into the SAS chose to return to their regiment. For officers who were set on a career path with the Guards, however, it was necessary to go back after a suitable period of time to resume their progression. The Guards battalions were reluctant to give up their top men to G Squadron but recognized that only their best could pass the SAS entry standards. Indeed, eventually it was necessary to take non-Guardsmen into G Squadron to maintain its strength. It is also a fact that G Squadron, like all SAS units, completed tours of Northern Ireland, one of which was in the latter stages of Nairac's time there.

Nairac worked with individual members of the SAS assigned to other intelligence units to which he was attached during his second tour in 1974. He was assigned to a top-secret Special Duties unit, and later specifically as the link man between the SAS and the RUC Special Branch to smooth difficult relationships when the SAS finally went in to Northern Ireland as a regiment in 1976. But he had never passed through the SAS selection procedure, and in fact, because he was an 'outsider', he was to an extent resented by some in the SAS. The more hard-line in the regiment who saw him in operation often complained that he was allowed to wear the SAS beret. 'Who is this guy?' they asked.

Clive Fairweather was a seasoned SAS officer with the rank of major at the time of Nairac's disappearance (today he is HM Inspector of Prisons for Scotland). He had been detached temporarily from his regiment to take up a role in Military Intelligence, as a general staff officer grade two, in Northern Ireland, partly because of his experience there dating back to 1969. It was not an SAS job but one that was generally filled by Special Forces personnel. On the question of Nairac's position with the SAS, he is quite clear:

> There was lots of speculation that he was a member of the SAS. He was not. To be a member of the regiment you would have to pass the SAS selection course and wear the badge and beret of the regiment. He was a Grenadier Guardsman who had been through special training, some of which had been given by the SAS. Part of their role is training soldiers from other units in certain specialities for particular jobs. He had been trained in a number of techniques, but he was there in Northern Ireland on a staff appointment, which was a new appointment, as SAS liaison officer. That does not mean you are a member of the SAS.
>
> I know that at times in the past it has sounded as if the SAS has been trying to cover up, trying to deny that one of its soldiers was killed by the IRA. The SAS always claims its dead. Later, when Captain Richard Westmacott [also from the Grenadier Guards] was killed in Belfast, we never denied he was a member. The SAS are soldiers, not members of some secret organization.

Nairac was an intelligence gatherer; a man who became a 'walking encyclopedia' on Ireland and who knew far, far more about its people and the Troubles than the majority of the soldiers who went there. At the time of his death, he was even attempting to learn the Irish language to help him in his undercover work.

He died because he deliberately exposed himself to the greatest possible risk in the area of greatest possible danger to British troops, an area in a Republican stronghold so remote that all strangers were viewed with suspicion. He had, as one of his officers said, 'stuck his head in the tiger's mouth'. Many still ask the question, why?

In the ensuing pages, the answers are revealed.

# 1

## A LOVE OF THE IRISH

SAS Captain D (who cannot be identified because he is still in a sensitive security role outside the military), a man with serious experience of hard combat and who was awarded the Military Cross for action in the Falklands, was one of the last to see Robert Nairac alive.

He identified a trait in Nairac that had been evident from his schooldays: 'He was a romantic and a bit of a loner – one of those guys who, if it had been the late 1800s, you could imagine wandering about on his own on the North-West Frontier, face blacked up, dressed as a native, gathering intelligence. The only frontier left in the Empire in the 1970s was Northern Ireland and it was just as dangerous, if not more so.'

One of his tutors at Ampleforth College, near York, had made the same observation years earlier. He believed that in his youth Nairac looked for heroes of a particular kind and, as he was a student of history, one of those he chose to emulate was T. E. Lawrence, the eccentric Anglo-Irish soldier whose student days and early career had striking echoes of Nairac's. Lawrence, like Nairac, went to Oxford, studied history, was recruited into Military Intelligence and immersed himself in his role so deeply that he became a legendary figure who had great affinity with the native people he was supposedly observing. Nairac, to a lesser degree, seemed intent on pursuing a similar course in Northern Ireland. The tutor also felt it worth recording that he was insecure – as indeed was Lawrence – and always trying to prove himself in all that he tackled, especially in his sporting prowess. The need to come first went deeper than a mere competitive edge. That tutor would later remark: 'I always expected him to come to a sad end because I always saw a sad end to his nature.'

Whatever passions Nairac held for Ireland – and passions they certainly were – they were not born solely out of his military experience. They had roots in his childhood, his religious experience, his schooling and his schooldays' friendship with the siblings of a prominent Irish family.

Born in 1948, Robert Laurence Nairac was the youngest of Maurice and Barbara Nairac's four children. His father was a doctor in the north of England who later specialized in ophthalmology and became a distinguished eye surgeon, eventually taking the family to Gloucestershire. There he became consultant eye surgeon at Gloucester Royal Hospital.

Maurice was Catholic and his wife Protestant, and although there were no difficulties about that within the family itself, Robert Nairac experienced first hand the significance of a religious division that tore into the communities that became his prime focus as a serving soldier. As the progeny of a comfortably-off middle-class family, he moved into the private education system allied to his father's religion. At the age of ten, he was sent to Gilling Castle, a school nestling close to the Howardian Hills on the edge of the North Yorkshire Moors. Gilling Castle is the preparatory school for nearby Ampleforth College, regarded as the Eton of well-off British Catholics. It is supported largely by the descendants of those who clandestinely kept their faith alive during the Reformation, when acknowledgement of Catholicism was a criminal offence, to be revived as conditions permitted. A year later, he transferred to the Ampleforth College itself, attached to the Benedictine Abbey of St Laurence. It was then presided over by Cardinal Basil Hume, who later became Archbishop of Westminster.

The young Nairac is remembered as an excellent student with a span of interests far wider than only academic ones. He gained nine O levels and three A levels, and was head of St Edward's House at the age of seventeen. He excelled at sports and his name went on to the college sporting honours board for his achievements in athletics, rugby, shooting, cross country and boxing; he especially loved boxing and became captain of the school team. 'He was the sort of boy who was good at everything,' said Father Patrick Barry, who was headmaster at the time Nairac was murdered.

Outside school, Nairac was a perfectionist at fly fishing and wild fowling. He adored the countryside and the terrain surrounding Ampleforth, and he took every chance to explore in the wilderness of the Moors, especially in winter. This growing fondness of the outdoors and all its pursuits, including fishing, shooting, bird watching, rambling and especially falconry, were to be enhanced by the friendships he made at school.

Among them were the Hons John and Redmond Morris, sons of Lord Michael Killanin, one of Dublin's most prominent public figures for much of the twentieth century. A former war correspondent for the *Daily Mail*, Michael Killanin, MBE, was also a sportsman, a businessman associated with a string of companies, an author, a film producer of note and president of the International Olympics Committee, to name but a few of his many interests. He was also the holder of many international medals, including the Legion of Honour. He naturally moved in exciting circles, with intriguing and famous friends who were often around him in Ireland, including a number from Hollywood. One of them was the great director John Ford, with whom Killanin collaborated on several films. They included his classic Irish comedy, *The Quiet Man*, starring John Wayne, Maureen O'Hara and Victor McGlaglen, which won an Oscar for Ford in 1952. Michael Killanin managed to inject much-needed Hollywood backing into the ailing film industry on this side of the Atlantic for more than a decade. Another film he co-produced with Ford was *Gideon's Day*, starring Jack Hawkins. Others which Michael Killanin personally produced included *Alfred the Great*, filmed in 1968 with David Hemmings and Michael York.

They were stirring times for the Killanin family and Robert Nairac was witness to some of them, travelling to Ireland in the school holidays to stay at the Killanin homes either in Dublin or, more usually, at St Annin's, in Spiddal, an Irish-speaking district on the wild Atlantic coast on the north of Galway Bay. It was an experience that he remembered well and would use years later in his career as an undercover soldier. One day, in his plain-clothes role in intelligence, playing the part of a man visiting the region of Crossmaglen, he was questioned in a bar about his accent and his origins. What was he doing there? The questioner was undoubtedly a member of the IRA. Nairac told him he was born in Spiddal although he had later left, moved north and then got a job in Canada. Now he was back and looking for work. Within a few minutes, an old lady was produced by his challengers. She too hailed from Spiddal and they chatted for a while. 'This boy is who he says he is,' she said. 'He knows Spiddal as well as I do.'

Lady Killanin remembers: 'Robert came over quite often. He was very interested in falconry, an interest he shared with my younger son. They used to fly the birds over the bogs, and he seemed to revel in all things Irish. He was very taken with the country.' This was confirmed by another of his friends. 'He often spoke of his love of Ireland,' said publisher Martin Squires, who met him in later years and became a good friend. 'The place was clearly instilled in his psyche somehow. He developed a great knowledge of Ireland generally. He talked about it often with a kind of romantic intensity that went far deeper than the love of a country or town you might have visited and remembered from your schooldays or holidays. He was captivated by the people, he adored the landscape – he loved being on the western coast, especially. He was fascinated by the history and, of course, he knew all the lovely songs – and the rebel ones too.'

It was from his early connections with the Killanin family that Nairac's knowledge of Irish culture and its ballads stemmed. There was to be an ironic twist in the tale of this connection, which did not materialize until long after his death. The Killanins' interest in film-making was to be continued by the Hon. George Redmond Fitzpatrick Morris (Morris is the family name), who was in Nairac's year at Ampleforth. Redmond Morris, as he became known professionally, followed his father into the movie business and, at the time of writing, he has been associated with almost two dozen films in roles ranging from assistant director to producer. The films include *Scandal*, the story of John Profumo and Christine Keeler, and *Gorky Park*, with Lee Marvin playing the lead in Dennis Potter's screenplay. His best-known movies, however, are those which – like his father – he made in his collaboration with a fine writer-director, the Oscar-winning Neil Jordan, including *Interviews with the Vampire* (with Brad Pitt and Tom Cruise) and *The Crying Game*, the complex and brilliantly portrayed film about an IRA gunman who befriends a black British soldier who is taken hostage. The film, starring Stephen Rea and Miranda Richardson, won an Oscar for Jordan as its writer. Undoubtedly, however, the highlight of Redmond Morris's film career to date has been his association with the controversial award-winning film depicting the life of IRA hero Michael Collins, for which Morris was a driving force as co-producer with Stephen Woolley, again with Neil Jordan directing. With Liam Neeson in the leading role, it depicted the life of the man who led the IRA against British rule and founded the free Republic of Eire in 1921 before he was ambushed and killed. The subtitle to the film contained a poignant echo of the era of Robert Nairac when the legacy of Collins was re-emerging: 'His dreams inspired hope, his words inspired passion, his courage inspired a nation's destiny.'

The life and times of Michael Collins revived even as Robert Nairac prepared for an all-too-short adult life that would eventually lead him to head-on confrontation with the inheritors of Collins's dream. After his youthful experiences in the south of Ireland, Nairac studied the legacy of Collins. Those early connections with Ireland inspired him to discover some of the complexities of Irish republicanism, the career of one of its most vehement protagonists and the tensions of the religious divide in the north. At the time, he had no thoughts about his own career. Far less did he realize that he would eventually choose a path that would take him almost immediately back to Ireland.

The groundwork for that path was being laid then, although without any clue as to the possibility of where it might be used. His mimicry of the Irish accent, his knowledge of the country, his repertoire of Irish songs, his strength and toughness (he was able and willing to take on the best), his ability to act out a part, not on stage but in adopting the role of any character or person, like Lawrence of Arabia, who happened to take his interest at the time – all these talents were to become part of the collected accoutrements of the undercover soldier he became. The rest of his skills were gleaned at Oxford and in his specialist Army training over the next few years.

He left Ampleforth a tall, strong and handsome young man of eighteen, who appeared to settle with ease into Lincoln College, Oxford, where he studied medieval and military history. He was by no means a bookworm. He kept up his sporting activities and played for the Oxford second rugby XI. But he was best noted for two other achievements: he revived the Oxford Boxing Club and gained four blues in matches with Cambridge, and he had the distinction of becoming the only student at Oxford to keep a bird in his room – the feathered kind – which he kept for hunting. One was used in the film *Kes*, about a boy in a northern town who learns about life from his pet bird. At home, he kept at various times a collection of animals and birds, which included a polecat, a ferret, a buzzard and a kestrel.

Julian Malins, QC, was with Nairac at Oxford and considered himself his best friend. They first met in February 1969.

I walked from Brasenose across the Broad from Trinity to seek out the then captain of the Oxford University

Amateur Boxing Club. I found him. We had a most disagreeable conversation. 'The Boxing Club is dissolved,' he said. 'Bugger off.' I pressed him, somewhat timidly, as to whether this could really be the case. In the end and only to get rid of me, he said, 'You're the second person to come round here about the Boxing Club.'

'And who was the first?' I asked. And I can still hear the reply ... 'Someone called Nairac, at Lincoln.' Within a minute, we had met. Within five, we were friends, and before the sun set, we had recruited a team, revived the club and kept the fixture with Cambridge. It was, indeed, action this day.

I understand that in the Army, Nairac was known as Bobby and it is true that there were many who called him Bob. But though we shared a flat together at Boar's Hill, boxed together, played rugby together and, if I had not had a brother, he would have been my best man, he was always Robert. And my memories of him ...

The Oxford class of '68 was good-looking, confident and unlike any previous generation since the 1930s. We came after austerity and before the shadow of stress had fallen on the young. We parked our cars on Radcliffe Square. We dined at the Elizabeth. The sun shone and the girls were sensational. Work was not on the agenda. In this third year, Robert's car was stolen and though it was recovered, his history notes had mysteriously disappeared. Of course, the Rector of Lincoln allowed him a fourth year. It made no difference that his notes had been his A level notes. Undergraduates were chosen by a different criteria in those days. It was the Swinging Sixties. Even against such a backdrop, Robert stood out. He was the most handsome of his generation. He had a terrific aura. No one could be in his presence without feeling the better for it. That is a great and rare gift. He never once indulged in a biting or satirical jest, which is always remembered by the victim long after it is forgotten by the speaker.

Apart from his skill in the ring, Robert was an expert falconer. He kept – indeed he lived with and expected his friends to live with – a variety of ferocious hawks. I recall one particularly large and violent bird which used to perch on his wardrobe. This monster was normally kept hooded but if Robert thought that a guest was getting above himself – as rugby players usually do in the presence of boxers – he would unhood the beast and demonstrate the Nairac method of feeding. Robert would place a small cube of raw steak on the bridge of his nose, between his eyes. Then he would approach the creature and put his face about twelve inches from the hawk's and, holding its gaze, remain motionless. After an agonizing wait, the hawk would strike and take the piece of steak, leaving Robert's eyes and the rest of his face unscathed. This was not a trick. There is no method of training a hawk to do this – on-the-job training would not, as it were, admit any error. It was sheer incredible nerve.

And then ... I see Robert in the ring ... he was fast. He had a lovely style; he was fluid and he never seemed to retreat. I do not recall that he was ever beaten but if he was, it must have been a crooked verdict, no doubt at Cambridge! I fought him once in a bare-knuckle fight which was the main attraction at a riotous summer party held on the college barge. We were roared on by the Fancy and though he gave me at least a stone, I took some terrible punishment.

I see him as the Greyhounds' open side wing forward, springing across the pitch at Grange Road to tackle the Cambridge winger in the corner. I see him turning up at my future parents-in-law's house with two pheasants for dinner, and my fiancée, now my wife, asking him if he would be an usher at our wedding. I hear his still charming reply that he hoped that we would not mind if he was late, and this was before we had fixed the date, let alone the time.

And in front of me, the OUABC Captain's book containing Robert's account of the revival of the Club. He wrote: 'I decided to get a team together, try and get permission to revive the Club, get Blue recognition and box Cambridge. Looking back on it, I think it was mad.'

I reply as follows: 'Robert, you were not mad. You were a star.'

Robert was a romantic, an enthusiast, simple-hearted, brave, a charismatic leader and quite without guile. He wanted to be a soldier and especially to join the Grenadier Guards. A connection with the regiment was needed, so my father proposed him.

Another piece of Oxford-time history was recalled by one of his military colleagues. During his boxing days, he was in a competition in which he was matched to go three rounds with a young Ulsterman named Martin Meehan, who was soon to become one of the most notorious of IRA leaders in the early 1970s, before he was interned and later imprisoned.

Nairac completed his final year at Oxford in 1971, in uniform, having been accepted for the Royal Military Academy, Sandhurst, with the sponsorship of the Grenadier Guards. He left one of his tutors with the feeling that the romanticism observed by others remained with him. Nairac, he said, seemed to have little sympathy for much in the modern world. The pursuits that most interested him were hardly those of sixties' youth or seventies' young adults – running across Irish peat bogs, flying kestrels, standing on the edge of Galway Bay allowing the windswept swell to splash against his face; nor even were the concentration of fly-fishing or the skill of tickling trout. The Army would engage his romanticism, perhaps, and have the dual role of providing a career and an opportunity to participate in the other aspects of life that most interested him.

After Oxford, he moved directly to Sandhurst, where he had an above average assessment from his tutors in both his further studies and his aptitude as officer material. During this time he took part in an exercise in which he was given a platoon and told to take a hill which was being held by the Gurkhas, who knew from experience to expect an attack from a particular direction. Nairac impressed his superiors by choosing an unorthodox route for a successful attack which involved taking his men through arduous terrain. The incident proved, it has been suggested since, that he was not foolhardy but took only calculated risks.

# 2

## DESTINY CALLS

That the life of Robert Nairac would come to an abrupt and sad end was predicted by several who knew him in his youth and early adulthood. It appears with chilling regularity among those whose reflections of him were sought both at the time of his death and for this book. Some, like one of his tutors, thought it long before he joined the Grenadier Guards.

It became so even as the Troubles began in Northern Ireland in 1969, observed by Nairac from his Oxford rooms, because of his personal interest born out of his earlier contact. The escalating violence, bombings and killings both depressed and intrigued him. He had studied the history and knew well the personalities of the past and the divisions and boundaries that existed, both physically and spiritually. He would, for example, contradict those who referred to Northern Ireland as Ulster, although it is a term generally used as a description of the province. Factually, he was quite right, too. Many overlooked the fact that Ulster was originally the name of one of the four provinces of Ireland as a whole, and included nine counties in the north of the country. However, when partition came, the Unionists, who formed the political majority in the north, opted to take only six of the nine counties. The other three counties of Donegal, Cavan and Monaghan, they astutely observed, would have brought with them a greater proportion of Catholics and Nationalists who might in time challenge the Unionist majority. They chose to give them away to the Irish Free State and opted instead for control of the remaining six: Londonderry, Antrim, Tyrone, Fermanagh, Armagh and Down. The six would assume the title of Ulster under the Protestant majority and the Catholics would get not protection from the law but sanctioned by it.

By the time Nairac sought an Army commission, the Army recruiters could confirm that service in Northern Ireland was an absolute certainty. Everyone in the British Army who had an eye on his career would seek to go there – it might be said by cynics that it was the only place left for serving British officers to win medals and achieve rapid career advancement. Nairac chose to try for Sandhurst not for the prospect of medals, but to establish himself as a career soldier, but all the time with an eye on Ulster. It was for that reason that after Sandhurst he undertook postgraduate studies at Dublin University and honed his knowledge of the whole island to a degree matched by few brother officers, unless they happened to be natives of Ireland. By the time he was available for service in the Guards, the situation in the province was already dire.

The beginning of the modern Troubles has been well documented by many, most notably Martin Dillon and Tim Pat Coogan. But for the purpose of gleaning some perspective on Nairac's eventual involvement, it is as well to remind ourselves of the chronology of events. The sixties' era of protest was in full flight across the world when it rose in Northern Ireland. The protest there rose almost unnoticed, dwarfed initially by the high-profile demonstrations Europewide that had spread from the civil rights upsurge in America. In 1968, dubbed the Year of Dreams, there were massive anti-war demonstrations in London, the students' revolt in Paris, which pitted 30,000 young people against an army of police, the Prague Spring of Freedom crushed by Soviet tanks in August, the shooting of Martin Luther King and Bobby Kennedy ... and a less prominent headline later in the year: '100 Catholics hurt in Londonderry riot'. Why should Northern Ireland be any different? But the events in Ulster were later, of course, to outdo them all in their impact.

Intellectuals, journalists and trade unionists formed the initial committee to steer a civil rights movement in Northern Ireland. They began their campaigns to raise international awareness to conditions in what was effectively a one-party state, run by Protestants with the object of keeping the Catholic minority firmly in its place as second-class citizens. The festering sores arising from this regime had been left unattended too long. Unacceptable discrimination in housing, jobs and services; gerrymandering; the absence of one-man one-vote; the outbreak of fire-bomb attacks on Catholics and assassination attempts by the Ulster Volunteer Force (UVF), which began in the mid-sixties – all these provided causes enough for demonstrations. The year of international protest provided the springboard.

The fateful 5 October march by a mere 800 protesters, organized by the Northern Ireland Civil Rights Association (NICRA), largely made up of Catholics but with significant support from Protestant liberals, was met by the boots and batons of the Northern Ireland police and the dreaded B-Specials, whose partisan reputation was such that they were considered to be as bad as the so-called loyalist gangs – hard-line Protestants who opposed Nationalism and supported the British monarchy – who had been terrorizing Catholic areas for years.

So the cause was just, but the horizons of the civil rights campaigners soon became blurred, hijacked to some extent by young bloods of the Republican movement, which had been relatively quiet in recent times. Indeed, the element of the widespread protest by civil rights campaigners that was overlooked, or ignored, by pundits and even the campaigners themselves was the Irish Republican Army (IRA), whose leadership was lurking in Dublin and busily reassessing its own political strategy.

Inspired by discussions with the Communist Party of Ireland and left-wing intellectuals – and watched, incidentally, by MI6 – influential leaders of the IRA had veered away from its founding principles of working for a united Ireland and protecting the

Catholic populations in the armed struggle against the Protestants and the British in the north. In fact, the IRA had more or less renounced violence in 1966 and it was the Protestant UVF who forced it back on the agenda with the first attacks of the current Troubles in that very year.

The traditional Republican cause, it was argued from within, could be replaced by a wider brief based upon Marxist theories. The sectarian barriers would be broken down by a communal appeal to workers throughout Ireland to create a following largely detached from the Catholic faith. This policy did not have the universal approval of the IRA membership. It was the cause of a rift between the Marxists and the traditionalists, and eventually led to a split.

In Northern Ireland, vociferous opponents to the Marxist view, particularly among the young activists, were looking to reassert some of the original principles of Republicanism born so long ago and boosted by the martyrdom of Michael Collins. They saw the civil rights movement of NICRA as a suitable Trojan Horse and many IRA members joined the movement without identifying the true nature of their ambitions. In his book *The Enemy Within*, Martin Dillon quotes one IRA member who said that the organization was used clandestinely to provide funds for the IRA, with money being siphoned off to purchase weapons which, it was claimed, might be needed to protect Catholic areas as the NICRA protests gathered momentum. In the early months of 1969, IRA activists were exerting considerable influence on the civil rights movement, which they gradually turned towards their own aims, bolstering the demonstrations with increasing levels of violence. Many in the civil rights movement left, disenchanted and feeling they had been betrayed. Some said the IRA had been there, in the background, all along.

As the months passed, the evident tensions on the streets of Northern Ireland rose dramatically and towards the end of the Protestant marching season they rose to boiling point. The fuse to the explosion of violence that erupted was the outbreak of the worst street fighting the province had seen for many years. Rioting flared in Londonderry towards the end of the Orangemen's Apprentice Boys' march. In three days of battles, five people were killed and more than seven hundred injured. Police used tear gas to disperse the riots.

Londonderry's Catholic population, under attack from marauding gangs, protested at the actions of the B-Specials and the Royal Ulster Constabulary (RUC) who, they claimed, allowed the Protestant gangs to go about their business unfettered. They were also angered by the IRA's failure to protect their communities from nightly attacks by petrol-bomb-wielding mobs. More than 1,500 Catholic families, compared with 300 Protestant families, would be forced to leave their homes because of fire bombs, looting and intimidation from loyalist gangs.

Trouble spread to Belfast, where hundreds of rioters came on to the streets, hurling petrol bombs, backed by hidden sniper fire. As gun battles raged, the inevitable dispatch of British troops to restore law and order was approved by the British government on 15 August 1969.

The first detachment from the Prince of Wales' Own Regiment arrived on 19 August for what the government described as a 'limited operation'; they would be withdrawn as soon as order was restored – but it never was. From then on, in terms of deployment numbers for the British troops, the only way was up, reaching in excess of 20,000 troops by 1972 – Ulster's bloodiest year ever, which saw 468 killed and 5,000 injured.

For the people of Northern Ireland, when the troops moved in there was initially a sigh of relief. But it was a temporary feeling that would soon turn to hatred in many quarters as the British troops floundered miserably, poor on intelligence, inexperienced in handling trouble among its own people and run by a hierarchy whose most recent experience of urban unrest was in the wild colonial campaigns when Britain extracted herself from the last remnants of empire. The Army seemed to believe that the same principles that were used in the fetid alleys of guerrilla-packed Arabian cities, the running battles in the mountains and deserts of the Middle East or the jungle terrain of Asia and Africa could be applied to the streets of its own counties. The government and its forces also failed to understand both the depth and reasoning behind the divided communities, and based their response on the belief that the issue was religion and the solution simply civil rights. They were nothing of the kind, extending far beyond those two areas into nationalism and history. Religion merely provided the badge of affiliation.

The Army was confronted by two increasingly vicious elements, which gradually sub-divided into many more. The IRA was being pressurized by activists in the north to renew its war on two fronts: for a united Republic of Ireland and for the protection and enhancement of Catholic communities in the north. On the other side were the Protestant groups and gangs, who had a head start on the IRA in the current upsurge, in that they had been actively engaged in modern terrorism since the mid-1960s. One such was the UVF, which was formally outlawed in 1966 following a number of sectarian attacks and its declaration of war on the IRA, later unbanned during an IRA ceasefire, and outlawed again in 1976. By the beginning of the 1970s, however, there were other Protestant paramilitary groups, who were as indiscriminate in their violence as the IRA but unlike the Republicans in that they did not generally attack the British 'forces of occupation'. They went for softer targets – civilians, prison warders, IRA members and occasionally policemen. They made great play of their 'loyalist' alignment but in those early days, the direction of that loyalty was never quite apparent.

It was Protestant gunmen who claimed the first RUC victim of the current Troubles, at a firefight on the Protestant Shankill Road, Belfast, on 11 October 1969, in demonstrations over the disbandment of the Protestant-dominated B-Specials. That day was also the first time the British Army opened up with return fire.

The IRA had, meanwhile, split. Two wings emerged: the 'Official' IRA and what became known as the Provisional IRA, which, as Tim Pat Coogan put it, rose from 'the mists of history ... moved not by hatred but by an instant bid for freedom'. With the IRA physically based in Dublin – although with many members in the North, activists in the repressed Catholic areas in the North felt isolated, restrained and let down. They were also under increasing pressure from their own communities for greater protection from the marauding Protestant gangs and with virtually no political voice to put their case, direct action was viewed as the only route open to them. The Provisionals, in effect, declared their own war and dragged the Official IRA along behind them. New volunteers quickly came forward, for the most part young, working-class, idealistic nationalists, increasingly from the north and from Catholic backgrounds. Between them, the IRA and PIRA gradually pushed their fight through three definable stages.

First, they marshalled their own army, run on military lines with an army council, local commanders and an intelligence division, with the initial priorities of defending nationalist and Catholic communities. This stage moved swiftly into the next, in which a serious and effective response to the loyalist terrorist gangs was organized and, at the same time, the British security forces were baited so as to alienate them from the IRA's own people in the north.

The last stage was to move towards guerrilla warfare, in the towns and in the countryside, or wherever the British troops or forces of law might be found. They achieved every one of their aims within two years, against a backdrop of almost frantic efforts by the government and the security forces to keep up.

In 1970, the death toll reached twenty-five. The Ulster Defence Regiment (UDR) was formed in April 1970 to replace the B-

Specials. The Catholics saw it as the B-Specials in another uniform. Very few checks were made to ascertain the motives of this volunteer force, whose soldiers were predominantly Protestant and many of whom doubled as members of terrorist gangs. In conjunction with the RUC, the British Army put into effect stronger tactics, introducing curfew and search operations that were last tried in Cyprus during the battles against the EOKA terrorists.

In 1971, the death toll shot up dramatically, to 174. The first soldier, Gunner Robert Curtis, was killed. Then, in March, the first multikilling brought the Troubles directly to the British breakfast tables when three Scottish soldiers were lured from a bar by girls and shot dead. The IRA stepped up its city-centre bombing campaign and was responsible for more killings. The Protestants responded with the formation of the Ulster Defence Association (UDA), a coming-together of various vigilante and paramilitary groups, which soon began to match the IRA, shot for shot, bomb for bomb. The introduction of internment and the rounding-up of hundreds of men from both sides – though mostly IRA suspects – merely turned up the heat and proved to be a totally ineffectual weapon against the violence.

The year ended in horrific, bloody carnage. The IRA bombed a bar in the Protestant Shankill Road, killing two and injuring many more, several maimed for life. The UVF responded by bombing McGurk's Catholic bar in North Queen Street, Belfast, killing sixteen. A week later, a Protestant shop on the Shankill Road was bombed, killing four, including a seven-month-old boy.

And so it went on … The new year of 1972 began with a frightening escalation, which also put the spotlight firmly on the British security forces. It was the year of Bloody Sunday when, on 30 January, the Parachute Regiment, confronting a violent demonstration in Londonderry, opened fire and killed fourteen people. None of those who died was found to have been in possession of a firearm or bomb. The controversial Widgery

Report placed no blame on the Paras for firing somewhat indiscriminately at a crowd running from them.

As these words are being written, this whole episode is being re-opened as part of the peace process with a new inquiry. At the time, the consequences of Bloody Sunday were cataclysmic, politically and on the streets. The security forces were thereafter identified with the Protestant cause and there was good reason to suspect that the British government and a good many in the military hierarchy still had not grasped the underlying currents in Northern Ireland, nor how to respond.

The IRA issued an order to all its combatants to kill every British soldier they could, and set the ball rolling by bombing the Paras' headquarters at Aldershot. 'Legitimate' targets included a nineteen-year-old Londonderry youth, William Best, who was a private in the British Army. When he came home to visit his parents while on leave, he was 'arrested' by the IRA, 'tried' and shot.

In July, Bloody Friday pushed the spiral of violence off the graph. The IRA exploded twenty-two bombs in Belfast, killing nine and injuring dozens more. The one-party Unionist government in Stormont resigned when Edward Heath's Conservative government transferred control of security to the government in Westminster. The year 1972 saw the worst violence since the current troubles began, with hundreds of bombs reducing city-centre and urban areas to rubble. Then there were the turf wars. The Official IRA and the Provisionals began shooting each other. The UDA mushroomed into a sprawling Protestant paramilitary organization, which, according to Michael Farrell in *The Orange State*, was heavily infiltrated by petty crooks and gangsters involved in protection rackets, extortion and intimidation: 'Many mysterious beatings, shootings and bombings in the Protestant areas were simply the UDA enforcing their levies.'

Shootings were so frequent that they no longer made the news headlines and many were ignored by the London-based newspapers. The British Home Secretary William Whitelaw agreed to secret talks with the IRA in London. A truce was agreed, but it quickly disintegrated. The struggle resumed with a vengeance, extending to targets throughout the United Kingdom and Europe. Arms and funds were flowing in from IRA and Catholic supporters from the United States and Middle East. Included in the 468 dead in 1972 were 103 soldiers, 24 RUC officers and 3 of their reservists. In 1970, there were 213 bombs planted in the Six Counties; the following year, there were 1,756. The statistics make stark reading compared to those of the period of 1956–69, when no soldier was killed and six RUC men lost their lives.

The Protestant paramilitaries, enraged by the proposal of Harold Wilson, leader of the Labour Party, for transitional negotiations for a United Ireland, stepped up the fight against Britain to stay British. His view, incidentally, was shared by an influential rightist faction in MI5, in direct conflict with MI6, which favoured a political solution – meaning power sharing, talks with the south and the reopening of a dialogue with Sinn Fein and the Official IRA. Sinn Fein, long ago recognized as the political wing of the IRA, is in fact Ireland's oldest political party. Founded in 1905, it takes its name from the Gaelic expression for 'we ourselves' and its statute is 'to work for the right of Irish people as a whole to attain national self-determination'.

These, then, were the very visible elements in play as Robert Nairac prepared to enter the fray. Less visible, as will become apparent, was a much dirtier struggle, supposedly a secret war. And it was to that effort that Nairac's deployment would eventually be diverted.

# 3

## FIRST IMPRESSIONS

Robert Nairac was on the streets of Northern Ireland in the early months of 1973, to experience first hand both the tough, uncompromising regime of the British military and the ruthless conflict between the Catholics and Protestants and their rival paramilitaries. All that now followed – for him, the communities in which he worked and everyone concerned with upholding the law, or falling foul of it – could be aligned to a statement by British colonial counter-insurgency specialist General Frank Kitson: 'Everything done by a government and its agents in combating insurgency must be legal. But this does not mean that the government must work within the same set of laws during an insurgency that existed beforehand.'

Some quite clearly misinterpreted this to mean that you made up the rules as you went along. The counter-insurgency planners did, the RUC and the British Army did, and the intelligence services of MI6 and MI5 certainly did. As a result, they received occasional directional touches on the tiller from Westminster and quite a few broadsides from the Commission for Human Rights and Amnesty International.

For Nairac, the rules of this game presented something of a dilemma that had to be quickly overcome and pushed to the back of his brain, never to be thought about; otherwise he might as well have walked away right there and then.

From a boyhood and youth of devout Catholic upbringing alongside the Protestant faith of his mother's family, he recognized the divisions. His own persona, moulded at Ampleforth, had experienced the strong religious faith instilled at every level by the priests who were his tutors. But initially he had difficulty coming to terms with the situation confronting him. It was not a straightforward issue of Catholics versus Protestants. There was, in the well-off circles of English Catholicism from which he came, a resentment of the large intake into the priesthood and Roman Catholic hierarchy from those of Irish descent.

Even Ampleforth's strong military connections, stemming from its army cadet force and famous old boys, did not, according to one of his former colleagues, fully prepare him for the local issues of the religious killing fields and the centuries-old paradox that was no nearer any kind of solution in Northern Ireland – that the God they had all been taught was the inspiration of love and justice seemed to have deserted the streets of the Six Counties. There were many on both sides of the Irish Sea who wished the British Army would do the same.

The complexities of being first the referee, then a participant and finally a target in the three-sided struggle would have taxed even the mind of one of Ampleforth's most famous sons who went on to military glory, David Stirling, founder of the Special Air Service and another of Nairac's heroes. It might be possible to compare Stirling's spectacular exploits in the Second World War to those that engaged the SAS in the next three decades, but in fact they bore no comparison to the Ulster confrontation. Most of the SAS officers recognized that; but others outside that regiment apparently did not. Wars that spawned the SAS legend in the deserts of the Middle East or the jungles and swamps of Borneo, far away and out of sight, had little in common with battles among their own people on the streets of the United Kingdom. That realization, however, was slow in dawning to some of the military commanders running the show and especially in the intelligence arena, long before the SAS came on the scene.

Robert Nairac arrived in Northern Ireland in back-up No. 1 Company, the 2nd Battalion Grenadier Guards. The battalion had just completed an eighteen-month commitment to British Honduras, the far-flung British colonial outpost below Mexico that became part of the Empire in 1786. Belize, as it was then known, was facing the threat of invasion from Guatemala, which had long claimed sovereignty over the country. Because of the emergency, recent recruits were deployed there before they had completed their basic training. As the situation eased towards the end of their posting, the battalion commanding officer Lieutenant-Colonel J. R. S. Besly chose to utilize their time in British Honduras training his men for their next engagement, which would be in Northern Ireland. He had already served there and training, he perceived with some understatement, was essential.

On return to the United Kingdom, the battalion was posted to Belfast for a two-week stint in March 1973 to bolster existing troops during a plebiscite in which the people of Northern Ireland were being asked to vote for or against staying in the United Kingdom. Since the Catholics had already said they would boycott the referendum, the result was a foregone conclusion, 90–1 in favour. But it enabled the British government to press ahead with proposals for a seventy-eight-seat Northern Ireland assembly elected by proportional representation. The week of the referendum was also marked by the discovery of a boat carrying five tons of arms for the IRA from Libya and the planting of five bombs around London, which killed one person and injured 250 others.

After this brief deployment, the 2nd Battalion returned to London for its public duties and provided Guards for the Queen's Birthday Parade while the rest of the battalion lined the Mall. They had just two weeks' training for their first and full tour in Northern Ireland before taking up residence in Belfast on 5 July. Their first major duty was to stand guard along the Shankill Road and protect the shopfronts during an Orange Day parade on 12 July.

After that, the battalion settled in to what had become the harsh and relentless routine of patrolling the streets of Belfast. The Grenadiers were given responsibility for the Protestant

Shankill Road and, later, the Catholic Ardoyne areas of Belfast, both of which had seen some of the most ferocious riots as the Six Counties slumped deeper into chaos and catastrophe. The Ardoyne was noted for the militancy of its women, hordes of which attacked soldiers with no greater weaponry than their hate and dustbin lids. Far from their original thoughts of relief that British troops were on the streets of Belfast to protect them, the Catholic communities were now convinced that they were merely the enforcers of the Protestant establishment.

In recent times, one Army unit covering the same area had lost eight of its men, killed or seriously wounded, and one commanding officer had suffered a nervous breakdown. The Grenadiers replaced the 3rd Battalion of the Parachute Regiment, whose own tough approach had won them no friends, and the Guards inherited that hatred. In his book *Contact*, Tony Clarke, a member of the departing parachute regiment, recalled the arrival of Robert Nairac into the fray:

> The Grenadier Guards advance party arrives and I have to show the platoon commander assigned to me the Shankill in all its glory. I'm still at the ops desk at ten in the morning, having had a brief respite for a wash and shave followed by breakfast, when the OC comes in with the Grenadiers to introduce me.
>
> 'Tony, this is Bob Nairac, who will be assigned to you for the handover period.' I shake hands with a stocky guy with curly black hair, far removed from the normal type of Guards officer you usually meet. I take in the broken nose and cheerful grin and think, Thank God I haven't got one of those guys with a mouthful of marbles. The pleasantries over, he goes off and dumps his kit …
>
> Bob is the one with all the questions, insatiable for knowledge, expressing disappointment that his company is not in the Ardoyne, and is not convinced when we tell

him that we, the Shankill Coy, have had far more finds and by far the biggest contact of the tour. He is no sooner in the place than he wants to go out on his first patrol. It just so happens that I'm due out with one of my sections in an hour's time so he goes away happy, to get his kit together. Clive and I look at each other in disbelief. There's no way we would be so keen to get out there and certainly not at this stage in the tour. In fact, the OC had to hound us to get us out into the street. Well, each to his own … right now I want to stay safe.

Out on the street, Bob is like a foxhound, digging into everything, questioning everything, wanting to cram five months' knowledge into one, short, two-hour patrol. The lads are working well, putting on their best performance to impress the 'crap-hats', and two hours goes quickly past without incident.

The reality of it all came later when Robert Nairac and his Grenadier colleagues began their work in earnest and experienced their stark initiation to patrolling the streets of Ulster. Nairac joined the others to form the notorious Army patrols, out twenty-four hours a day, faces blackened, weapons cocked, occasionally nervous, often under a good deal of strain and subjected to a constant stream of venom and hatred.

They had been warned that they could expect their presence on the streets to attract every kind of response, from sniper fire to spit, petrol bombs to booby traps – always under the watchful eye of the IRA, whose intelligence system in some areas was better than the Army's. Indeed, everything about the Army's operations in Northern Ireland was still rather unsophisticated. For months the Westminster politicians had harboured the hope of a decline in the violence, thus relieving the need for so many troops and eventually enabling them to withdraw altogether. So purpose-designed equipment was still not plentiful.

For the most part, they were making do with gear that really had no place in the inventory of internal security forces confronting their own people. It was only when it was clear they were to be there for the foreseeable future that more suitable equipment began to arrive. The Grenadiers were still wearing their brown cloth berets; they did not get helmets with visors until three years later. They wore flak jackets, which offered only partial protection against low-velocity gunfire or bomb shrapnel. They carried heavy-duty 7.62mm self-loading rifles designed for front-line combat, perhaps on the Soviet borders with Germany or some other flashpoint. Each patrol had men carrying 9mm Sterling sub-machine guns, and pistols were carried selectively, usually at the time of roadblocks.

Like all servicemen who experienced this situation in the early 1970s, Nairac's patrols also carried batons and weapons that fired rubber bullets or CS gas for riot control. Gas was also used on house searches where violent opposition was used against them and this naturally alienated entire communities; gassing them in their homes was hardly conducive to cooperation. These indiscriminate weapons were used for three years, and heightened considerably the alienation of the Army from the people of Northern Ireland.

By 1973, these weapons were being used less and less, partly as a result of international criticism and partly because by then if gunfire broke out, it came from well-armed snipers who invariably vanished into the ether. If a firefight developed, both sides would use their full armoury. Land Rovers were in reasonable supply for mobile patrols but the armour-plating then used on the vehicles was light and inadequate for the strength of IRA weaponry.

Ferret scout cars and Alvis Saracen armoured personnel carriers were also much in evidence. The Grenadiers' mobile units would patrol using two men standing precariously in the back of a Land Rover with rifles, and a third in position in the front passenger seat with a rifle pointing out through the open door. It soon became clear that the soldiers were sitting ducks for snipers or rock-throwers. One of the battalion's company commanders, Major H. M. L. Smith, described the scene for Oliver Lindsay in his history of the Guards, *Once a Grenadier: the Grenadier Guards 1945–1995*:

> When we took over from the Parachute Battalion it was too dangerous to drive down Old Park Road in Belfast; we could only patrol on foot. I never allowed more than four Irishmen to group together. At night I switched off all street lights with the master key so the IRA couldn't see us. But they had a key too, so switched them on to set up ambushes for us. I twice shot out the lights, just as we shot at petrol bombers. There were a lot of butterflies in tummies as there was on average a shooting incident in the battalion's area each night.

The Grenadiers' policy was similar to that followed by most of the Army patrol units and established in those desperate times during the tours of Northern Ireland of the 1st and 2nd Battalions in 1969–70 and again in 1971–74. In bars and public houses where suspects were thought to be present, the men would be taken outside, lined up against a wall and questioned, and have their names and addresses taken and checked. Anyone on a particular list might be arrested on the spot. If the patrol was shot at from a house or had reason to suspect it was being used as a safe house, weapons' store or IRA medical centre, the Guards 'took the house apart within a few hours'.

While local residents crowded around, hissing and screaming their protests, locked doors would be smashed down, attics and lofts would be searched for escape routes, floorboards would be ripped up and walls that had signs of remedial works or sounded hollow would be demolished. Motorized diggers from the Royal

Engineers would be called in to plough up gardens. The Army was supposed to pay 'full and fair' compensation for damage, and residents whom they disturbed in this way were given forms to lodge their claim before the soldiers left. If the Army had broken windows with the use of rubber bullets or had smashed down doors, the Guards' Pioneer Platoon would be called in to make immediate repairs. 'It was a very tough policy but fair. The locals soon got the message,' said Major Smith, rather naïvely.

The Grenadier patrols pursued the established pattern, utilizing intelligence passed down the line by other Army units and in liaison with other security services such as RUC Special Branch and MI5. There were two priorities: searching for weapons and hunting known IRA or Protestant extremists. But in its hefty programme of patrolling, the battalion – like its predecessors – began to build up a detailed portrait of inhabitants of the areas they patrolled and a mass of other information. They regularly checked names of residents in a particular street, noting movements of strangers or non-residents, noting basic details such as milk deliveries to see if the order had been increased and even clothes lines for any out-of-the-ordinary appearances.

Robert Nairac was frequently engaged in both mobile and foot patrols involving an entire company. They would move out of camp at speed, with half the section in covering stance, weapons cocked, while the rest exited towards the patrol area. They operated in an irregular pattern, never to any set routine, and organized their deployment so that no single patrol could be isolated without back-up. The golden rule was: always make sure of your back-up.

No vehicle ever travelled singly. The patrols worked to a clearly defined brief, operating a 'net' in parallel streets, each patrol maintaining radio contact throughout. They never followed tracks, because invariably they led to an ambush or booby trap. They had to look up for snipers and down for trip wires. It was a pressurized existence for the young and relatively inexperienced junior officers and NCOs in command.

They operated largely to a blueprint drawn up by the battalion intelligence cell, which remained in constant radio contact to advise on operations, and especially on 'P' checks (personal identification verification). These began as soon as the patrol hit the streets, often with an intelligence officer on hand. They would confront anyone they had a mind to stop. That person would be asked for identification, which would be relayed to the intelligence cell for a hasty match against their 'P' cards, an index system which contained the names of all IRA suspects or criminals in the area. If the person being interviewed gave cause for suspicion, the intelligence group would pass on a series of carefully worded questions to gain a more precise view of whom they were dealing with.

In the meantime, precious minutes were ticking away. A stationary patrol was a sitting target. Therefore a time limit was set – three or four minutes at the most. If the suspect did not check out, he or she was arrested. Speed was of the essence, both for the protection of the troops from snipers and to avoid the attentions of hostile crowds, who often materialized with remarkable alacrity.

The communications system used by the Army was not safe, either. The IRA were known to be listening in, with their own radio installations strategically positioned. This was a lesson learned early on and by 1973 when Nairac was on patrol, the Army always worked on the principle that its radio communications were insecure.

By then patrols routinely used code words and numbered map references that gave no clue to the true position for 'enemy' eavesdroppers. Not that that stopped the IRA from discovering the patrol whereabouts, since spotters and runners would report pretty well every movement to IRA intelligence units. IRA combat units also staked out areas where Army patrols were expected or known to be approaching. The spotters gave the signal of their imminent arrival: a youth kicking a football ... a man running his hand through his hair ... a bedroom window closing – any one of them might have been a signal to the IRA.

If the patrol ran into an ambush, the radio operator would report the action and the location even as the bullets thudded around the patrol. Within minutes the back-up platoon would move in and probably a helicopter would arrive overhead. The area would be sealed off with roadblocks, houses searched, arrests made. Invariably, the gunmen got away.

Towards the middle of their 1973 tour, when the violence had quelled somewhat, the Grenadiers also initiated a 'hearts and minds' (or community relations) operation, ostensibly to improve their image and try to forge links with the community – for which, incidentally, they were thanked by local Catholic leaders. Lieutenant Bob Woodfield ran a special patrol group to make forays into the Ardoyne, attempting to reduce the tension and reach out to the communities. They found themselves doing unfamiliar tasks, such as unblocking sewers and helping with a severe rat infestation. The operation served a dual purpose as it also aided the overall intelligence picture.

Robert Nairac was among those who volunteered for community relations missions and was given the task of establishing contact with youth organizations. Lieutenant Woodfield told Oliver Lindsay that his work in this area was excellent:

> Robert was fantastic with Irish youth. I used to visit the Sporting Club in the Ardoyne with him. He introduced me to all the club's committee and sang Irish rebel songs with them, knowing more about Irish history than all of them. He also knew most of the fourteen- and fifteen-year-olds in our area, and how crime was in their blood. He used to give talks to their mums and dads on where their children were going wrong.

When the 2nd Battalion completed this tour of duty on 31 October 1973, Nairac was one of five Grenadiers who stayed on as liaison for the incoming 1st Battalion of the Argyll and Sutherland Highlanders.

The replacement troops were given a baptism of fire. Barely had they unpacked their kit when, on the first evening on patrol with Nairac and Lieutenant Woodfield along for company wearing Argyll berets, a young officer, attracted by a flickering light, happened to peer into a car parked in the Crumlin Road. It turned out to be a burning fuse. He yelled out a warning to his patrol and they dived for cover just as a massive explosion tore the car to pieces, took the roofs off four nearby houses and blew out all the windows in the vicinity. The sharp-eyed lieutenant saved his patrol from certain death and in the event no one was hurt. Nairac stayed on the scene until 3.00 a.m., helping local residents, generally organizing the evacuation of surrounding houses and joining the hunt for more bombs.

The second night was also eventful. The Argyll patrol set off again, with blackened faces, when an irate local reported that one of the young men from the area had just been abducted. Nairac and Woodfield led the investigation, taking the Argylls into local bars and clubs crowded with drinkers in an attempt to extract information. When they went in, weapons cocked ready to open fire if necessary, Nairac covering Woodfield as he led the way and six Argyll platoons providing back-up, they were met by nothing more damaging than streams of abuse – but they succeeded in finding the youth. He hadn't been abducted at all; he was playing snooker.

The tour of the 2nd Battalion Grenadiers was judged a success, as was usual, by the 'score' – rather like a soccer match. In their four months of duty, they took possession of 58 weapons, 9,000 rounds of ammunition and 693 lbs of explosives, and put 104 men in prison. 'This', concluded Lieutenant-Colonel Besly, 'compared very favourably with our predecessors and successors.

Incidentally a good proportion of our arrest and finds were from the Protestant areas, which did not endear us to the police and local authorities. Luckily no Grenadier got seriously hurt. I am also glad we didn't shoot any gun-toting IRA youngsters – our priority was to arrest them and put them, with their godfathers, in prison.'

For Robert Nairac, the tour proved a turning point in his military career. Several of his colleagues are convinced that the experience pushed him towards a deeper involvement in the problems of Northern Ireland. He could easily have opted for a regular career pattern in the Guards, which had many compensations and a fairly full social life. Soon, his battalion would be posted to Hong Kong, where a good time would be had by all, with ample opportunities for sport and recreation, including some of the pursuits that Nairac most enjoyed – canoeing, combat survival, judo and diving, quite a few cocktail parties and no threat of military action other than exercises.

He rejected that path in favour of Northern Ireland, volunteering for special duties, with an emphasis on intelligence. He already knew the score, long before he came to the Six Counties as a soldier. Now he had witnessed for himself some of the dire conditions confronting Catholics, surrounded by the Protestant estates, and the gangs and pseudo-gangs of the so-called loyalist paramilitaries. It was, he judged, not difficult to see why the Catholics in the worst-hit areas believed that the British troops were there merely to aid Protestant domination. Nor was it difficult to see why there was such support for the IRA. Nairac hated extremists, whatever their religion. No one interviewed for this book suggested that his personal faith got in the way of his soldiering; if anything, he overcompensated against it. There is little doubt that what he saw on that first tour of duty convinced him that he should try to make some sort of contribution to the resolution of the Troubles. It was naïve, some said, but they admired his courage.

Nairac saw that in the operations in which he had recently been involved the object of the Army patrols was to dominate an area, quell the violence, round up the weaponry, take out the ringleaders and, they hoped, leave a more peaceful community. It was the oldest of military tactics, born in the days of colonial expeditions when wild natives with charismatic leaders at their head had to be 'pacified'.

Those aims had been achieved in some areas, largely by sheer weight of numbers, but that alone was insufficient. The key to all the troop manoeuvres was, as always, intelligence – identifying the leaders. Nairac had worked closely with his battalion's intelligence cell. He had seen intelligence officers debriefing soldiers for minutiae about the people in houses they had raided; often photographs were taken. Confirmation of identities was paramount. Personal identification cards were linked to house cards, street cards and car cards. In an age before mass computerization, it was a laborious process of cross-checks, with more and more detail crammed in after each debriefing so that suspects or known extremists could be tracked and monitored.

The battalion, like others who made successful contacts with their quarry, linked up with the RUC Special Branch, whose ultimate responsibility was formal arrest, charges and trial. It was not unusual for an Army patrol to return for their debrief in the early hours of the morning, and on the basis of the information they brought in a specialist search team might be deployed immediately to a particular address, perhaps at 3.00 a.m. It would be made up of a patrol to cordon off an area and break down the door at the target house, interrogation officers, a dog trained to sniff out explosives and a woman officer from the Royal Military Police, WRAF or UDR to attend to any female at the 'attack' address. While the patrol kept guard outside, the occupants would be herded into one room, invariably protesting loudly, while a thorough search was made. Even if nothing was found –

and often it wasn't, the gradual attrition of the IRA was judged to be succeeding.

Nairac decided that this was his forte and on his return from his first tour he went forward for specialist training, such as it was, to equip himself for whatever role might eventually be assigned to him. There were numerous courses and training routines through which special duties volunteers would proceed. At the time, undercover soldiers, intelligence officers and those to be attached to the special units operating in the province were badly needed.

Most of the appointments were anonymous, thankless, dangerous and no place for glory hunters. Most went through the Army Joint Intelligence College at Ashford, Kent, where they learned the rudiments of intelligence defined by key words – estimation, re-assessment, collection, interpretation, evaluation and dissemination. He trained in the well-tried spy games used by the college such as using dead letterboxes, practising surveillance and making clandestine contact with agents. In fact, according to SAS Captain D, the set-up at Ashford – like many of the intelligence training units on the British mainland – had little in common with the needs of Northern Ireland:

> Frankly, it wasn't up to much. They still hadn't cottoned on that Northern Ireland was like no other place. In the early 1970s, they did not have enough experienced tutors to teach the particular type of intelligence operations required there. Very few had had the opportunity of field work. Ashford was still geared ostensibly to the Cold War, with a training manual that was largely concerned with conventional wisdom regarding espionage and counter-espionage. Northern Ireland was something else; it was a very hard area.
>
> Walking about with folded newspapers under your arm may have been OK in London or Berlin, but in

Belfast there was a different style of intelligence – a different game altogether and dirtier, too. I know that those members of the SAS who went to Ashford had to be retrained before they went to Northern Ireland. The province was a big learning curve for everyone concerned – not least the managers at Ashford, who had to find ways of adapting their training methods to the requirements of tracking terrorists, using informers, agent handling and some pretty duplicitous stuff targeting people who were for the most part British nationals.

Nairac also received the benefit of an SAS training course at Hereford geared specifically to the province. He was honed in the use of the Ingram sub-machine gun, increased his proficiency in the use of handguns and the famous SAS weapon, the pump-action shotgun. He also took instruction in the use of electronic surveillance gear, night sights, directional microphones – which were to become extensively used, all kinds of other bugs and a very handy new gallium arsenide laser with opto-electrical linkage that could pick up conversations from the vibrations on window panes.

His intelligence training also included field work in London, getting jobs on building sites that employed large numbers of Irishmen, in whose company he practised his accent. He was sent to the Army's top-secret training facility in Kenya for a lengthy survival course. When he returned, he told his friends that he had been forced to live off whatever he shot. His parents were convinced that their son was undertaking a military role, which was best suited to his talents and ambitions.

His physical fitness assured, he later attended an Army course at Warminster, Wiltshire, which honed his psychological fitness and tutored him in techniques of a kind that were used across a whole raft of operations almost exclusively in Northern Ireland, for which the course had been designed. His course controller at the time was not particularly impressed. He told me:

I was a major, directing staff at the Junior Division of the Staff College at Warminster ... Robert Nairac was one of my students. I don't remember him as shining particularly academically but I do remember him being great fun, attractive both intellectually and physically and very good company. Because we took to each other, he spent quite a lot of time at my house (with my then wife and myself), often arriving at odd hours looking more like a poacher than anything and as often as not with a pocketful of brown trout which he had just tickled somewhere. He was excellent company and the trout delicious. He had a well-developed, but also cultivated, degree of unconventionality. It was I believe the cultivated bit which led to his ultimate downfall.

# 4

## 'ANYTHING IS POSSIBLE'

Although it has been said by some who knew Robert Nairac well that his experiences during his first tour of Northern Ireland with the Grenadiers had a serious impact upon him and pointed him towards the role he eventually took on in Army intelligence, in fact, those experiences merely scratched the surface, and, said his friend Major A, he had no idea what he was coming to when he volunteered for special duties.

It is difficult not to take into account his religious views in assessing his personal feelings. Nairac had taken a close interest in the events unfolding across the Irish Sea – more so than most of his colleagues transferring from university into military life. In the relatively cosy, occasionally hallucinatory atmosphere of late 1960s and early 1970s Britain, it took some time for the mainland to notice what, exactly, was going on in Northern Ireland. As for the impact of the tour, few could come through it unscathed, especially those who had been close witness to the barely credible scenes – not to mention those living permanently amongst them – since the Troubles began. The political shenanigans, the sectarian issues, the rivalries, the war lords, their soldiers and the indescribably inhuman acts of viciousness from virtually every one of the contending groups provided an urban scenario matched, perhaps, only by the Lebanon in this last half century. Major A who, like Nairac, completed four tours, two with his parent regiment in 1973/4 and two with his eventual SAS squadron in 1976/8, said:

> 'You could see houses being torn to shreds either by the Army patrols or the bombs of the paramilitaries. You

would see day after day the victims of the beatings and the shootings and the endless bombings. We, the security forces, which included the RUC, were also effectively torturing people in the cause of gathering intelligence. But it was Northern Ireland. Did anyone in England care? Did they even know? We actually used to ask ourselves that question and by and large they didn't, not until the IRA began their bombing campaigns on the mainland, which is about the time that Robert Nairac came in.

There was so much going on that was either being ignored, overlooked, covered up or lost in the welter of extremist violence. People were going haywire; some were going slightly mad. There were mean and petty jealousies within the intelligence business and especially between the Army and the RUC where communications all but broke down at one stage. At times, it was chaotic. There were rumours of unauthorized shootings, secret graves, crime gangs mixing and matching with terrorists and the UDR alike so that you never really knew who the fuck was your true enemy, and the people of Northern Ireland were swept along in the tide. Looking back now with the knowledge of hindsight, I know that anything – perhaps all of these things – was possible, more likely probable.

There was the fact, also, that hardened and experienced media people in London were slow to grasp the intensity of it all in the early days; and it is certainly true that even some of those on the ground, reporting events, did not at the time believe the rumours that not all atrocities were committed by the extremist gangs: that a shoot-to-kill policy existed within the Army's Special Duties units, sometimes using locally recruited pseudo-gangs they themselves had set up, and that torture and psychological abuse was being routinely meted out by trained interrogation teams upon those brought in for questioning, largely from the

Catholic regions. Much propaganda and disinformation delivered from both sides had to be treated cautiously. Inevitably, a lot was swallowed.

The general thinking among the Army hierarchy in those days was that the Catholics were allied to the IRA and vice versa, so if patrols were chasing suspects or looking for weapons, they deluged the Catholic areas. It was, therefore, not difficult to understand why the Catholic's original relief at the arrival of the British troops evaporated virtually overnight and turned to spitting hatred.

Conversely, when Westminster wrested political control from the Unionist administration in Stormont in 1972, the loyalists believed that the British had surrendered to the bombers and their gangs emerged on the streets for a killing spree that cost hundreds of lives, mainly Catholic and often innocent. Nor did Dublin escape. Bombs were exploded there too, at a time when new laws to restrict the activities of the IRA were being discussed. The IRA denied responsibility for these and put the blame on British intelligence, reasoning that bombs close to home would force Dublin to impose firmer measures. As far as the British Army was concerned, the principle enemy was the IRA, and the areas of attack were the Catholic strongholds.

This was the situation that confronted Nairac and the many others of his faith in the British Army. Some were simply unable to come to terms with it and retired emotionally hurt. But Colonel G, an SAS officer who was a major at the time he first met Nairac and later a Lieutenant-Colonel and commanding officer of 21 SAS, remembered: 'I never felt that religion was any kind of a consideration in the way of [Nairac's] work. As an Ampleforth lad and a committed Roman Catholic, he had an understanding of the religious issues in Ireland that ran far deeper than most.'

G would become closely involved with Nairac when he came back to Northern Ireland, equipped for his new role in intelligence. Nairac knew full well he was stepping into an exceedingly murky world in which, by the time he arrived, the truth of the torture techniques and generally heavy-handedness of Army and RUC interrogators on terrorist suspects was beginning to surface. Methods that had been perfected by Britain's colonial security forces and used on the indigenous population they were attempting to quell at the time had lately been applied to those unfortunate enough to have been arrested in the Six Counties. Many of them, incidentally, were never charged with any offence and were never proved to be members of the IRA, PIRA or any other paramilitary organization.

Some of the practices were outlawed – officially, at least – pending an investigation by the European Commission for Human Rights, while senior military figures and politicians claimed they had not given approval for these tactics in the first place. But there was still plenty going on, including training in psychological warfare in which Nairac would himself become involved and which became subject to a scathing Amnesty International Report in 1978.

It might be helpful to summarize the events of the very crucial couple of years prior to Nairac's return, in order to establish what had gone before and how the framework of the intelligence community that he entered came into being. It was, by the end of 1973, a very crowded arena with a great deal of rivalry on both sides. In fact, intelligence gathering as a whole was to some extent a mess, largely because of the number of agencies involved, half of whom did not know what the others were up to, and some of whom spent time digging holes for their rivals to fall into. There were also a fair number of bounty hunters around – soldiers and civilian operatives looking for medals, honours or, at the very least, a career boost.

Although he did not admit it, the disorder of intelligence gathering was one of the reasons Colonel G and intelligence specialists from other regiments were drafted in to individual appointments long before the SAS arrived on the scene as a fully operational unit. One of the key problems arising from the disorder was the use of informers and agents, who might become double agents or triple agents, with one intelligence group being played off against the other, or indeed attempting to scupper the other's work.

The unit to which Nairac was assigned on his first posting as an intelligence liaison officer already had bloody hands and its history went back to the very heart of the Northern Ireland military response, which emerged with renewed vigour in 1970 when Edward Heath led the Conservatives to a general election victory. Army commanders were certain that a Tory government would commit themselves to an altogether tougher line in Ulster than the previous prime minister Harold Wilson had allowed. New proposals were already written up, awaiting presentation. The Army's top brass had been deliberating for months on the fact that the military was driving headlong into a situation from which it would be difficult to extract itself, with the result that the 'war', far from being brought to a swift conclusion, could drag on for years.

All the elements of a historical conflict were in place and every piece of intelligence pointed to an increase in IRA manpower and arms. That the two wings of the IRA were still at loggerheads was barely a consideration. At some point in the very near future they would join the struggle as a single entity and in consequence the Protestant/loyalists would escalate their own response.

The Army had little experience of how to handle war on the streets of its own country, and the methods of approach would, by necessity, be based almost entirely on past experience of British military tactics in Cyprus against EOKA, in Aden against the Communists and Kenya against the Mau Mau. Chief of the General Staff George Baker had been Director of Operations and Chief of Staff in Cyprus in the 1950s. His methods were controversial enough there, and now he was to use them as the basis for dealing with the Ulster crisis.

The new Home Secretary who came in with the Heath government, Reginald Maudling, more or less gave the Army a free hand. The Army's high command was told to do whatever was necessary to resolve the Troubles in Northern Ireland. Maudling, one of the most cynical politicians of the age, saw it as a military problem and virtually walked away. He did not like Northern Ireland and visited the place only on three brief occasions in the two years before he was forced to resign over his connections with corrupt architect John Poulson.

The new tough line was visible within a month of the new government's arrival, following the shooting of six Protestants by the Provisional IRA. An RUC informer led the police to a small cache of weapons – fifteen pistols, a rifle and a sub-machine gun – in Official IRA territory, in the Lower Falls area of Belfast. The following day, 3 July, soldiers began a full-scale search and were met with a hail of stones and petrol bombs, and then gunfire from snipers. More than 2,500 troops moved in and fired hundreds of CS-gas canisters with a makeshift catapult into the streets where the rioters had refused to disperse, releasing a huge cloud of choking smoke. More than fifty streets were placed under curfew and low-circling helicopters were used to broadcast a warning that anyone still on the streets after 10.00 p.m. would be arrested. Four civilians were shot dead, another was killed by an armoured vehicle and seventy were injured.

Afterwards, the Army patrols moved in to search the houses in their usual fashion. Civil rights leaders protested loudly at the damage caused, and churchmen noted that many objects of religious significance in Catholic homes were wantonly destroyed. The Army public relations department claimed, however, that the results of the operation vindicated the Army's firmness, as more than 100 weapons, including shotguns, rifles and machine guns were found, along with a quantity of gelignite – proof of the Army's belief that many weapons were being stored in Catholic areas. But this skirmish added considerably to the standing of the Provisional IRA.

In September 1970, as the bombings and shootings increased, the Army chiefs of staff agreed upon a significant addition to their military strategy. Counter-insurgency specialist Frank Kitson had been appointed to command 39 Infantry Brigade, which covered Belfast and the east of the province. The move was significant because Kitson was a veteran of colonial campaigns, notably using turncoats against Mau Mau terrorism in Kenya in the 1950s. At that time, he was twenty-eight years old, operating as a district intelligence officer. He later fought in another terrorist war in Malaya, and took command of a battalion in the Cyprus campaign in the early 1960s. Kitson was an intellectual, a defence fellow at University College, Oxford, and before his posting to Northern Ireland he had spent time researching and writing a book, *Low-intensity Operations*, which was a follow-up to his 1960s offering, *Gangs and Counter-Gangs*. Both were to become the manuals for anti-terrorism in the Six Counties. He was acclaimed as one of the most knowledgeable soldiers around on intelligence, interrogation and urban warfare, although his arrival went almost unnoticed by media military watchers. His appointment pleased the hawks among the military because as he – and they – saw it, the Army was restricted in its ability to attack the real terrorists. It could arrest those caught in the act of violence but not the organizers, i.e. the IRA battalion commanders.

Brigadier Kitson's study of the province drew on key words derived from his book. His recommendations dealt first with the Army's general approach. He recommended 'de-escalation' in the Catholic communities by using community projects, hearts-and-minds campaigns and propaganda to undermine the IRA and unlock it from its religious base. He proposed a concerted programme of attrition, targeting IRA strongholds and rounding up extremists. As Nairac experienced in his first tour, his recommendations were closely followed, although it must be said that others had already put forward similar views. These were given a full airing at Edward Heath's Cabinet committee, GEN 42, set up specifically to deal with Northern Ireland.

The most important development, however, came in the early months of 1971, when Kitson was given permission to form a new unit, whose concept was based upon the gangs and counter-gangs principle so successful in Kenya. There, members of the Mau Mau terrorists were turned against their own side by threats of imprisonment and other forms of intimidation and used as spies and in direct action, leading the British to round up large numbers of the subversives. The British Army also sponsored counter-gangs, setting terrorist against terrorist.

The Army's own intelligence-gathering capability in Northern Ireland in 1971 was pretty thin – and they did not trust the RUC, a feeling that was entirely mutual. So Kitson created his own secret intelligence group, which was called the Military Reconnaissance Force (MRF). Initially staffed by forty men and women, it became a multi-faceted organization, which invented numerous seemingly ingenious ways of gathering intelligence, mostly within the Catholic communities, which they believed would ultimately lead to the capture of large numbers of senior figures in both wings of the IRA. It was also the forerunner of an intelligence operation that would eventually employ the talents of Nairac and many other undercover soldiers.

MRF was manned by volunteers from Army regiments and the UDR, who were trained by officers and NCOs from the Special Forces. Both the SAS and the Special Boat Service were involved in training, some of whom also remained as unit commanders. It was not, and never became, an SAS operation. They were generally non-uniformed operatives whose identity was kept secret. The very fact that members of the SAS were taken individually into the unit gave rise to great public speculation that the regiment was operating in Northern Ireland long before it was admitted in 1976.

Although attached originally to 39 Brigade, the MRF was basically a law unto itself, and selective in which of the British intelligence agencies was given access to its information. Distrustful of the RUC, the MRF kept much to itself and it was not uncommon for both the RUC and regular British army units to barge into an MRF operation, unaware that they were actually dealing with plain-clothes British soldiers.

The first projects launched through MRF focused on turning captured IRA members against their own side. Though few in number, these men were to become an important source of intelligence. Known as 'Freds', they were drawn from the ranks of IRA men arrested on the streets. They were interrogated and usually threatened with a long prison sentence (and, later, internment) if they refused to cooperate. Initially, there were ten 'Freds', including a recently demobilized soldier from the Irish Royal Rangers. They were kept in safe custody in heavily guarded quarters at the Palace Barracks in Belfast. Although they saw each other, they were not allowed to associate. All were subjected to long periods of interrogation, or debriefing as the Army preferred to call it.

They were used extensively for the purposes of identifying both people and locations. They were shown extracts from a mountain of photographs that the Army intelligence had on file and they were taken out clandestinely on to the streets. They would routinely travel inside armoured personnel carriers or other vehicles from which they could not be seen, pointing out the 'players' (the Army term for IRA) and houses and buildings for surveillance or raids.

They even travelled with their intelligence minders to the mainland – to Liverpool, Manchester and London. Some were given special training in surveillance work and went back into the communities from whence they came, where they continued to send messages back to the MRF. It was a lethal business and many did not survive to die a death of natural causes.

The MRF also carried out long surveillance missions, sometimes lasting weeks on end, as well as local watches on people and places of interest, attempting to get one step ahead of the bombers. Among the many other tactics used in the early days by the MRF were two of particular note: a bogus laundry service and a heavily bugged massage parlour, both operating from Belfast.

The Four Square Laundry was a fully operational profit-making venture which provided intelligence opportunities on a number of fronts. It operated from 15 College Street East. Trained laundry staff were, it turned out, placed in considerable jeopardy when they accepted a contract to work for the undercover operation at the laundry. They had no idea as to the true nature of the Four Square Laundry. Plain-clothes operatives, men and women, drove around collecting laundry. The Bedford laundry van, touting for business or collecting and delivering laundry, made a perfect surveillance vehicle. Its motif of four squares was cut into the top front of the vehicle. It was fitted with a roof compartment from which operatives could observe in areas where it was otherwise virtually impossible to carry out unnoticed observation. They could take photographs from the van and keep watch on who went where while driving around the estates. The other advantage came from the laundry itself – providing the MRF with the opportunity of examining clothes and linen for possible evidence of their customers' involvement in IRA activities. Any suspect item was subjected to forensic examination.

Similarly, the massage parlour operating from premises at 397 Antrim Road provided a constant flow of information. Under the name of the Gemini Health Studio, it was staffed by attractive women under the proprietress who ran the business with her husband. The women were apparently unaware that rooms above had been rented to a young couple and were in fact a base for the MRF unit. A similar operation, set up in July 1970 by MI5 with the advice of a London man experienced in the business and run from premises in Stranmillis Road, had proved very successful. The MRF's operatives wired the massage parlour for sound and collected some very useful material on tape and photographically over a period of more than fourteen months. It also proved to be an effective source of gossip from unsuspecting relief seekers.

The MRF managed to operate successfully without the knowledge of others in the field, and indeed the extent of its operations came as a surprise to the RUC when they stumbled across the MRF on 22 June 1972. Four Catholics standing at a bus terminal on the corner of Glen Road in Andersonstown and another in his bedroom at a house opposite were hit and wounded by a hail of bullets from a Thompson sub-machine gun, fired through the rear window of a passing car. Initially, it was thought that the shooting had been carried out by the IRA, who, according to general mythology, used the gangster-style Thompsons with their circular magazines.

The incident would have been put down to the terrorists but for the fact that on this occasion, an RUC police car happened to be coming up behind and gave chase. The police arrested the driver and his passenger. They turned out to be a British army captain and a sergeant. Both admitted to the RUC that they were part of an MRF unit but denied the shooting was in any way a premeditated act. They said they came under fire from the group of men and simply returned the fire to protect themselves. The inquiry naturally reached the highest levels of the military establishment, and efforts were made to keep it under wraps. That was impossible because some of those shot had reported the incident to civil rights activists, who were pressing for explanations since none of the men at the bus stop was apparently armed at the time.

On 27 February 1973, eight months after the shooting, the two soldiers were charged with unlawful possession of a Thompson sub-machine gun. The sergeant who fired the gun was also charged with attempted murder and causing grievous bodily harm. On 2 May, the firearms charges against both men were dropped, leaving only the attempted murder and wounding charges against the sergeant. In court, a year after the shooting, he repeated his defence that he had been fired on by the men at the bus stop and was merely responding, fearing his own life was threatened. The main thrust of the Crown's evidence was that none of the five men injured was armed. The judge directed the jury to acquit the sergeant on the charge of attempted murder since there was insufficient evidence. The jury returned to acquit him on the remaining charges.

Regardless of the facts of that particular case, the question of the Army's ability to shoot someone on the streets of Northern Ireland whether or not they thought they were being shot at was raised at the highest level in a GEN 42 meeting at 10 Downing Street in the summer of 1972. Army Chief of Staff Sir Michael Carver was confronted with a proposal that he believed to be unlawful, one apparently floated by a senior-ranking MI5 adviser to Heath. Lord Carver, as he had become, described the situation in his memoirs:

> It was being suggested that it was perfectly legal for the army to shoot somebody whether or not they were being shot at because anybody who obstructed or got in the way of the armed forces of the Queen was by that very act the Queen's enemy and this was being put forward ... I said to the Prime Minister that I could not under any circumstances allow a British soldier to be ordered to do such a thing because it would not be lawful. He did say his legal advisers suggested it was all right but I said, 'You are not bound by what they say. What I am bound by is my own judgement of whether or not the act of the soldier concerned would be legal because in the end it is the courts that decide.

No one in the media, it was pointed out to me, linked the Glen Road shooting with the fact that on that same day, 22 June 1972, both wings of the IRA were 'responding favourably' to ceasefire negotiations secretly initiated by the Northern Ireland Secretary William Whitelaw. There was a real chance of at least a temporary ceasefire, because the IRA was facing growing pressure from within the Catholic community for peace.

Whitelaw was given approval by Edward Heath's GEN 42 committee to open a limited dialogue with the IRA leadership. He also agreed to the release of a young activist in the Provisional IRA, Gerry Adams, from the Long Kesh internment camp to lead the negotiations on behalf of the PIRA.

Two of Whitelaw's staff met Adams and David O'Connell, a senior member of the Provisionals' Army Council, on 20 June for exploratory talks. The meeting was arranged without the knowledge of the Army chiefs of staff, but they were soon to learn of it from sources in the security service.

The ceasefire was largely engineered by MI6. MI5 was strongly opposed to it, on the grounds that it was merely giving breathing space to the terrorists, allowing them to stock up with arms and get their people into strategic locations for a fresh onslaught. MI5 was also strongly opposed to the IRA demands that all prisoners and internees should be given prisoner-of-war status and that the Army should halt its raids, arrests and destruction of houses.

The negotiations continued, however, and the ceasefire came into effect on 26 June – in spite of the shooting of the five men in Glen Road on the 22 June. On 7 July, under extreme secrecy, an IRA delegation, which included Gerry Adams and Londonderry commander Martin McGuinness, were flown aboard an RAF plane to London, and on to a house in Chelsea for discussions with Whitelaw's aides. Their mood was tough and uncompromising. The IRA demanded a statement of intent that the British troops would be withdrawn by 1 January 1975. No agreement was reached but the two sides agreed to meet again. They never made it.

Fresh outbreaks of violence flared up within two days as the UDA, fired by rumours of a deal with the IRA, quickly put about by its opposers, who, we must remind ourselves, included MI5, began anew a concerted campaign of intimidation in Catholic areas. By the end of the month, new barricades were going up in Protestant areas of Belfast. On 31 July the Army launched its massive Operation Motorman, involving 12,000 troops supported by tanks and bulldozers, who smashed their way into no-go areas, with assistance (whether asked for or not) in Belfast by paramilitaries of the UDA. The operation was carried out with the assistance also of intelligence supplied by the undercover agents of the MRF. So ended the Whitelaw peace bid.

The MRF drive-by shooting involving the Army sergeant and his captain was the first time the organization had been exposed to IRA gaze. It was to be finally and fatally compromised by two of the men the MRF had arrested and turned into agents, who turned back to inform their PIRA commanders of what had happened.

The PIRA hit back. On 2 October 1972, the laundry, the massage parlour and the surveillance flat were put out of operation for good. At 11.15 a.m., the Four Square Laundry van was doing its rounds on the Twinbrook Estate, Belfast, staffed by a 'young hard-working couple' whom the locals had got to know quite well. They both had Belfast accents. The van turned into Juniper Park and one of the laundry staff, in reality the MRF's Lance-Corporal Sarah Jane Warke (Provost Company, Royal Military Police) was at a house collecting laundry, chatting on the doorstep to a mother with her two children, when a blue Cortina drove by. Seconds later, she heard shots and turned to see two men in a crouching position unleash bursts of fire from automatic weapons at the van. One of them turned and saw her, and aimed at her. She dived into the doorway, pushing the mother and her two children out of the way.

The male driver of the laundry van was in real life Sapper Ted Stuart, aged twenty, from County Tyrone. He was hit with five bullets and died instantly. Warke escaped unhurt and was later awarded the Military Medal for her bravery in undercover operations. On the same day, PIRA gunmen entered premises in Antrim Road, looking for the offices which they believed were connected to the laundry. They were, apparently, unaware of the massage parlour operation. They found themselves at the wrong door, heading into an office block. One of them tripped up a step and accidentally shot himself, and they all ran off. Later, the streets around Antrim Road were cordoned off by uniformed Royal Marines commandos, who proceeded to empty the MRF's apartment of all its contents, carrying out boxes, beds, furniture and clothes.

The laundry and the massage parlour were effectively put out of business. All that remained for the PIRA was to tidy up a couple of outstanding matters. Later that day some of their volunteers went missing from their homes in Belfast.

At 7.00 p.m. on the night of 2 October 1972, Seamus Wright answered a knock at his front door. There were two men there. His wife heard him shut the door, and walk to their car and get into the back seat. He was wearing his slippers and no jacket. The car sped off.

Seamus Wright was one of the so-called Freds. He had been a volunteer in D Company of the Provisional IRA, which operated in the Lower Falls area. He had been arrested as an IRA suspect on 5 February 1972. After two days, his worried wife had heard nothing and got a priest to phone the RUC. They knew nothing, but eventually the priest discovered that Wright had been released from custody some time earlier. In fact, he had been taken first to a military post in North Howard Street and then to Palace Barracks, Holywood, for interrogation by MRF officers. The captain who was in the car involved in the Glen Road shooting was among those who interviewed him. He was told that there was evidence to connect him with a bomb explosion in which a member of the security forces had been killed, and that he would face a long prison sentence unless he cooperated.

Wright's wife, in the meantime, received a message supposedly from her husband, by way of a telephone call to their corner shop. He said he had 'scarpered' – not a word he normally used. A day later, she received a letter from him stating that he had escaped from custody with another fellow and had gone to England. He would telephone her the following day at the corner shop. The call duly came through. Her priest had arranged to tape their conversation. Wright, it transpired, was in Birmingham. He gave her an address to write to, and then hung up. Mrs Wright and her father immediately got on a plane and went to Birmingham.

They found the address, a ground-floor flat at which her husband eventually arrived with another man. Wright told her that his companion's name was Colin and that he was in the SAS. Mrs Wright had about ten minutes with her husband before Colin became agitated. Seamus said she had better go. He told her they were taking him back to Palace Barracks in the next few days and that they would then release him. Over the next seven weeks, she received letters from Wright postmarked Manchester or London. They gave no clue as to what he was doing, except that he was working at his trade, which was as an asphalt layer. In fact, he was already back at the Palace Barracks, where he was being given training in one-to-one surveillance.

When he finally arrived home, on 31 March, he explained to his wife that he could not tell her much, because of the secrecy, but he had been questioned about everything he knew and cooperated as far as he could to save himself from prison. At the Palace Barracks, he was billeted with others, including two other young men, a young girl, her mother and two children. They had been under constant guard by an armed man.

On his release from Palace Barracks, Wright reported back to the local commander of PIRA's D Company, as he had been told to do by his MRF handlers. He explained to his commander that he had been questioned about guns and explosives and had been forced to give names of those operating in the Lower Falls and was then released. D Company's intelligence officer took over the Seamus Wright case and, intrigued by his story, allowed him to go back home and continue as if nothing had happened.

The PIRA men judged that by sending Wright back they could secure an insight into the operations of the security forces, and what exactly was going on at Palace Barracks. Some weeks later, Wright disappeared again for a short while and upon his return, he was picked up by his PIRA friends and interrogated for two days. In the course of that questioning, he volunteered the name of another Fred named Kevin McKee, who was related to a well-known Republican family. McKee, he said, knew something of a particularly large MRF operation.

McKee was eventually picked up by the PIRA unit and interrogated for forty-eight hours before he finally cracked and told the wide-eyed PIRA intelligence officer about the Four Square Laundry. McKee was removed to a safe house in South Armagh, where he was detained. Wright was allowed home and throughout August and September continued to make visits to his handlers at Palace Barracks. The PIRA set him up with fake intelligence to check that it was going back to th MRF. It was.

Wright returned to his family and life settled down again – until the night of 2 October, the date of the PIRA attack on the Four Square Laundry. Seamus Wright was last seen by his wife, being driven away in the car. In spite of appeals for information by Father Brian J. Brady of the Association for Legal Justice, delivered to General Tuzo, the Army Chief of Staff, Edward Heath, Harold Wilson, William Whitelaw and virtually every other senior politician of the day, no news was forthcoming as to what happened to Wright.

Both the British Army and the IRA denied any knowledge of him. In fact, he was put before an IRA court martial and executed the day after his arrest by IRA men and buried secretly. They were happy to allow speculation that Wright had been killed by the British Army or, more specifically, by the SAS.

Kevin McKee was also sentenced to death by the IRA for being an informer. His family was told of what had happened and two gunmen from 1st Battalion of the IRA were appointed to execute him. A priest was in attendance to give the last rites and to say prayers at his secret burial. As with Robert Nairac, almost five years later, the bodies of the two men were well hidden and have never been found.

The events of 2 October 1972 spelled the end not only of the Four Square Laundry and the Gemini Health Club but also of the MRF. The MRF was, however, judged by the Army commanders to have been far too valuable to let drift. Although its founder, Frank Kitson, had ended his brief sojourn in Northern Ireland months earlier, his manual for gangs and counter-gangs and his ideas on counter-insurgency would long remain part of the British intelligence operation in Northern Ireland.

An organization replacing the MRF came into being in 1973. It was to be far more sophisticated, less reliant on risky ventures such as massage parlours and laundries, and had far more highly trained specialist operatives on board. Among them would be Captain Robert Nairac.

# 5

## THE REAL THING

Robert Nairac returned to Northern Ireland at a crucial stage in the intelligence war. The MRF was chalked up as a successful enterprise from which lessons had been learned in what one of its Army opponents had described as 'an unfortunate series of cock-ups'. Despite these, statistically, the IRA appeared to be on the run. By 1974, many leading members of both wings of the IRA had been rounded up and either interned or sent to prison on criminal charges. Various military and intelligence experts were saying that the IRA was virtually beaten, and that in some areas – especially in Belfast – internment had mortally wounded key IRA brigades. Many arrests resulted from information supplied by agents such as Wright and McKee.

To outsiders, the methodology of the MRF was suspect, open to severe criticism from politicians and accusations of a shoot-to-kill policy by local civil rights activists. Because of the publicity given to some of the 'cock-ups', for years the MRF and Kitson became the focal point of protest and propaganda, long after the MRF had been shut down and Kitson had departed the scene. But, in a nutshell, it was the Army's first real attempt at fighting fire with fire. Even though the IRA had gleaned so much about the organization of the MRF in so little time, the score was, as one of its former operatives put it, 'evened up a touch'.

Its demise, however, created a large hole in the Army's intelligence-gathering capability at the very time when the 'war' was moving into an even more vicious phase. Predictions that the IRA was on the floor were well wide of the mark. The Provisionals, admittedly badly hit by the detention of key personnel, were growing in their skills alongside the international terrorist movement, sponsored by the likes of Libya's Colonel Gaddafi. In fact, 1973 ended with a crescendo of violence, and dire warnings of escalation were proved correct, with 3,206 acts of terrorism recorded within the Six Counties in the following twelve months.

The MRF's replacement was slow off the mark and did not become operative until the early months of 1974. The results of the MRF had been so good that Frank Kitson's original blueprint for intelligence gathering provided the basis for continued operations under a new heading, more focused and specifically targeted. These operations moved onwards and upwards with increasing sophistication through new technology, intermittent saturation of Republican areas with troops and long-term surveillance operations of IRA suspects. What evolved was a secret Special Duties company that remains in operation to the present day. It was, and still is, a third wing of the British Special Forces – and was recognized as such in 1987, when it was placed on the same pay footing as the SAS and SBS. Its area of operations was at the time exclusively Northern Ireland. Known within as The Group, its official title was the Army Surveillance Unit, but it became far better known among journalists and writers on issues relating to Northern Ireland and the Special Forces as 14 Intelligence and Security Company, abbreviated to 14 Int.

This title was in itself very similar – deliberately so – to that of a unit of computer programmers, report writers and data specialists who bore no comparison to the undercover soldiers being recruited to the new company.

The name 14 Intelligence did not come into official use until the 1980s; but, as prior to that confusing cover names were used for the company, for the purposes of this book the term 14 Int will be used. The cover names in the early days were deliberately chosen to sound like other units within the Army, usually engaged on more innocuous tasks. The secrecy was not merely a security screen to fool the IRA. From the outset, this was to be a long-term intelligence strategy and its founders were desperately anxious for their new grouping to remain totally undercover. Army chiefs went to great lengths to hide its existence and the identity of its operatives even from other regiments and, to some extent, from the political hierarchy. Certainly the leaky UDR and the RUC were shut out, although in the short term, individual officers from both those organizations were used as intelligence feeds to 14 Int.

Army intelligence needed input from the RUC's own intelligence-gathering specialists and reciprocated by training anti-terrorist units within the RUC's Special Branch. Conversely, 14 Int made every effort to disguise its operations and especially to prevent any understanding of its wider brief. It was intended that neither its purpose nor details of its operations were allowed to seep into either the RUC system or even the British military community as a whole. They wanted to protect it from infiltration by agents who were likely to spill the beans, either under pressure or voluntarily, to the IRA. These precautionary measures, according to numerous sources, meant a tough, new approach to intelligence gathering, utilizing some extreme techniques.

Robert Nairac was 'attached' early on to what became known as 14 Int, and at one time specifically linked with one of its section commanders, Captain Julian 'Tony' Ball, a tough SAS hard-liner who later became a lieutenant-colonel commanding the Sultan of Oman's Special Forces. He was killed in a car accident in 1981 at the age of thirty-eight. Ball was one of a number of SAS personnel drafted to the special duties units long before his SAS regiment was sent to Northern Ireland. He, like Nairac, was working to an intelligence command under the banner of 14 Int and not to his SAS regimental command. But because the SAS supplied and trained staff for major roles in the operation in the early days, 14 Int was later often mistakenly described as an SAS unit.

Many writers claiming inside knowledge have described Nairac as a member of 14 Int, or whatever name the unit had at the time. Some still persist in stating he was also SAS, which I have shown, without doubt, that he was not. When I was attempting to establish his exact role. Brigadier C, a former SAS colonel and also a later commander of the Sultan's Special Forces, insisted: 'You asked me whether I had known Robert N when he was a member of what you (and most press) described as 14 Company. I said No for two reasons: one, that when he was in Northern Ireland, I was elsewhere and two, as far as I know, he was never in '14 Company', whatever anyone else may tell you. I was and I know.'

However, let us defer to Colonel G, who was an SAS major at the time. G was posted to Northern Ireland in a hurry in 1974, to take up a post with the title of G2/Int Liaison in the intelligence corridor at the Northern Ireland Army headquarters in Lisburn, County Antrim, just a short drive along the M1 motorway from Belfast. He told me (referring to Nairac's subsequent work in South Armagh):

Mine was an Army Intelligence appointment, not SAS, but it suited people from our background. I was delighted to be there because it got me out of Germany where I had been for a year. I became a sort of central coordinator of intelligence. There existed already the Army's special intelligence, elements of which Robert Nairac was by then a part. He had worked down in the very troublesome region of South Armagh. He was the liaison officer for the 3 Brigade area covering South Armagh and as such was attached to intelligence in Northern Ireland long before 22 SAS was ever there [in January 1976]. He was the liaison man to the RUC, the RUC Special Branch and the Army units in the area. He also liaised with HQ Northern Ireland in Lisburn on intelligence matters.

Meeting up with Robert, I certainly felt he was one of the most effective of our liaison officers. Not least because he had a lot of charm but most particularly because he'd also studied at the university in Dublin and had this very real love and understanding of the Irish people. That was abundantly clear, right from the beginning. He was very much a people person. He wasn't a bureaucrat and there was an evident rebel streak in his persona.

He identified very strongly with the problems and the people whilst at the same time he was very much against the IRA and all the extreme elements. He probably had a better understanding than anyone I met of the IRA, their history and motivations and the Republican cause, along with the communities which supported it. He had studied it in great depth and by identifying with the south and the whole Irish situation, he had both the knowledge and, to some degree, empathy with the wider picture that confronted us.

He also had that certain unique Guards' smooth charm that works wonders in Army circles. He got along famously with the RUC, which was very, very important because the Army and the RUC were too frequently at loggerheads. There were degrees of competition in all areas. Army units came and went. In the early years, units were often trying to grab their own little share of glory to varying degrees, some more than others, and the RUC had been there for ever and was constantly catching the flak of all concerned with security in the province. Robert did an extremely good job in those early days setting up the intelligence process down there.

Nairac's exact job description, then, was liaison officer – the link man between Army units, Intelligence HQ, RUC Special Branch and, occasionally, other agencies, which included the secret service and the security service. His work, however, seems to have expanded substantially into other areas, usually at his own bidding, to enable him to become more deeply involved. Perhaps if he had kept within the parameters of that job description, i.e. liaison, he might never have become entangled with the IRA men who took him away and shot him, as we shall see.

At the beginning of 14 Int's life in 1974, Nairac's was a unique role, one that was shared with few undercover soldiers, in that he had access to information gathered by both RUC and Army intelligence operatives in Northern Ireland at the time. While most saw only part of the jigsaw, he was more likely to be able to view the wider picture.

As Colonel G identified, he was especially valuable to the Army in one particular aspect – the rapport he developed (through his Guards' charm) with officers of the RUC Special Branch, which cut through troughs of deep antagonism between the two groups. (His popularity was marked when he departed Northern Ireland briefly at the end of one tour of duty with a presentation to him by RUC Special Branch officers of a silver tankard.)

RUC sources were vital. The Army's relationship with the force had been patchy at the best of times and downright distant at others. Many Army officers of the 'old school' were openly hostile to the RUC over its much criticized methods of interrogation, which brought it into international disrepute, and were horrified by rumours of the association of some of its officers with loyalist killer squads. The continual arrest of British soldiers in the course of their 'duty' was a particular bone of contention and, conversely, many senior officers in the RUC were not backward in expressing their opinion that the MRF was run by a bunch of cowboys. However, the Special Branch still ran the largest network of informers and agents.

With a new intelligence force starting out, and with the Army determined to prevent it from being compromised like the MRF, Nairac was one of the link men who smoothed the path for the Army's special units to tap into RUC sources, borrow its informers and, if possible, secure access to some of the better intelligence that the Special Branch had at its fingertips. The Army had built up its own massive database on its complex card-index system, but it was so vast as to be unwieldy. Its huge and interminable census checks, which had caused so much anger among the communities in the province, had similarly produced masses and masses of documentation that, in the end, became almost impossibile to transfer effectively to an instantly accessible database. A new £500,000 computer was delivered in 1974, but, as ever with such equipment in the 1970s, it took time to set up and make an effective contribution.

The Army had decided that its priority task was to open up a fresh window into the IRA, in ways never previously attempted, through 14 Int and with the definite aim of ultimately eliminating any reliance on the RUC/Special Branch whatsoever. The company, 14 Int, was an umbrella organization to, initially, three smaller intelligence groups, whose exact functions were to remain beyond the scope of public scrutiny or revelation; they are today buried in the deepest chasms of the Official Secrets Act, and will undoubtedly remain so. There are no documents, no formal regimental records and no governmental statistics in the public domain that relate to them.

The three detachments or Dets, into which the company was at first divided, were each commanded by junior officers, usually a captain and when available a second officer. The second officer would be either a lieutenant or a captain, generally appointed to fulfil the role of liaison or operations officer. Nairac was one of three liaison officers. The Dets were manned by volunteers from various army units, who were trained to exacting standards on a par with the Special Forces, although initially there was insufficient time to bring them fully to that level.

Priority was given to training for long-term surveillance of terrorist suspects, utilizing all the latest accoutrements of observation. Operatives had to become proficient in covert signals procedures, photography, wiring for sound, use of night sights, telephone tapping and a selection of internal and external eavesdropping devices. In addition, they took two intensive courses designed to indoctrinate the volunteers to these units in the general procedures for Northern Ireland and its particular requirements.

They were tested in their ability to undertake these demanding surveillance tasks which, as every special forces operative knows, can be exceedingly traumatic. They would then move on into static and mobile surveillance exercises. They had to demonstrate their ability to withstand interrogation and their reaction to simulated terrorist interrogation, which itself can be psychologically stressful, was monitored. All this training was pretty well as published in the Special Forces training manuals.

There were around 80–100 operatives attached to 14 Int, drawn from across the Army regiments throughout the UK, with the SAS and SBS providing operatives for key posts and as instructors. Those who came from the Special Forces were taken out of their regular units and assigned to specific roles, and although they had no supervisory contact with their parent unit while in 14 Int, many of them became key operatives when the SAS was eventually sent into the province.

The very presence of Special Forces in these teams brought renewed and constant allegations from Republican politicians and the media that the SAS were already in Northern Ireland, and had been secretly posted there to mastermind undercover assassination squads and the use of special techniques in police interrogation centres.

The accusation became an established part of the IRA propaganda war, in which it would subsequently be claimed that virtually every unsolved killing was the work of plain-clothed SAS patrols. The SAS had a very bad press, which had flared up when the British security forces were heavily censured by the European Convention on Human Rights Commission over the interrogation techniques used in the early stages of the struggle, between 1971 and 1972, which amounted to torture.

These involved hooding the victim, subjecting him to 'white noise', making him stand for long periods with his fingertips touching the wall, constant and loud harassment, deprivation of sleep and other tricks learned in Cyprus, Aden and elsewhere. Witnesses to the Human Rights Convention told of being made to stand for twenty-three hours, and in one case, twenty-nine hours with fingertips touching the wall. This, along with widespread allegations of beatings, was laid heavily at the door of the SAS by IRA propagandists and was fodder for left-wing activists. It was true that the SAS had been involved in the training of RUC officers in certain elements of anti-terrorism, but the interrogation centres came into being following a seminar in Britain in April 1971 under the auspices of the English Intelligence Centre, at which RUC officers were given an oral briefing into methods of interrogation that were eventually used against terrorists in police barracks.

The sensory methods of interrogation used by the RUC in the early 1970s by interrogators were approved during the era of Frank Kitson, although it was MI5 that promoted their use. A special police interrogation centre at Castlereagh in which these techniques were used was ready for operations some time before internment was approved by the Heath government. The exact nature of the interrogation methods to be used, when the time came, was withheld from the Cabinet committee for Northern Ireland by Sir Dick White, former head of MI5 and Chief Coordinator of Intelligence for GEN 42. Lord Carver, the former Chief of Staff, maintains that the committee was 'misled' and he personally would not have approved the operation, which, he said, was crude and brought unnecessary criticism and embarrassment for the political and military authorities.

It was, therefore, not without some justification that a frenzy of scaremongering arose among the Catholic and nationalist communities and human rights campaigners. It became almost impossible for the British Army to admit even a limited presence of Special Forces men (which is exactly what it was in 1974) for fear of giving weight to the IRA allegations. In the situation that faced the Army and the British government, it was hardly feasible that the Special Forces would not have been active in some role or other, and in fact it was the Special Boat Service, allied to the Royal Marines, that took the brunt of early service missions both in direct action and covert activities in relation to tracking weapons shipments and unearthing the arms caches.

In spite of the rumours, however, the only Special Forces operating as a unit up to January 1976 were those assigned to 14 Int and its detachments. Such was the importance of their operatives – and especially those like Robert Nairac seeking intelligence on dangerous guerrilla warfare commanders in border areas of South Armagh, which was too dangerous for standard Army patrols and virtually a no-go area – it was not unknown for some special operations to be controlled directly from London, thus cutting out local contact.

Nairac was linked to a unit that had the cover name of 4 Field Survey Troop, Royal Engineers, based in County Armagh. Its tasks were to be more wide-ranging than the Army's regular intelligence corps and it took on a robust set of ambitions aimed specifically at identifying leading personalities in the terror business and effecting their removal (preferably to prison) as soon as possible by whatever means necessary but, officially, within the letter of the law.

When MP Ken Livingstone raised questions about this unit in the House of Commons in 1988, he was informed by the Parliamentary Under-Secretary of State Roger Freeman that there was no information available on the troop. It was formed, he said, in 1973 and disbanded in 1975 when there was no further use for it. All documents relating to that period, Freeman claimed, had been destroyed 'as is normal procedure'.

Volunteers for the new intelligence units were trained at a special camp set up in 100 acres of terrain surrounded by razor-topped wire just outside a village. The fence became something of a joke, however, because the village road ran straight through the camp and efforts to get it closed were rejected following complaints by local farmers.

Closed-circuit cameras covered the area and, like most of the Ministry of Defence's sensitive installations, any lingering traffic brought immediate reaction from camp patrols. Behind the security barriers, the 14 Int volunteers received their training in specific procedures, along with other covert personnel from the police and military police.

In terms of general training, Robert Nairac was in a different class. He was already well versed in much of what the 14 Int operatives were being taught, and more. He brought to his job knowledge and experience that few others possessed, as a member of the RUC Special Branch confirmed to me:

Take it from me, Robert was no fool. He soon learned to move around the place with ease, but always he was alert. He had to be, of course, because this was dangerous country. Strangers were noticed. The word would quickly pass down the line to the Provisionals' own local intelligence officer if there was someone suspicious in the locality. They weren't fools either. Newcomers were watched, perhaps even photographed, just the same as we were doing. In those early days Robert wasn't so much of the loner he later became. He was attached to a particular unit and operated within it as a liaison man, although I believe he often went out on operations and surveillance. He also began, at that time, to practise his Irish accent within the community and was, I think, a bit nervous about it. His attempts weren't too bad, but not 100 per cent. His cover story was that he'd been away, working in Canada. That didn't matter so much then because he was running the link between us [RUC SB] and the Army. He was more important to them than he was to us, but he was a decent guy, well liked, I think, by most of us.

He operated from the base at Castledillon. His unit was in a separate compound to the rest, and out of bounds to everyone without top-level security clearance. I had a good deal of respect for Robert. He knew much more than your average forces intelligence officer, not on routine matters but about people and history. That was important, and it helped with the rapport. He was pretty cool, level-headed I would say, and certainly not naïve, although when he'd had a drink and started singing one of the old songs he could only have been drawing attention to himself. I never went out with him, but I heard about it. Even then, he was pushing out into the most violent place in the province. He was supposed to be liaison but it appeared to us that he was also going out in the field, on covert operations, and he was certainly in contact with informers, some of whom he snitched from us. Agent handling itself is a skilled and dangerous business. I could never be certain, but Robert appeared to be involved in that, too.

The RUC man identified one of the aspects of Nairac's behaviour that was to cause much debate among his colleagues both before and after his death. He seemed almost determined to get noticed in the pubs in a locality that was fervently anti-British. The very fact that he was out there, often without back-up, propping up bars, often with his black Labrador, Bundle, at his feet and attempting to engage serious Republicans who were probably IRA men in conversation and then actually standing up and singing, loudly and gustily, the rebel songs he learned in his youth and had swotted up since, took extreme courage. It was a huge risk.

Eventually, he went out of his way to adopt a totally different style to that of other soldiers, almost to the point of becoming high-profile, which is an odd stance for an undercover soldier. As Colonel G noted, he possessed an empathy with the Irish and he extended it towards the people he came into contact with. His reasons were not wholly clear to those around him.

It seemed to many of his colleagues that he was going one step too far in the intelligence game, but with the benefit of hindsight, it can be seen that a pattern emerged whereby he seemed intent on setting himself up as a man who could be trusted and who would be accepted in Catholic areas and by the Provisionals themselves. His friend Martin Squires, who was with him in London just before he began what would be his last tour, had his own theory:

> I am pretty sure that Robert believed he could and would infiltrate the IRA by some means or other. It would have been a marvellous coup but bloody suicidal and I told him as much. But, of course, I had no way of knowing whether he was under orders to do so. There came a cut-off point in all our conversations whereby the detail of his work was strictly taboo.

That may have been his ambition, the ultimate in an intelligence mission, but realistically it is unlikely he could have pulled it off, and in any event he would never have been given permission from his superiors, unless of course he was working for MI5 or MI6 as well – 'if he was, and that's always a possibility, it would have been MI5 but I have no evidence of it,' one of his senior officers admitted to me.

Regardless of any higher ambitions, Nairac did pull off some creditable intelligence achievements in those difficult months of 1974. He was noting everything around him – the people, the mood of the locals, the swing of their general conversation, picking up the pub gossip and eavesdropping on the whispers of any forthcoming action.

He instilled sufficient confidence among those around him to let them drop their guard and allow him to perform an interrogation of his subject without them knowing. He could pick up valuable intelligence, discover suitable cover for other Army intelligence operatives who might be moved in as spies and even pick up vibes that could lead to a man being turned into an informer.

To reach even the point of opening a conversation with a fellow drinker at the bar in such areas, Nairac had to draw on a capability that one of his tutors at Ampleforth had identified years earlier – of being able to act out a part, slightly disguise himself, adopt an Irish accent and dissolve his real self into his imagined character in such as manner as – like a true actor – to suspend disbelief. The role-player thus became accepted as the character he was portraying. He must have been successful; otherwise he would have been killed in those opening months of 1974.

The big question that remained, however, was why did Nairac get himself noticed like this? As just a liaison officer, he was going way beyond his brief and into a much more specialist area. Gerald Seymour's Harry (in his best-selling novel *Harry's Game*), so realistic as to be treated as a real-life character, went undercover, alone, specifically to glean intelligence of a particular terrorist act. The book was published in 1976, nine months before Nairac went missing. The similarities were uncanny. Few in Northern Ireland knew of Harry's existence, which is why he was inadvertently killed by his own side. Thus when Nairac was killed, certain comparisons would be drawn, not least of which was the conspiracy theory that he too was accidentally compromised by his own side.

For Nairac to take on that kind of role for multi-directional intelligence gathering seemed, on the face of it, beyond comprehension. But then, as 14 Int opened up for serious business, nothing was impossible, however unrealistic, unbelievable or unachievable it seemed.

# 6

## AGENTS ABROAD!

The partnership of Robert Nairac and Julian 'Tony' Ball, according to Army sources, produced some 'spectacular' results during some 'fine' intelligence work against the IRA. They joined forces in 1974 in the fictitiously named survey troop that Ball commanded during the period he was on detachment from the SAS. They worked together for almost nine months and met up again later, in 1976, when Ball returned to Northern Ireland with his regiment. In the course of their time together, Ball and Nairac were involved in some controversial activities. Subsequent claims of their association with notorious sectarian murders in an era that saw many unattributed killings continue to arise. But there are two sides to every story in Ulster.

Tony Ball, one of his then senior SAS officers, Colonel G, told me:

> He was sharp, aggressive and streetwise. He was very tough and hard, but a super chap to be with and completely admired by most of his contemporaries. He had come up through the ranks of 22 SAS and obtained a commission with the King's Own Scottish Borderers in 1970. He was awarded an MC with them and won an MBE for his intelligence work in Northern Ireland. He was with 22 SAS for many years, having previously served in the Parachute Regiment.

After his death in 1981, his obituary in the SAS magazine *Mars and Minerva*, as ever, provided little illumination upon his career but none the less contained some significant pointers:

In a very short space of time, he established an unequalled reputation for being an original thinker, an outstanding leader and tactician ... he became one of the Service's foremost authorities in Northern Ireland. The personal contribution which he made to the fight against terrorism and his cool gallantry resulted in him being awarded a number of unique decorations for the campaign. He was also recommended for several others.

The obituary went on to say that Tony Ball was as compassionate as he was ruthless, and he showed a great sympathy for the problems of the people of Northern Ireland.

His loping figure will be missed by many different areas of Belfast as well as in more familiar places ... he made a considerable and long-lasting impact, both on operations and training. Always restless, he elected to leave the Army and had just started to establish himself as a tough, uncompromising commanding officer of the Sultan of Oman's Special Forces when he was tragically killed in a road-traffic accident. He was only thirty-eight.

G described him as a 'very upfront guy' who could put senior officers' noses out of joint very easily, whereas Robert Nairac could smooth things over and keep them all happy. 'They made a very good pair,' said G.

Other sources also confirmed that the activities of Ball and Nairac were 'outstanding' in the war against the IRA, at a time when a lot of 'silliness' was going on in various areas, a result of the very crowded intelligence arena in Belfast. Apart from the newly created 14 Int, there was 12 Intelligence Company, staffed by 210 people, which was attached to the Intelligence Corps mainly for data processing, report writing and cross-checking, although some of its officers were also involved in agent handling. Then there was the Army's Special Military Intelligence Unit (Northern Ireland) (SMIU) which had a staff of around fifty officers and NCOs who formed the main plank of intelligence transfer between the Army chiefs and the RUC Special Branch, servicing all brigades. The growing antagonism between the two organizations was no better, apparently, than relationships between the Special Branch and SMIU. Next, there was MI6, who had a relatively low active involvement through its sole representative, a dour Scot in a tam-o'-shanter named Craig Smellie. His reports were linked to those of its operatives in the Republic and used as ammunition for MI6 in London as they attempted to influence ministers' thinking on the emergence of a possible ceasefire. MI6 influence took a severe jolt, however, from allegations in a Dublin court that it had encouraged two agents, Keith and Kenneth Littlejohn, to rob banks in the Republic of Ireland.

MI5 was altogether stronger on the ground in the north; it ran its substantial bank of agents, and steadfastly and resolutely opposed any attempts to lure the IRA into a ceasefire. The rivalry between the two groups, however, continued well into the late 1970s, by which time MI5 was generally recognized to have achieved supremacy.

All these intelligence groups were to be found represented in a dingy intelligence corridor at the Army's headquarters in Lisburn, and elsewhere. Though supposedly on the same side, intense rivalry for the 'limited human sources' available to act as agents and spies also developed. A new staff appointment of Director and Coordinator of Intelligence found his job virtually impossible because of the feuding by the resident intelligence groups.

The Dirty War had a side element of internal strife, which did not preclude attempts to nobble each other's operations. 14 Int came into the arena partly to offset the Army's problems in this direction, and to give it an exclusive line of intelligence that relied on few other sources except its own. However, often it would be dealing with informers and agents who, not necessarily known to the Army, were also working for others and, in some cases, reporting the whole scenario back to the IRA.

In the mid-1970s, the undercover teams of both the military and the RUC were highly protective of the detail of their work and few discernible facts have ever emerged of specific operations.

Robert Nairac and Tony Ball were, quite clearly, key operatives in the emergence of 14 Int, whose arrival – quite apart from the intelligence rivalry in Belfast – was also set against an incredible backdrop of shambolic government in both Westminster and Stormont, assisted in its state of chaos by a rampant dirty-tricks department operating on both sides of the Irish Sea. All around Robert Nairac and the rest of the burgeoning intelligence units, 1974 was shaping up to be a big year in every respect.

The Sunningdale Agreement, which sanctioned a power-sharing executive to run Northern Ireland, was billed as the most dramatic moment in Irish history. Almost immediately, it was reduced to total disarray, with deep divisions within the Protestant movement refusing to share power with Catholics who were, said Protestant hard-liner Dr Ian Paisley, really the IRA. Police were called to forcibly remove him from a meeting of the new council.

On 4 February, eleven people were killed on the mainland when a bus carrying servicemen and their families was blown up on the M62 near Bradford. Britain as a whole was on the rack and reduced to a three-day working week through the miners' strike. Edward Heath called a general election and lost. Harold Wilson's Labour government was installed with an unworkable majority, which ensured a weak and timid administration until a second election was called later in the year. The new government wasn't much better.

The Sunningdale Agreement, the flawed forerunner of the 1998 Good Friday Peace Agreement, finally collapsed in the wake of the loyalist-inspired Ulster Workers' strike, which brought the province to a standstill in May. The hawks in the upper echelons of the British Army and MI5 were said to be delighted that the power-sharing executive had foundered, because administration of the province would be transferred back to Westminster, thus alleviating the tedium of having to deal with the sectarian demands of Northern Ireland politics.

Thirteen years later, the *Sunday Times* published a report by Barrie Penrose on the case of an Englishman married to an Irish Protestant. The report said he was recruited as an agent for MI5, infiltrated the UDA (which was far easier to do than the IRA) and became a military commander. From this trusted position, he was asked by his MI5 case officer to help promote the Ulster strike. The story had some kind of confirmation when the government's D-Notice committee asked the *Sunday Times* not to reveal the man's name and present whereabouts.

On the fourth day of the strike, the Republic of Ireland also suffered its worst day since the Troubles began when twenty-eight people were killed by a car-bomb explosion during the rush hour in Dublin. Five died in a similar attack in Monaghan, the worst bombing outrage in the modern history of Ireland; it would remain at the top of the league table of carnage until the Omagh car bomb in August 1998. Both cars used in the attack came from the north and the bombs were widely believed to have been the work of a joint force of UVF and UDA paramilitaries. A loyalists' press spokesman issued a statement that they were 'very pleased' about the bombings. There were strong rumours of clandestine assistance from the security forces. Later allegations that Ball and Nairac were involved in the pre-planning of these attacks in conjunction with an officer of the RUC Special Branch have, naturally enough, never been confirmed by UDA, the UVF or any other sources for that matter, though strongly suggested by many. There is, however, not a scrap of evidence to confirm it.

But, without doubt, the Dirty War was about to get much dirtier. The Provisionals never had much faith in the Sunningdale

Agreement and had already stepped up their efforts to protect Catholic communities from the loyalist terrorist gangs. They had also been concentrating on improving their own intelligence system, more or less at the same time as 14 Int came into being, and this included a remarkable plan to bug the Army headquarters in Lisburn. According to Martin Dillon, who revealed it, this was achieved with the aid of equipment acquired from within the HQ, which unscrambled the Army telephone conversations. The tapping of the Army phones continued only long enough for the PIRA to discover that Military Intelligence had a highly placed source in their midst, and it was he who tipped off the Army about the bugging operations.

The source also pointed his handlers to some major IRA properties. It is impossible to place Robert Nairac in this intelligence coup, but given that he was working in one of the heartlands of the Provisionals' command structure it is more than likely that he was involved at some point along the line. It is known, for example, that he and Ball were frequently in Belfast around crucial stages of this story.

On 10 May 1974, the RUC Special Branch and Army intelligence raided an IRA house in Myrtlefield Park, where some of the vital tape recordings of the bugged conversations were stored. Two men were arrested and the Army took possession of four rifles, a sub-machine gun, two pistols, 3,600 rounds of ammunition, bomb-making equipment and detonators. Far more interesting to the Army, and subsequently to MI5, was a cache of documents found at the house. These were to become known as the IRA's Doomsday Plan, a hypothetical scenario in which it documented an ambitious plan to take over the city of Belfast in the event of increased attacks from loyalists, especially during the Ulster Workers' strike, which was accompanied by a great deal of brutal intimidation in the Catholic areas.

Maps of the city were marked with all important buildings, which were coded into offensive and defensive targets. The plans were taken to the fullest degree and included the setting-up of the IRA's own radio station through which broadcasts would be made to the people of the city. Even press statements were drawn up explaining the necessity for harsh measures.

The Army made much of its discovery of the Doomsday Plan, and the extent to which the IRA was prepared to go in order to achieve its ends. It did not, however, mention that also recovered from the house were tape recordings of bugged Army HQ phone calls, although not all of them were stored there. Nor did it mention that it had also uncovered a large arms' dump, packed with explosives of all kinds. The Army secretly took away the explosives and kept the place under surveillance. The IRA, now aware that it had an agent in its midst, could not go near the arms' store to check whether or not it had been discovered, and it was abandoned.

The agent within the IRA ranks remained undiscovered for another eighteen months before he was finally unmasked by a long process of elimination. The IRA trapped him into confessing. He was put before a court martial, found guilty and shot. He was buried in a secret grave.

It was easy to get a conviction in Northern Ireland, according to a hard-hitting Amnesty International Report in 1978. It complained that many suspects simply confessed under duress. The same system sent the Birmingham Six to prison for bombings they did not commit. Young men and women picked up off the streets for possible IRA-linked offences were placed under enormous pressure to become informers. Some agreed to cooperate, even though the risk of imprisonment was often outweighed by the knowledge of certain death if they were discovered.

In May 1974 two young men who perhaps did not fully appreciate that prospect were hauled in for questioning by the RUC over the killing of two policemen. A liaison officer (probably Nairac) of 14 Int learned of their presence through his Special Branch contacts. The two were soon to become the central figures of a counter-insurgency operation that ultimately cost their lives.

The two – Vincent Heatherington, aged eighteen, and Myles Vincent McGrogan, nineteen – were arrested separately, along with three other youths, the day following the murders of the policemen. The other three were released without charge; Heatherington and McGrogan were remanded in custody on a number of charges. They had both been in trouble before when they were members of the IRA's youth brigade – they had been tarred and feathered by the IRA for theft from their neighbours.

The two youths were sent on remand to the Crumlin Road gaol where, as a matter of course, they were offered the choice of which section of the prison they wished to be housed in – either the Republican section or that for non-political crimes. They chose the IRA wing and were locked up with terrorists and bombers. The IRA officer commanding the IRA prisoners apparently became suspicious and sent for word from the outside as to the history of the two young men.

In due course, a message came back: Heatherington and McGrogan were not IRA. Furthermore, they had not killed the two policemen. Those murders had been carried out by members of the 1st Battalion of the PIRA and 'those kids had nothing whatsoever to do with it'. They were both brought before the IRA's commanding officer for interrogation. Heatherington held out for while and then broke down and admitted that they did not shoot the policemen. He said that he had been told to enter the IRA wing of the prison by the British plain-clothes soldiers and there were probably others inside who had done the same.

He claimed that after their arrest, he and McGrogan had been taken by two RUC officers to a football match, where a gun was produced and handed to Heatherington. He was told to fire over the crowd. He refused and one of the policemen, wearing gloves, took the gun, fired the shot and told the two youths they now had the evidence of a gun with fingerprints upon it; they would be convicted of murder. Heatherington claimed that they were then taken to a British Army base, where they agreed to cooperate and were given instruction by British-accented operatives. They were shipped out to 'somewhere in England' for continued tuition, and were given money, alcohol and the services of prostitutes.

At this stage, the IRA's interrogation of Heatherington was halted by an incident elsewhere in the prison. A warder had been attacked and the governor ordered that all prisoners should be locked in their cells pending an investigation. The following day, when the prisoners were let out once more, Heatherington and McGrogan were nowhere to be found. They had been moved out of the Crumlin Road gaol and did not surface again until February 1975, when they were brought to trial on the charges connected with the shooting of the policemen.

After a long-running case, they were acquitted and disappeared once again. They were both eventually tracked down by the IRA and shot.

The discovery of their involvement with British intelligence had caused mayhem in the prison community. The IRA ordered a check by all its commanding officers in both the prisons and its organizations on the outside for possible agents working for Army intelligence. A witch-hunt developed. Suspected agents were rooted out and subjected to brutal interrogation, in one case using piano wire and an electric current, which forced some to admit to being turncoats when in fact they were not. The IRA were not averse to using even more horrific methods of interrogation than the Republican movement had complained of among the security forces.

As a direct result of these interrogations, a killing spree broke out and lasted for a year or more. Those murdered by their own side included a number of prominent Belfast Republicans, all on the basis of the evidence drawn initially from the prison interrogations.

It was only much later that the Provisionals learned that they had been set up by 14 Int (although they were still unaware of which intelligence group it was). Heatherington had not, as it appeared, broken under pressure during the questioning but in fact had been 'programmed' during his time in England to release his information to his IRA interrogators in prison – thus feeding them with information that was to tear them apart from within. And it worked. A PIRA source admitted to Martin Dillon: 'We realized by then that we were had ... it was very much in the mould of the MRF operations, only better planned and, it must be said, brilliantly executed. It created paranoia in the ranks and the IRA found it difficult to admit that British Military Intelligence was so good. It almost destroyed us.'

The Heatherington/McGrogan episode, however, seriously undermined the intelligence system of using forced agents, not least because they were among the many who were discovered and executed by the IRA. In the mid-1970s, the equally dubious practice of paying informers large sums of money to testify against terrorist suspects, loyalist and IRA, gradually began to replace the carrot and stick. The plan to use paid informers, which bore similarities to the long-running American witness protection programme and that adopted by anti-Mafia forces in Italy in the 1980s, was soon to become an integral part of RUC and Military Intelligence policy. From these tenuous beginnings, the supergrass phenomenon emerged and by the early 1980s, more than 300 suspects had been thrown into prison on the word of the highly paid informers.

The police preferred to describe the system as the 'converted terrorist process' – another variation on the theme brought to Northern Ireland by Frank Kitson – and although leading judicial figures severely criticized the system as being against the principles of British justice and encouraging the telling of lies for money, it continued with the support of politicians in Westminster at a cost of millions of pounds, funded by the Home Office. Justice, in Northern Ireland, could be moulded to suit the needs of those in charge of its security and provide whatever evidence the police required for a conviction.

Potential supergrasses were offered a new life and identity in the country of their choice, education for their children, a good pension and the services of a speech therapist to diminish their Irish accents. By 1986, twenty supergrasses were living on the mainland because no other country would take them. Some left under their own steam, with the benefit of a one-off bounty, and fled to America.

In March 1987, the *Belfast News Letter* published a report that two loyalist paramilitary leaders who had been working with British agents in the mid-1970s were living safely with their families in Scotland. One of them, it was claimed, was connected with the 1974 Dublin bombings and both were involved in murders of Catholics in what became known in that era as 'the triangle of death' in County Armagh.

This, in turn, linked back to allegations made by Captain Fred Holroyd, a former intelligence officer with the British Army – and, it must be said at the outset, a man with a grudge. He had earlier produced a list of six people who he claimed were involved in plotting the Dublin bombings. He sent their names in a written statement to the RUC. The content opened up a can of worms that is still wriggling around years later. He said:

To my certain knowledge Sgt X of the RUC Special Branch was controlling key members of the UDA/UVF. These included the nominal UDA commander for County Armagh and the most active terrorists [three names] ... I can also state from first-hand knowledge Sgt X abused his authority by protecting these people from prosecution. During the years mentioned Sgt X worked closely on operations with a special unit of SAS-trained soldiers, the second in command of which was Robert Nairac, who personally related to me his participation in the murder of John Francis Green. The weapons used in the Miami Showband murders of military origin were obtained from a cache of weapons whose location I revealed to Sgt X ... at least two members of the Portadown UDA have identified Nairac as being with them on planning sessions for terrorist outrages ostensibly initiated by [two names]. The SAS unit was controlled through SAS ordinary staff officers attached to HQ3 Infantry Brigade based at Lurgan and SAS officers based at Lisburn. There were two similar units in Belfast ... and Ballykelly. Nairac's unit posed as an SAS survey team and the Ballykelly unit as a signals squad.

On one occasion while on duty with Sgt X during a surveillance operation, he confided in me that the Portadown UDA/UVF were responsible for car bombs that detonated in Dublin and Monaghan.

John Francis Green, mentioned in the statement, was an Officer Commanding, 2nd Battalion, North Armagh Provisional IRA. He was assassinated at the time of the IRA ceasefire that came into effect at the end of 1974 (as described in the next chapter). He was just one of a number killed over an eighteen-month period between early 1974 and the autumn of 1975. Several of the killings were those executed by their own side, the Provisional IRA, in reprisal for allegedly working for British intelligence or the RUC. Others have been put at the door of loyalist terrorist gangs drawn from the UDA and the UVF and, some would have it, linked in some way to Robert Nairac.

The story will be familiar to all who have followed the repeated allegations made by Holroyd, regarded as a good officer who had spent his life in the military. Educated at a Yorkshire grammar school, he enlisted as a lowly private and was commissioned three years later in the Royal Corps of Transport. He volunteered for service as a Military Intelligence officer and, like Nairac, attended the Joint Services School of Intelligence at Ashford. He was then sent to Northern Ireland, attached to the Special Military Intelligence Unit, which provided intelligence officers to act in liaison with the RUC.

These intelligence officers were in contact with the RUC Special Branch and the Army's intelligence corridor at Lisburn. Holroyd's duties included the recruitment and the handling of sources. The intelligence gleaned was generally passed through Special Branch channels down through the intelligence operatives of 3 Brigade.

Holroyd was also in regular contact with Craig Smellie, the MI6 representative in Northern Ireland at the time, who also ran cross-border operations and was in constant battle with MI5, who he claimed wanted to maintain their own superiority and influence in Northern Ireland.

Holroyd's claims became a subject of much scrutiny in the 1980s and beyond, by a variety of interested parties ranging from some of Britain's most respected investigative journalists to rebel MPs looking for a cause, who all latched on to them. But it should be noted that Holroyd's account was made some years after he had left the British Army in disgust at his personal treatment. He was moved out of his post in Northern Ireland intelligence because of what the Army described as mental strain, dispatched to hospital for psychiatric evaluation and subsequently offered a less demanding role on the mainland. The Army said he could no longer cope with the strife of Northern Ireland. His life was in fact turned upside down. One who worked with him at the time told me:

Fred was a basically a nice guy, well respected and very hard-working. Like anyone close to the hub in those days, he was under very heavy pressure. He also had some terrible family problems during his time in Northern Ireland. He and his wife weren't getting along too well, largely I believe because of the unsociable hours and the nature of Fred's work, always looking over his shoulder. As anyone in undercover work knows, you are never able to talk about it other than to your colleagues. Outside the work environment, when you're on your own or with the family, it is always there in your mind and you have to be careful that it does not take you over. Just think about it – every time you went out you had to check your car for a bomb. Part of our training, of course, was to help us to deal with that – and much more emphasis was placed upon that aspect in later years – but few of us who were married escaped that without some scars. There were some rare old shouting matches in Fred's house and lawyers were consulted. The work situation was aggravated by other personal problems. His mother had died of cancer and then his father came to stay with them – he was also dying from cancer.

All these things were running alongside Fred's work, which in some respects was the forerunner to Robert Nairac's. It involved dangerous contacts and undercover manoeuvres, running agents and, yes, the dirty tricks he has spoken of; I don't see how anyone could not be feeling out of sorts with all that going on. He insisted, and always has, that he was doing the job he was paid to do and more. Frankly, I would have jacked it in voluntarily. Life's too short – and even shorter in that situation. Unless you were sharp and had your ears and eyes wide open to everything that was going, you were an easy target. Dead meat, in fact. Fred, I reckon, was definitely feeling the strain.

Holroyd did have a glowing reference from RUC Assistant Chief Constable Charles Rogers, later to become head of the RUC's anti-terrorist campaign, who described him as a man of 'unquestionable loyalty, outstanding courage and a devotion to duty that one rarely finds today'.

Bitter over his treatment and the slur of mental instability on his record, he subsequently left the Army and moved to Rhodesia, served for a while in the Army there, returned to a succession of jobs in Britain and was living in some poverty with his then unpublished book, *War Without Honour*, under his arm when the media began to take an interest in his claims in 1984.

As he fought for recognition of what he believed was rough justice by his former employers, he had named numerous people in the Northern Ireland hierarchy as being part of a conspiracy against him. It was also Holroyd who first brought forward the story that was to tarnish Nairac's reputation. In a long list of dirty tricks and other acts of a criminal nature by the intelligence services and Army personnel the main thrust of his allegations was that Nairac boasted to him that he had organized and carried out the assassination of the IRA captain, John Francis Green.

His story was first given a public airing in a Channel 4 documentary, *Diverse Reports*, by Christopher Hird and Duncan Campbell. The programme was linked to a series of articles by Campbell published in the *New Statesman* in May 1984. The journalist, well known for his thoroughness, spent six months conducting his own investigations and he was able to confirm many of Holroyd's claims. He also discovered that the RUC had completed a 900-page report of its own investigations of the Green incident, and other claims Holroyd had made to them. It remained unpublished. By then, however, Nairac himself had been murdered, Tony Ball, Nairac's unit commander, had been killed and Craig Smellie, who left Northern Ireland in 1975 and who passed on to Holroyd some of his agents, had also died. In fact, the truth was more complex than Holroyd seemed to be aware.

# 7

## ACCUSED!

The question is still being asked: did Tony Ball and Robert Nairac track IRA captain John Green to a remote farmhouse on the other side of the Irish border and then, waiting until he was alone, kick in the door and empty the contents of two pistols into his body?

The saga of John Francis Green had its beginnings towards the end of 1974, when sectarian killings of Catholics and Republicans, in the so-called 'triangle of death' close to the border, increased taking the year's overall death toll to 216. Loyalists were running with the larger total 'hits', and a succession of underground pamphlets and other literature appearing on the streets of Belfast repeatedly named names, accusing members of the UDA and the UVF as the killers – thirteen names in all repeatedly appearing. There were pointed references linking one UDA commander to a certain officer of the RUC Special Branch and even then rumours were rife that British Army special intelligence groups were clandestinely backing loyalists by encouraging members of the UDR to infiltrate the terror gangs. Encouragement was not always necessary. Many of them were already members and had been when they volunteered for the UDR.

The IRA, in the mean time, had been badly hit in the previous months, more than anyone outside the organization knew, by the three-pronged attack of the RUC, the British Army with its Special Duties squads, and loyalist murder gangs. The H-Blocks of the Maze prison were being filled by its young volunteers, gathered up in ever increasing numbers by the security forces and the police. That policy in itself was actually backfiring, because the packed prisons were training grounds, plain and simple, for short-stay prisoners to continue the war upon their release.

The intelligence units, and the troop under the command of Tony Ball with Robert Nairac at his right hand, had inflicted real damage in South Armagh. There were continuing allegations of a shoot-to-kill policy among the security forces, which included the RUC, and they were investigated at various times. None of these inquiries was more controversial than that which ultimately became the nadir of John Stalker, the former Deputy Chief Constable of Greater Manchester. He focused on the shooting of six terrorists in a farm shed. From the outset, his investigation was strongly opposed by undercover operatives of the RUC and MI5. He faced obstructions at every turn, was removed from the inquiry at a critical stage and then suffered a smear campaign aimed at discrediting him and his years of unblemished police service. The hands of MI5 and the RUC could not have been far away.

A spectacular response by the IRA was already gathering momentum for a show of force on the mainland to demonstrate that the IRA was alive and exceedingly dangerous. Two teams of bombers had arrived in England by various routes in the spring to await orders. They settled into lodgings and flats, assuming the lifestyle of ordinary working people, but all the time surveying and planning. Explosives and detonators, shipped into the south of Ireland courtesy of the PLO, Libya and ETA, the Spanish terrorist organization, were moved piecemeal on ferries across the Irish Sea and hidden close to the area of operations.

No prior warnings were to be given. The intent was maximum damage and maximum loss of life. On 5 October 1974, the first team moved to their target zone. The sites selected were two public houses in Guildford, Surrey, frequented by soldiers, and the bombs exploded at the busiest time of the day. Five people, two of them soldiers, were killed and fifty-four injured. One month later, the same team hit a public house close to the Woolwich Barracks, killing two and injuring twenty-five.

On 21 November the second team, led by a 26-year-old IRA captain born in Dublin, was activated. They were to attack

Birmingham, placing bombs at the Tavern on the Town and the Mulberry Bush public houses. Warnings were telephoned to the local newspapers but exact details of the bombers' targets were not given. The devices exploded simultaneously, killing 21 people and wounding 160.

The horrific scenes shown on television shocked Britain into abject revulsion and generated a massive anti-Irish reaction. In their haste to show due punishment for the horrendous crimes, the police quickly arrested the Guildford Four (who remained in prison until 1989) and the Birmingham Six (released in 1991), all of whom were wrongly convicted. The Birmingham bombers had, in fact, travelled individually to the Irish Republic not long after completing their task. The London team remained, preparing to bomb the London underground during the peak of the pre-Christmas rush.

The scale of the IRA carnage, and the threat of more to follow, moved the Wilson government to a state of virtual panic. MP Tony Benn said they should get the troops out of Northern Ireland as soon as it was feasible. Northern Ireland Secretary Merlyn Rees authorized Michael Oatley, an MI6 officer, to hold secret exploratory talks with the terrorists, and intermediaries fixed up a meeting with the IRA. A peace deal was supported and in part brokered by MI6, whose policy towards the IRA had remained constant. Their view continued to be that by drawing it into the political arena, recognizing Sinn Fein and making concessions such as the ending of internment and a commitment for at least a reduction of troops, the need for violence would be terminated, leading to the demise of the IRA.

MI5 and the Army were not keen. MI5 claimed to have far more experience on the ground in Ulster than MI6 and the support of many of the Army's top brass. A ceasefire, they continued to caution, would simply give the IRA the opportunity to recover, regroup and replenish, ready for a new wave of violence. Could there be any better evidence, they argued, than the Doomsday documents, recovered from the flat in Belfast earlier in the year? They failed to explain to Wilson that the documents were of a hypothetical nature.

Wilson wasn't very friendly with MI5 at the time. His house had been broken into in October, and a batch of personal papers and tax documents stolen. He blamed a right-wing faction of the security service. Some of his friends said he was imagining things. Peter Wright, the former MI5 officer who came to fame with his book *Spycatcher*, said he wasn't and so did one Colin Wallace, whom we shall meet shortly, who wrote to Wilson warning him of a conspiracy emanating from Ulster.

MI6 felt vindicated, however, when moves to open lines of communication precipitated a giant step towards a ceasefire. A group of leading Protestant churchmen made contact with the IRA and implored them to call a truce. This they duly agreed to do a few days later. All hostilities would cease at midnight on 22 December. A bomb attack on the London underground was called off but as a last defiant demonstration of IRA capability, the London bombers who had blown up the pubs in Guildford and Woolwich tossed a bomb on to the balcony of Edward Heath's London home. The young bloods of the PIRA, like Martin McGuinness and Gerry Adams, were still wary of British intentions. And, as McGuinness said, there was nothing like a good operation to encourage local volunteers to the cause.

Even so, the ceasefire took hold and negotiations between Foreign Office officials and representatives of the IRA began almost immediately, attempting to turn the truce into a more lasting peace. There was already talk of extending the ceasefire into a permanent arrangement and the Army was ordered to put on a show of goodwill by halting house searches and other harassing activities.

In the middle of these negotiations, John Francis Green, officer commanding the 2nd Battalion, North Armagh Provisionals, was assassinated. Green was something of a local hero in the border regions. A jolly 28-year-old, married with three children living at Lurgan, he was, according to his brother Gerry, a priest, a clean-living man who did not drink and took strong action against crime in his neighbourhood. He had been arrested in December 1971 and interned on suspicion of IRA membership, but he had escaped when brother Gerry came to visit. The priest was tied to a chair and Green made his escape in his brother's clothes. He had been dodging the RUC and the military ever since, and there were plenty of neighbours in Lurgan who were willing to whisk him away when the searchers came.

Robert Nairac and his 14 Int unit had been attempting to keep tabs on Green for months. They knew from their own intelligence that he had been largely responsible for cleaning up the PIRA organization in South Armagh. At the time, Green had just completed an inquiry into the Provos' internal affairs and had typed up a report concerning the possible misuse of funds. It was found in his car. He was apparently upset by having to go through these procedures because the people who were being accused of taking the cash were close to him.

Green was at home for Christmas, joined by a number of other Provos who had been released from internment as part of Harold Wilson's concession to the ceasefire. According to Green's wife, the Army called at their house over the Christmas period and asked if her husband was at home. They did not, however, push inside as they would have done at other times. Green decided to return to the other side of the border soon after Christmas, staying as he often did with friends in Castleblayney. There were a number of safe houses in which to billet, including a family with ten children who had a very large home. Green spent his time working on his report on the IRA cash and visiting friends. There was no pattern to his movements, and visits to other homes were generally casual and not previously arranged.

He was obviously under surveillance by someone for some time. A white Mercedes or Audi was spotted twice with three men inside. Green brushed it aside but was none the less cautious about his movements. The houses in which he was staying were, curiously enough, close to a belt of Protestant country which stretched from Castleblayney to the border and beyond towards the community of Newtownhamilton. In that particular region, there were more Protestants than Catholics and there were no outward signs of animosity between them.

On the night of 10 January 1975, he left the little town of Castleblayney and drove off in his green Volkswagen towards Mullyash Mountain to visit his friend Gerry Carville, who lived in a remote farmhouse. The weather was cold and wet with a strong wind blowing across the barren countryside. Green went to his friend's house, and sat and chatted over a cup of tea. Carville left around seven, as he had been doing every night for the past month, to travel to a neighbour's farm to do the milking. As he returned an hour or so later, he could see the lights of his own farmhouse blazing. At the house, he saw the door virtually hanging off its hinges. Inside, Green was lying full out with his back to the floor – 'well shot'.

The IRA put on a big show for Green's funeral. On 12 January, 3,000 people lined the route for the removal of his body from the local morgue for the journey home to Lurgan. Relays of pall bearers carried the coffin through the streets, accompanied by a guard of honour provided by the PIRA, in their dark glasses and black suits, marching to the beat of a single drummer. The president of Sinn Fein addressed the crowds and said they should not have revenge in their hearts. John Francis Green was killed at a time of peace, which showed there were people in Northern Ireland who did not want it.

A similar crowd awaited the funeral cortège in Lurgan. Even RUC officers saluted as it passed. Green was buried with full IRA military honours, his coffin draped in the tricolour.

The shooting of John Francis Green passed into history. To the outside world it was just another sectarian killing; to the British public, freshly horrified by the IRA's bombing campaign, his murder merely rid the nation of another vicious thug – and why didn't they kill them all? To the Green family, it deprived them of a loving father and husband. The gamut of emotions experienced in Northern Ireland, repeated every day of every year since the Troubles began, were no better summed up than by this particular death. And like most before and after him, his name is remembered only by his family and the *Republican News*, which pays tribute to those who died 'on this day'.

Or at least, that would have been the case but for the persistence of Captain Fred Holroyd in bringing his own gripe against the British Army and the Ministry of Defence into the public arena. Green's killing, along with his other revelations, became the hobbyhorse that carried Holroyd to notoriety and, at the same time, blackened the reputation of a George Cross hero. Holroyd was to repeat the story often, and has never departed from the original version he told to Duncan Campbell.

He said that not long after Green had been assassinated, Nairac called on him at the Army's Mahon Road camp in Portadown. It was a routine visit in which intelligence matters were usually discussed, leads noted and gossip exchanged.

Towards the end of the conversation, when an SAS sergeant major who had been in the room left, Nairac boasted that it was he who had killed John Francis Green. Holroyd said Nairac must have noticed the look of disbelief on his face because he produced a Polaroid photograph of Green, taken after the shooting. It showed the corpse from the waist up, lying flat on his back and covered with blood.

According to Holroyd, Nairac said he and two other men had jumped the border to kill Green. They had had him under observation for some time and noticed that he occasionally visited the farmer Gerry Carville. They also noted that Carville left the house at a particular time each evening. They followed Green to the farmhouse, waited for Carville to leave, and then, while the third man waited in the car with the engine ticking over, Nairac and his comrade kicked down the door and shot Green. Holroyd's account does not give room for any other possibility than the fact that Nairac did the shooting or, at the very least, was present when it happened. According to Martin Dillon, he also mentioned privately that Tony Ball was the 'other man' who went to the house with him.

The sequence of events described by Holroyd was virtually as it happened and for many years journalists anguished over his claims, some supportive and others attempting to demolish them. There were a couple of instantly recognizable errors in the account published by Duncan Campbell. He wrote that Nairac was a member of the SAS, although 'new to it'. He said that he first arrived in Northern Ireland early in 1974, with a troop of about thirty men from the SAS regiment's Hereford base at a time when the Government was denying that the SAS was in Northern Ireland at all. He added that Nairac left the SAS in 1976, although remained in Northern Ireland as an intelligence liaison officer.

It is perhaps being pedantic to mention again that Nairac was never SAS and up to that time, 1975, he had never been attached to an SAS unit. The SAS men were there individually on secondment. And, of course, it was not Nairac's first visit to Northern Ireland; he came there in 1973, after which he volunteered for special duties. He did not leave the SAS in 1976, as he was never in it, and in fact that was the year he became attached to the first SAS unit to arrive in Northern Ireland as 3 Brigade liaison officer.

Campbell also drew his readers' attention to SAS operations: according to the official ('Restricted') manual on Counter-Revolutionary Operations, the SAS's tasks included the 'infiltration of ... assassination parties ... into insurgent held areas' and 'liaison with ... forces operating against the common enemy'. The training manuals and the general *modus operandi* of the SAS were indeed utilized in the training of the Special Duties operatives, as we have seen, and the infiltration of and liaison with forces operating against the common enemy (i.e. the IRA) was not only acceptable, it was widely practised.

This aspect of Duncan Campbell's series was overlooked by many other journalists, who preferred to concentrate on the more tangible evidence in Holroyd's account – the Polaroid photograph that he said Nairac gave to him, allegedly taken immediately after the shooting.

The two (the tasks defined by the manual and the Polaroid) are linked, in that if Nairac possessed a photograph taken immediately after the shooting, then either he was present when it happened or he was given the photograph by the killers. The killers, therefore, were either himself and his unit or a loyalist gang who brought back the photograph as proof of the deed done against the common enemy. If that was the case, Nairac could be shown to have been directly involved in the killing or at arm's length from it.

In the somewhat frantic debate that followed in the media after Holroyd's revelations, there was some heavy support for the RUC's version of events (the preferred version of the Army) surrounding the Green killing, which asserted:

- that Nairac was a braggart (and, presumably a liar);
- that his claim to have killed Green was nonsense, because the act was performed by a deranged Protestant named Elliott (now dead) who believed his brother had been killed by the IRA on Carville's farm and shot Green in mistake for Carville;
- that the Polaroid photograph was taken by the Irish police the following morning (the RUC had a copy and said it was the same as the one that an RUC detective claimed to have given Holroyd, who was a collector of such items and kept a scrapbook noting times, dates and places).

The debate developed into something of a row in print between Duncan Campbell and David McKittrick, a journalist formerly with the *Irish Times* and by then with *The Independent*. McKittrick, an acknowledged expert on loyalist terrorism, more or less followed the RUC line over the source of the photograph, thus discrediting Holroyd's version of events. He revealed also that the RUC had taken possession of the photograph in question, which they obtained from Holroyd's wife, then living in Zimbabwe. McKittrick said he had seen a copy of the photograph and it did not match Holroyd's description of it. Campbell countered that he had established that the Irish police did not possess a Polaroid camera at the time – and so, in effect, the RUC was lying.

To pursue the argument about the photograph (or photographs) is futile now, because at the end of the day, it is a case of who does one believe – Holroyd or the RUC, or neither? What can be established is that there is every reason to believe that Nairac would have a copy of the photograph. He collected 'scene-of-the-crime' pictures as well as masses of other photographic evidence, partly out of personal interest and partly for his work. Much of it was found when his room was cleared after his death. We can conjecture that he had obtained a copy of the photograph and in the conversation, Holroyd perhaps misinterpreted what Nairac had actually said. Holroyd denies that, although he was shown to be hazy on other detail relating to the same period.

For instance, he said that when MI5 won the battle for supremacy with MI6 and took over their agents, ten first-class sources were given a 'head job by the IRA' within a week and the intelligence officer who handled them committed suicide. There are no records of ten such deaths in such a short space of time and even the IRA scoffed at the possibility. As to the soldier who shot himself, the reason was nothing quite so dramatic. In truth, he was stressed out, having just broken up with his girlfriend.

In any event, the source of the photograph proves nothing. It is circumstantial evidence, at best.

The solution to the Green/Nairac affair lies in the deeper investigation of whether or not Nairac took part in the shooting and even there, the murkiness has not yet begun to clear. I put the question to his one-time boss, Colonel G, who it will be recalled, went to Northern Ireland to take over as G2 Int/Liaison in 1974. He had returned to base by the time Green was killed, although he linked up again with Nairac later.

Of the Holroyd claims, he said:

> I knew Fred very well. We were officer cadets together but he did not make it first time round. We were then in Northern Ireland at the same time. Let's just say I don't place any great credence at all on what he said [about the shooting of John Francis Green]. Robert Nairac was always the clever, broader thinker who stood back and weighed up every possibility. In my judgement, Robert did not shoot Green. I wouldn't have seen him in the killing mode. He would perhaps in a firefight or confrontation … [but] Robert was more the man to have traced him, done a lot of lead-up work and fingered him.

This falls into line with a scenario offered to me by a Northern Ireland source:

> J. F. Green was just one of a number of people Ball and Nairac were tracking. I know they had followed him to Carville's farm and for a time, they had a hide down there. The farm itself had been photographed and mapped out. So were other places where Green hung out. There was nothing strange in that, except they were across the border, of course, but that happened all the time. Details on Green were originally handed to Nairac by one of his contacts in the police who, as a matter of course, did not generally go across the border.

Nairac in turn kept his RUC contact up to date with developments and the fact that they were expecting to pick up Green in the near future. At that point, a local man with UDA/UVF connections came into the picture, with another guy he'd worked with before on sectarian killings, a member of the UVF from Lurgan who was virtually a professional hit-man. He killed for both money and sectarian reasons. This hit was definitely the latter. He was a killer, known to the police and the military as an occasional informer and general handyman, if you get my drift – a very dangerous man – and he had worked with the UDA man on a number of occasions. He was picked up a couple of times but never faced a court, and was never charged with any serious crime. Now, I don't know whether Nairac's crowd ever intended to go into the south and hit Green. Why risk it, we might ask ourselves? The fact is that the UDA guy and his pal from Lurgan got there first. It was they who did the hit on Green. Nairac wasn't even there. If they took a photograph, then it probably came back to Nairac by the same route and frankly, I don't think anyone who was close to it then would express surprise at that possibility.

However, further light was thrown on the issue of the photograph in a letter I received after the publication of the hardback edition of this book in January 1999. It came from Major E, who requested anonymity because of the nature of his previous work and confirmed what I had been told by Northern Ireland sources. Major E wrote as follows:

I was a Military Intelligence Officer with the Special Military Intelligence Unit (Northern Ireland) between 1974 and 1976, based in Newry as MIO H Division. Later

I did a second tour as MIO J Division based in Craigavon. I knew Robert Nairac very well, and Fred Holroyd less well. Your picture of Robert is outstanding, better than anyone else has achieved. I worked very closely with him (and Tony Ball) during his time as 2IC and IO with 4th Field Survey Troop based at Castle Dillon. I am pretty sure that he belonged to the troop rather than 3 Brigade staff. A very great deal of their work was carried out on behalf of SB Newry and I saw them both weekly during this period. Robert was mostly involved in liaison, but he did carry out some surveillance work.

I can help spread a little light on the John Francis Green business. The Polaroid camera used to take the pictures was originally mine, or at least issued to me by the SMIU. It was given by us, that is SB Newry and myself, to the Gardai in Dundalk, who we were very keen to cultivate, sometime prior to the shooting. Photographs of the murder scene were taken by them and passed to us. Robert, as you say, collected such things and asked us for one – they had no evidential value and we gave him one; others went to other places, I couldn't say where, nor how many we had. Robert was not involved in the Green murder and I don't think he was involved in the Miami Showband murders either.

Fred Holroyd was a friend of mine as well but he started his tour before I did and we did not train together. As you have probably discovered, the role of the SMIU/MIO varied widely from division to division. My predecessor had done a great job and I was completely integrated in SB Newry. I had free access to the whole office and all the files except for the identity of their sources. They had free access to all my material. I ran sources on their behalf and they were aware of their identity. On the other hand, Fred's predecessor was a disaster who left behind a legacy of distrust. Fred had no access to his SB's file and was not even allowed into the office in Portadown RUC station. He was required to visit at set times and sit on a chair in the corridor until they saw fit to brief him. It is no wonder that he found other things to do, well outside his normal remit. He undoubtedly did some good work, but he also had a vivid imagination. I took over his files some years after he left and some were pure Walter Mitty stuff. Even at that time there was a legacy of distrust in the division which I was only able to overcome because my former chief inspector in H Division was by then Superintendent SB South based in Armagh and he banged some heads together.

Additional evidence on the shooting of Green emerged in January 1999, again prompted by the publication of the hardback edition of this book. Pursuing various aspects of this story, Liam Clarke, a *Sunday Times* writer in Belfast, conducted a series of interviews with former RUC sergeant John Weir who claimed to have a definitive identification of John Francis Green's murderers, based on information from Ulster Volunteer Force members in Portadown. Weir himself has a murky past. In 1980, after ten years in the force, he was convicted of the murder of William Strathearn, a Catholic pharmacist whom renegade police officers had falsely denounced as a former IRA man. He served fourteen years in gaol and emigrated to South Africa shortly after his release. He claims he is now an advocate for a South African-style truth and reconciliation commission to clear up murders and dirty tricks during the Troubles. In the interviews with Liam Clarke, he named Green's killers as Robin Jackson, a loyalist hitman known as the Jackal, Robert McConnell, an Ulster Defence Regiment soldier later killed by the IRA, and Harris Boyle, the UVF man who blew himself up during the Miami Showband murders.

According to Weir, the target of the cross-border mission was not Green but Carville. Although loyalists had long suspected that Carville's farm was an IRA safe house, Weir may have provided the information that led to Green's death. Weir had a tip-off shortly before the attack. 'My source told me there was a house at Mullyash [in Monaghan] in which a kidnapped UDR man, James Elliot, was held and tortured before his body was dumped across the border,' he said. Weir reported the tip-off to the RUC Special Branch. Perhaps suspecting his links to loyalist paramilitaries, it tried to put him off the scent. 'The officer I told said he knew the Carvilles, and they were decent people and he did not think they would be involved in that.' Shortly afterwards, Green was shot dead.

Holroyd's claims were to be given new impetus in 1987 when he joined forces with another intelligence whistle-blower, Colin Wallace, who was emerging as a *cause célèbre* with the media although some, it must be said, preferred to brand him as a latter-day Walter Mitty and still do.

He had just been released from prison after serving six years of a ten-year sentence for the manslaughter of his girlfriend's husband – which he claimed was a 'trumped-up charge' linked to his dispute with MI5, who had him removed from his job in Northern Ireland because he refused to take part in their dirty tricks. MI5, he said, wanted to take control of the province and boot out MI6 from any immediate sphere of influence, which more or less fell into line with what Fred was saying.

Wallace, while struggling to get his life back together after his release, was arrested in 1980, accused of battering to death Brighton antiques dealer Jonathan Lewis and dumping his body in a river. At the time, he was having an 'amorous but not adulterous relationship' with Lewis's wife. He always maintained his innocence and on his release from prison his case was taken up by my colleague at the *Daily Mirror*, columnist Paul Foot. He believed Wallace's claims and wrote a book entitled *Who Framed Colin Wallace?*

In 1996, after a long campaign, Wallace subsequently won a new hearing and the conviction for manslaughter was quashed by the Court of Appeal. On the way to that successful outcome he had made numerous allegations that went deep into the activities and rivalries between MI6, the RUC Special Branch and MI5 which, he claimed, struck at the heart of British politics, enhancing Prime Minister Harold Wilson's belief that MI5 was plotting against him in 1974–5.

There is no denying the significance of the underlying aspects of the claims of Holroyd and Wallace, especially when linked to the wider sphere of 'dirty tricks' launched by MI5, as set out by Peter Wright in his book *Spycatcher*, published in 1987. As Professor Ben Pimlott wrote in his acclaimed and searching biography of Harold Wilson, 'Taken together, the two accounts [Wallace and Wright] are almost impossible to dismiss, for although each may mislead or exaggerate on particular details, it is stretching credulity to reject as fabrication the key material ...'

The additional link provided by Fred Holroyd meant that in the late 1980s he and Wallace, by then good friends and combining their resources for the onslaught, became fellow travellers in the media clamour that finally engulfed them. It is not the purpose of this book to disseminate the claims of Holroyd and Wallace any further: that has already been performed at length on numerous occasions in the past. Regardless of the accuracy and truth of either men's recollections, they did open up a previously heavily curtained window upon the activities of the Army's Special Duties squads and the intelligence community in Northern Ireland in an era when truth and fiction were easily merged.

The misinformation and disinformation being pumped around the system at the time all left their mark. Spin doctoring as such was not yet invented, but there were plenty of operatives in intelligence circles who were making a pretty good fist of it, attempting to manipulate the media with false trails, red herrings and downright lies. The Ministry of Defence joined in with its own well-versed equivalent, commonly known in the trade as stonewalling.

The intelligence community, led by MI5, of whom everyone in official circles was, I am told, 'shit-scared', was playing its own hand with carefully placed leaks, in an attempt to influence reportage of events in line with the way it wanted a story angled. Wallace himself claimed to have become embroiled in the black propaganda effort, feeding journalists with information specifically designed to help operations against the IRA.

With concessions to the IRA widely expected to encourage a permanent ceasefire, the Army and MI5 began to engage in dirty tricks. They told selected journalists that the policies pursued by Wilson and Merlyn Rees (later Lord Rees) would lead to disaster. 'I discovered that the dirty tricks campaign included a list of politicians in all parties,' said Lord Rees. 'A psy-ops [psychological operations] was also run against politicians in both the north and south of Ireland. The Army was involved in that. It was out of control.'

The extent of MI5's involvement in the Wallace case will probably never be known. Apart from having his conviction for manslaughter quashed, he fought his dismissal from the Army, claiming that he was forced out by MI5. A 1990 inquiry into the affair ordered the Ministry of Defence to pay £30,000 in compensation, after finding that its 'representatives' improperly attempted to influence the outcome of the appeal board. The representatives were taken to mean MI5.

Wallace was a key player in the psy-ops, once known as psychological warfare, about which Lord Rees complained. The psy-ops were coordinated by an organization with the innocent-sounding title of the Information Policy team, which used Colin Wallace as one of its mouthpieces to the press. In early 1974, he said, the Information Policy team became involved in an MI5-led operation codenamed Clockwork Orange, originally aimed at isolating and exposing sectarian killers on both sides of the religious divide.

Amid widespread differences over policy between the new Labour government of Harold Wilson and both the Army and MI5, Clockwork Orange was to be used to undermine the government, Wilson himself and various other troublesome politicians using tactics which targeted misdemeanours in the three specific areas of sexual, financial or political misbehaviour.

Weighing against these propagandist efforts, attempting to present a balanced and as near factual account as possible, was a heavyweight band of Fleet Street's finest, swarming like ants over Northern Ireland – including the excellent Robert Fisk, then with *The Times* and in constant pursuit of the SAS; Simon Winchester and Tony Geraghty of the *Sunday Times*; Mary Holland of the *Observer*; Simon Hoggart of the *Guardian*; and many others. Locally, an equally impressive line-up of journalists from the newspapers of both the north and south of Ireland let nothing slip and often scooped their London rivals. Indeed, they had given early insight to some of the claims that were later made by Holroyd, Wallace and others.

It was because so many journalists recognized that they had been fed false or misleading information during that period of hyperactivity between 1972 and 1976 that Wallace's claims could be readily accepted by so many. He could be challenged on many points, no doubt, and he had certainly had plenty of time and lonesome hours to go over and over in his mind his experiences of the past, even those where he stood only on the periphery. It was not difficult to string together a very credible package of events – all based upon fact. Wallace knew the score and the gossip, which is why journalists found that much of what he disclosed struck a chord, even if he did push several of his claims to the limit of believability.

There was to be yet one more twist in this story when it became known that forensic scientists had proved that one of the two pistols, a Star, used in the assassination of John Green was also present in the massacre of the Irish pop group the Miami Showband six months later. In July 1987 newly elected Labour MP Ken Livingstone felt the connection was sufficient to state in his maiden speech in the House of Commons in July 1987 that having assassinated Green, it was likely that Nairac had organized the attack on the Miami Showband.

The relevant parts of Ken Livingstone's speech need to be given in full, in order to place his allegations in their proper context – which has seldom been done, apart from in Hansard:

> During my election campaign in Brent, East, there was an unusual public meeting. An individual was invited to it who has never been a Socialist, who will never be prepared to vote Labour and who thinks that the Tory party is the natural governing party of Britain. He was invited to share a platform with myself and some of the relatives of those who have been subject to miscarriages of justice by the British courts over issues of bombing here in Britain. We invited Mr Fred Holroyd.
>
> For those who do not know, Mr Holroyd served in Northern Ireland with distinction. As I said, he is no Socialist. He comes from a military family. He went to a Yorkshire grammar school. His whole objective in life was to serve in the British Army. He believed in it totally. He enlisted as a private in the gunners, and three years later he was commissioned into the Royal Corps of Transport. He volunteered for the Special Military Intelligence unit in Northern Ireland when the present troubles began, and he was trained at the Joint Services School of Intelligence. Once his training was finished, he was stationed in Portadown, where for two and a half years he ran a series of intelligence operations.

When he was recruited as an MI6 officer, he said of them [MI6] that they were not disagreeable; their ethics were reasonable; they were seeking a political solution. His complaint, which eventually led to his removal from the Army and an attempt to discredit him, which has been largely successful, was made when the MI6 operation was taken over by MI5 in 1975 – by many of the same people who are dealt with in Peter Wright's book, and many of the same people who are alleged to have been practising treason against the Labour government of the time. He said that once MI5 took over, the reasonable ethics of MI6 were pushed aside by operatives in the intelligence world who supported the views of Mr Kitson and the policies and tactics of subverting the subverters. I recommend Brigadier Kitson's words to those who are not aware of them. His attitude was to create a counter-terror group, to have *agents provocateurs*, to infiltrate, and to run a dirty-tricks campaign in an attempt to discredit the IRA.

Mr Holroyd continued to believe that what he was doing was in the best interests of the British state until early in 1975, when Captain Robert Nairac, who, as many Honourable Members will know, was later murdered by the IRA, went into his office, fresh from a cross-border operation – something that of course is completely illegal – and showed him the colour photograph that had been taken by Captain Nairac's team. Captain Nairac had crossed the border with some volunteers from the UDF. He had assassinated John Francis Green, an active member of the IRA who was living south of the border. As an agent of the British government operating across the border as an assassin he had brought back the photograph as proof of that operation.

103

When Captain Nairac showed the photographs, Mr Holroyd started to object, not because he objected to an active member of the IRA being assassinated in a highly illegal cross-border raid but because he realized that once the British state started to perpetrate such methods there was no way that, eventually, Britain would not alienate vast sections of the community and eventually lose the struggle for the hearts and minds of the Irish people.

Holroyd then started to object to the use of such illegal methods by MI5 officers. He was immediately shuffled to one side by the expedient method of being taken to a mental hospital and being declared basically unfit for duty. During the month that he spent in the British mental hospital, the three tests that were administered to him were completely successfully passed.

Certainly, over a decade later, having met him, I can see no evidence whatsoever that he was in some sense mentally unbalanced. He was a spy who realized that the operations of the British government were counter-productive. He started to object, and was pushed to one side for his pains.

I raise the link with Captain Robert Nairac because, as I said, Fred Holroyd had qualms about this but was not particularly shocked; these things happen in a war. The matter needs to be investigated. I cannot prove the claims but allegations are being made extensively here in Britain, in republican circles and on Irish radio and television. A particularly horrifying incident that many Honourable Members will remember was the murder of three members of the Miami Showband – completely innocent musicians with no political affiliations whatsoever. It took place in the midst of the ceasefire that had been negotiated by the then Labour Government and the IRA. The Right Honourable Member for Morley and Leeds,

South (Mr Rees) pushed it through and sustained it, although there was considerable opposition from within the security services and within many political parties. The Labour government did everything possible to make the ceasefire work, but it was not wholly accepted within the apparatus of MI5 – our operatives who allegedly were working on behalf of the British state in Northern Ireland.

What is particularly disturbing is that what looked at the time like a random act of maniacal violence and sectarian killing now begins to take on a much more sinister stance. It has begun to emerge that Captain Robert Nairac is quite likely to have been the person who organized the killing of the three Miami Showband musicians. The evidence for that allegation is forensic and members of the UDF are prepared to say that they were aware of the dealings between members of the UDF gang who actually undertook the murder of the Miami Showband musicians. The evidence is quite clear. The same gun that was used by Captain Nairac on his cross-border trip to assassinate John Francis Green was used in the Miami Showband massacre.

Earlier this year, the radio and television service of southern Ireland, RTE, showed a documentary in which the makers – not myself; no one could accuse RTE of being pro-IRA – allege that they now have contacts with members of the UDF in that area who say that Captain Nairac passed the explosives and the guns to the gang and set up the killing of the Miami Showband musicians. If that is true, it needs to be investigated. The allegation was made on the broadcasting network of southern Ireland. It is supported by men who served on behalf of Britain as spies in the area at the time. It needs to be investigated and disproved, or the people behind it rooted out. If one wanted to find a way of ending the ceasefire that had been negotiated between the Labour government and the IRA, what better way to do so than to encourage random sectarian killings? I believe that that was happening.

It is likely that many of the officers mentioned in Peter Wright's book who were practising treason against the British government at home were also practising treason against the British government in Ireland. If the allegations are true, they were prepared to murder innocent Catholics to start a wave of sectarian killing which would bring to an end the truce that the Labour government had negotiated with the IRA. No democratic society can allow that sort of allegation to go uninvestigated. It is made by people who served on our behalf as intelligence officers in the area.

Livingstone's speech was attacked by Robert Nairac's father Maurice as 'disgusting, disgraceful and without foundation'. His reaction was understandable. After all, it placed his beloved son and George Cross hero at the centre of some more very nasty allegations. But what was the evidence on which Ken Livingstone based his claim?

# 8

# THE SHOWBAND MASSACRE

Whatever remained of Robert Nairac's religion-based upbringing must have been pretty well torn apart in those days in the border regions of South Armagh where he spent so much of his time, an area that witnessed the most vicious sectarian struggles. It was perhaps a touch ironic that it was two Catholic priests, Fathers Raymond Murray and Denis Faul, a couple of human rights campaigners and co-authors of almost three dozen books and pamphlets, who drew attention to what they called an onslaught against Catholic communities in the area at the time the IRA were in ceasefire mode.

The priests published their pamphlet entitled *The Triangle of Death* in 1975, highlighting the number of killings and listing the victims in the area bounded by Portadown, Armagh and Dungannon, heartland of Republicanism and IRA support. The uneven balance in the statistics of death suddenly became exceedingly apparent in the summer of 1975. Of the 163 sectarian killings in Northern Ireland in the first seven months of the year, 72 per cent were Catholic; in due course the Provisionals would seek to rectify that situation. It was, as Murray and Faul pointed out in their various writings, no coincidence that the imbalance in the ongoing slaughter occurred during the IRA's engagement in talks.

By the use of the tactics of endless negotiations and the carrot of limited concessions such as the release of internees, Merlyn Rees's negotiators persuaded the IRA to extend its ceasefire well into 1975. In return, Rees agreed to a gradual rundown of the military and its street presence, a shutdown of the identity checks and the ending of internment. The IRA on its part agreed not to target the British forces or the RUC but 'reserved the right to protect Catholic communities against sectarian attacks'. The ceasefire did not, incidentally, include the bombing cells already in place on the mainland.

This and the agreed setting-up of monitoring stations to be manned by Sinn Fein and funded by Westminster, allowed one more important concession: that those involved in the management of the ceasefire could carry arms. This also applied to the UDA and the UVF who, for their part, would achieve political recognition. The result was that for a time, all the paramilitaries were openly carrying weapons.

While the writings of Murray and Faul are in the form of straight and presumably honest reportage, naturally slanted towards the Catholic cause, they do highlight certain aspects of those events in a way that the reader is left in no doubt as to their meaning or the views of the priests. They had no compunction, for example, in including in the term 'terrorists' – along with the IRA, the UVF, the INLA – the SAS. Father Murray clearly included Nairac in that category. In his very detailed book *SAS in Ireland*, he states boldly, 'Robert Nairac of the SAS was ordered to kill [John] Green' and later:

> If the murder of John Francis Green stands out amongst all the other tragedies from the publicity point of view at the beginning of the IRA ceasefire, the related murder of the Miami Showband captured the headlines in the mid-term ... the SAS organized the gang which was made up of members of the UVF some of whom were also members of the UDR, providing weapons and explosives. The murder of innocent Catholics was part of an officially approved counter-insurgency plan.

This statement represented a giant leap into supposition, as misleading as Ken Livingstone's statement to the Commons, as we will see. Martin Dillon presented a far more reasoned argument in *The Dirty War*:

> The Miami Showband massacre ... is one example of how collusion between Loyalist paramilitaries and members of the security forces, namely the Ulster Defence Regiment, has frequently been misinterpreted and has led to the widely held belief ... that Loyalist-inspired violence is often masterminded by British military intelligence in liaison with RUC Special Branch ... The Miami massacre best illustrates the degree to which Loyalist terror often depends on cooperation from dissident UDR personnel and not from British military intelligence or Special Branch.

Father Murray is more accurate when he quotes reports from a list of incidents which 'if investigated would demonstrate a background involvement of the security forces'. Number fourteen on that list is the assassination of Catholics in 1975 by Protestant groups backed by the military.

The security forces, as Dillon repeatedly points out, included the UDR, which was manned almost entirely by Protestants and which itself had suffered very heavy casualties from IRA bombers, snipers and stone-throwers. The number of UDR personnel killed or wounded was highest in the south of Ulster, which was also one of its major recruitment areas.

There was also an embarrassing 'other side' in its short history which includes not a small number of its past members, who themselves engaged in terrorist acts. Father Murray says of the 1975 period:

> It is interesting to see the tip of the iceberg of UDR/loyalist paramilitary involvement in the 'triangle' area in the 1970s by looking at occasions when they

came before the courts. The evidence illustrates the unsuitability of certain members and the laxity of vetting ... convictions among UDR men included stealing guns, possession of ammunition, discharging guns, possessing guns in public while under the influence of alcohol, arson and drunken driving.

The loyalists in the border regions saw the UDR as defenders of Protestants against the IRA and incursions from the Republican south. Protestant communities in the south of the Six Counties, often small and isolated, must have felt under constant threat. Conversely, the IRA saw as its heritage the defence of Catholics and the promotion of the cause of Republicanism, a united Ireland and getting the British out. Younger IRA members, especially among the less well-off and unemployed, were actively courted by the IRA regional commands, continually being informed that it was their duty to join the struggle. Likewise, Protestants in that region, where the two sides met with such ferocity, responded by either volunteering for service with the UDR, which ran full and part-time units, or joining the paramilitary groups.

That many joined both seemed to concern no one. As members of the armed forces, they were able to carry personal weapons for their protection. Loyalist groups such as the UDA and UVF encouraged their own members to join the UDR force and through this method were able to obtain all the accoutrements of being in the security services – weapons, passes, training – but, more importantly, access to details of upcoming military operations and, most important of all, files relating to Catholics, Republicans and the IRA. The UDR also suffered continual 'thefts' of weapons and uniforms from its bases and the homes of its members.

The Republicans and the Catholics screamed their unheard protests: it was nothing short of a scandal that through legally constituted military involvement, UDR men who doubled up with the UDA or UVF had access to important military information. No less of a scandal was the movement of troops and Army patrols in regions where the loyalist groups might themselves be active against the Catholic community, or, for example, transporting an arms cache.

South Armagh, where Nairac was by now (early 1975) operating for much his time, had developed into a front line between UDA/UVF groups, who had their base at Portadown, and the IRA, spread across the territory. The security forces were stretched to the limit. Since the Troubles began in 1969, some of the IRA's most committed activists and some of its most dedicated volunteers for active service came from or operated in South Armagh, so as to be able to make a swift retreat into the south when it became necessary.

The liaison between the RUC and UDR with the UDA and the UVF undoubtedly provided a valuable source of intelligence for the British military units, and for Robert Nairac, in his role as liaison officer, in particular. His contact with the RUC Special Branch in South Armagh had, as we have seen, been excellent, and through it was channelled intelligence against 'the common enemy', the IRA. The intelligence he gathered led him beyond the formalities of inter-agency exchange of information.

All the time, Nairac was gathering his own personal stock-in-trade of names, photographs, contacts, agents and associates that sometimes went beyond his brief. He could not restrict himself to the handling of information and to some extent his association with Tony Ball encouraged him to move into the areas of front-line activity, of going out with patrols and involving himself in 'the action'.

There is little doubt that he had contact with the UDR and undercover liaison with contacts who were also members of the UDA and the UVF, and there was every reason for him to pursue those contacts. The alleged association with the Miami Showband massacre, however, is not so certain.

The story of the massacre began on 30 July 1975. On that evening, the Miami Showband, which for a dozen years or more had enjoyed success as one Ireland's foremost pop groups, travelled to an engagement in Banbridge, a Protestant-dominated town in County Down. Although they were all Catholics, the band had always refused to allow the constraints of politics or religion to halt their tours of the whole island, north and south. That they courageously continued to brave the violence earned them great respect and a good following.

As usual, the evening had gone well with a large and appreciative crowd at the Castle Ballroom, who were starved, as these communities were, of much nightlife. It was after midnight before the six members of the band were packing up their instruments and sound gear in their minibus, ready for the journey home. Five of them were travelling in the bus, and the sixth, who lived in Antrim, left in his own car.

Trumpeter Brian Mccoy, driving the minibus, steered it out of the ballroom car park and headed off towards Newry, and onwards to the border. They had travelled only a few miles, reaching Buskhill on the Banbridge–Newry road, when Mccoy called out to the others that there was something up ahead. A red light was flashing in the centre of the road. As they drew nearer, they saw men in uniform and assumed it was a military checkpoint.

As Mccoy slowed to a stop, one man, in what was believed to be a UDR uniform and armed, approached and told Mccoy to pull over and identify themselves. When the minibus stopped at the roadside, the band was ordered out. There were now several shadowy figures around them, and they were told to line up at the roadside, facing the fields.

It was now apparent there were at least eight men surrounding them and Des McAlea, the band's saxophonist, thinking he heard an English-accented voice, believed it to be a UDR/British Army roadcheck, especially as the soldiers were armed with rifles and sub-machine guns. At that point, the band members had no reason to be suspicious and in fact a couple of the soldiers were chatting to them about that night's performance in Banbridge. But then things began to turn nasty. The 'soldiers' had opened the rear of the bus and begun searching and moving things around. The guitarist Stephen Travers asked them to be careful with his guitar and moved over to see what they were doing. He was punched and told to return to the others and not to turn round.

Two of the 'soldiers' walked over to the bus carrying a parcel. It contained a bomb. They placed it in the rear of the bus with the instruments and as they did so, it exploded prematurely, killing both instantly and cutting the minibus in two. They were later identified as UVF officers Harris Boyle, twenty-four, from Portadown and Wesley Sommerville from Dungannon.

The Miami band members, all in their twenties, were struck by the searing heat and thrown by the blast into the ditch. There was pandemonium all around and numerous bursts of machine-gun fire. The band's lead singer, Fran O'Toole, took eighteen bullets as he lay on the ground, Tony Geraghty was struck by eight and Brian Mccoy was fired upon by two separate gunmen, his torso riddled with bullet holes. Steve Travers was also hit and seriously wounded, but not killed. Des McAlea escaped serious injury; the blast of the bomb had thrown him clear and knocked him unconscious, and he lay in the ditch, coming round as a second burst of gunfire broke. The bus was on fire, and it was spreading along the ditch. He rolled out as the gang were leaving. McAlea took off down the road heading for Newry and managed to get a lift the nearest police station.

When the police and pathologists arrived at the scene, they discovered that the gang had left their own dead where they lay after the bomb had exploded prematurely. The remains of Boyle were lying twenty yards from the wreckage of the minibus. Sommerville's body had been cut in two, ten yards further on. An arm from one of the victims, found some distance away, bore a tattoo, Portadown UVF. The gang had also abandoned two sub-machine guns, ammunition and a .38 pistol, three green berets and a pair of spectacles.

The following day, Portadown UVF issued a statement that carefully hid the true facts, claiming that the UVF stopped the minibus as part of its vigilante patrols against IRA terrorists:

> A UVF patrol led by Major Boyle was suspicious of two vehicles, a minibus and a car parked near the border. Major Boyle ordered his patrol to apprehend the occupants for questioning. As they were being questioned, Major Boyle and Lt. Sommerville began to search the minibus. As they began to enter the minibus a bomb was detonated and both men were killed outright. At the precise moment of the explosion the patrol came under intense automatic fire from the occupants of the other vehicle. The patrol sergeant immediately ordered fire to be returned. Using self-loading rifles and sub-machine guns, the patrol returned fire, killing three of their attackers and wounding another. The patrol later recovered two Armalite rifles and a pistol. The UVF maintains regular border patrols due to the continued activity of the Provisional IRA. The Mid-Ulster Battalion had been assisting the South Down South Armagh units since the IRA's Forkhill booby trap which killed four British soldiers. Three UVF members are being treated for gunshot wounds after last night but not in hospital.

The UVF statement was worded to throw the police and the public off the scent. It was made to appear as if the Miami Showband was carrying the bomb, and that they opened fire on the UVF patrol. The presence of two vehicles, a car and a minibus, was simply untrue. The band's sixth member travelling by car had turned off in another direction.

The truth was not long in coming out. Sommerville had been arrested with his brother James and another in the past for terrorist offences. Significantly, he had been charged with capturing a bread delivery van in 1974, filling the back with explosives and driving it to a Catholic housing estate. It exploded injuring twelve people. The three men were all later acquitted of the charges.

It now became apparent that they had been intending to use the Miami Showband wagon for a similar operation, and to drive the bomb into Dublin. Sommerville and Boyle, it was later discovered, were also part-timers in the UDR – hence the uniforms and the green berets identified by the surviving members of the band. McAlea and Travers were also able to provide descriptions of others in the UVF patrol but a key to the further investigation came from the spectacles found at the scene. An optician took a reading of the glass and discovered that the prescription type was exceedingly rare, worn by perhaps only one person in half a million patients.

Files of local opticians were examined, and a South Armagh optician identified them as belonging to James McDowell, twenty-nine, whose description fitted that of the man who led the UVF patrol. The police investigation led them to Thomas Crozier, another UDR member. Crozier, twenty-five, was a lance corporal, stationed with the 11th Battalion of the Regiment, at Lurgan.

They refused to cooperate with the police, or give any clues as to their accomplices, but Special Branch detectives were convinced that several others were UDR members. They admitted that the explosion was caused by a bomb being planted in the minibus by Sommerville and Boyle. Crozier also admitted to being a member of UVF but said that it was entirely legal. This was true at the time. As part of the peace concessions made to the IRA in 1975, the UVF had been 'unbanned' by Merlyn Rees, and it was not reimposed until November 1975.

He also stated that membership of both the UDR and the other main loyalist group, the UDA, had never been officially barred as the UDA was not an illegal organization. This was confirmed by a UDR spokesman at the trial of Crozier and McDowell in 1976.

Investigations by the police revealed that the selection of the Miami Showband was for the purpose of getting a bomb across the border and past possible checks on both sides. The bomb's timer had been set to explode the device once they were well inside the Republic. The band would have been killed, apparently by the explosives they were carrying. The band would have been discredited and their high profile would have focused attention on lax controls at the border, which would have prompted greater action to harass the IRA in its largely unhindered passage to and fro. McDowell, Crozier and James Sommerville (brother of the UVF man who was killed) were each sentenced to thirty years' imprisonment for their part in the crime.

The police were convinced that there were ten men in the gang and it later transpired that one of them was also involved in the killing of John Francis Green. He had used guns from a UVF arms' dump on both occasions. This was not at all unusual. Every terrorist unit, anywhere in Northern Ireland and of whatever alliance, kept and managed its own weapons' store. No single weapon was assigned to a particular member of a terrorist unit, although some had their favourites and would select them time and time again. The Star pistol that had been used to kill Green was taken out on that night and the bullet markings matched some of those found in the body of Brian Mccoy. The police had arrested the man and questioned him on four occasions but found no evidence to link him with either crime.

With only half the story, the presence of the Star pistol at both scenes of crime was sufficient for those pursuing the theory that Nairac was responsible for shooting Green to say that Nairac was present at the roadblock where the musicians lost their lives. Nairac, it was concluded by some journalists, provided the mysterious English accent heard at the roadside and it was his identity the captured UVF gang refused to reveal.

The whole business was given such an airing that the public at large could be forgiven for overlooking the small print and believing that there was ample evidence to show that Nairac doubled as a terrorist killer during his pursuit of intelligence on behalf of the British Army. When examined closely, that conclusion had rather less a weight of evidence to support it than that which sent the Guildford Four and the Birmingham Six to prison for life. It was based entirely on supposition, assumption and circumstantial connections which, in a court of law, would have been blasted out of the water.

Having reached fever pitch in the imaginations of many, the story gathered momentum and was re-examined in July 1993 in a Yorkshire television documentary in the *First Tuesday* series. The programme achieved a significant departure, in that it included testimony from former officers of Irish military intelligence, which would have required official sanction. Once again, the subject of British intelligence backing for loyalist paramilitary organizations was discussed and the names of Tony Ball and Robert Nairac were mentioned. The programme included statements from former British agents to the effect that for some time, the UVF had background links with British intelligence. They stated that the loyalist paramilitaries would not, for example, have had sufficient bomb-making expertise to create the device used in the Dublin bombings, although others would wholeheartedly disagree: bomb-making skills were high on the tutorials of all terrorist groups.

The implications, however, were obvious and after watching a screening of the programme, the Taoiseach (Prime Minister of the Irish Republic) Albert Reynolds ordered a formal inquiry. The results were never made known.

It is, after the passage of time, difficult to improve on the case against Nairac. My own information concurred with that of Martin Dillon, who wrote:

It is, to say the least, highly dubious if not absurd, to conclude from such superficial factors that Nairac was present at the Miami murders. I was told by a source close to ... and another loyalist hit-man that Nairac was not present at either murder [of the Miami Showband or Green] ... the source I regard as impeccable was in a position to know who was involved in both episodes.

Other local incidents that occurred at the time in these dramatic killing fields in the border regions were lost and forgotten in the sheer weight of atrocity. However, in the spate of revenge murders carried out by the IRA that followed the Miami massacre, there was one that stood out: the killing on 14 August 1975 of William Meaklin, a mobile shop owner from Newtownhamilton and former RUC reservist. His van was found abandoned near Crossmaglen and his disfigured body was found on the road to Castleblayney (where Green was murdered). It was common gossip in the area at the time that the IRA had found out the names of the killers of Green and that Meaklin was one of them.

There were a number of other murders of Protestants and known members of the loyalist paramilitaries who appeared to have some connections with Meaklin. The IRA also took a heavy revenge on the UDR for the fact that some of its members were in the Miami shootings and the loyalists responded in turn, killing up to a dozen Catholics in individual incidents up to the end of 1975. For weeks and months on end, murder came thick and fast in tit-for-tat vengeance.

As to the position of British intelligence personnel, and Robert Nairac, in this terrible mêlée of violence, it would be absurd to imagine that they did not utilize every possible opportunity to unearth intelligence from whatever source. They were dealing with dangerous people in the paramilitaries, as well as informers drawn from society at large, many of whom were liars and cheap hoods. It would be naïve in the extreme not to imagine anything else in a period of such terror.

Contacts were undoubtedly maintained with the loyalist paramilitary units, as the UVF itself openly admitted. After the Miami killings, the organization's magazine carried tributes to its two members killed by their own bomb, which stated: 'We do not stop our members from becoming involved with the security forces. Some are attached to the RUC, UDR and several full-time Army regiments. They are not only active members of the UVF but they also feed us vital information on security and Republicans.'

A later interview claimed that the UVF even possessed Army photographs of 90 per cent of the 'people we take action against to go along with their obituary ... we must face it ... there are security personnel who agree with our standpoints. Let us say there is a thin line between UVF membership and security forces membership in certain cases.'

The depth of contact that Robert Nairac, Tony Ball and others established within these organizations will never be known. As we have seen, the penetration of terrorist groups by security forces cannot be denied. Nairac became the key name in unlocking allegations which, if true, painted a picture of incredible rivalries and conspiracies among the intelligence community. His name became synonymous with the linkage system of tales of dirty tricks as they finally emerged in the late 1980s and beyond.

The claims concerning Nairac's activities came long after his death, during the exposure of an 'information offensive' in 1974–6 which had been designed to smear and damage Harold Wilson. Every piece of 'evidence', regardless of its provability, was picked up and chucked into a veritable well of often uncheckable facts from which it could be withdrawn in support of a particular thesis in the ensuing years, in the full knowledge that the subject, Robert Nairac, could not sue for libel.

The most skilful and, perhaps, trustworthy of all the major investigations that followed was Paul Foot's account of Colin Wallace's experiences. This account, by its very subject matter, anchored many of the dirty tricks within MI5 to Northern Ireland. Foot reproduced Wallace's notes, purportedly written in 1974 as guidance for the dissemination of smears during his contact with journalists. Those notes, whose constant theme is that Wilson was being run by the Communist Party and the KGB, included the advancement of the theory that Wilson wanted to see a 'Red Shamrock Irish Workers' Republic'. This, coincidentally, was exactly what the Official IRA had set out to achieve in the late 1960s, long before the Troubles flared.

Wallace, presumably, was not the only officer receiving guidance in the art of becoming a smear tactician, and he was also a relatively minor cog in a wheel working towards a given aim. Professor Pimlott, in his biography of Harold Wilson, describes Wallace's account as 'a remarkable and alarming glimpse of the activities of what has been called the secret state. They appear to reflect a security quagmire in Northern Ireland in the mid-1970s which may or may not have affected the mainland to the same degree. There is some evidence that smearing ... was endemic in Northern Ireland.'

The evidence of Wallace ran parallel to the claims of Peter Wright. Even former MI6 officer Anthony Cavendish, who opposed Wright's views, found a measure of agreement over the smear campaigns that, he said, were organized against anyone of consequence who appeared to be sympathetic to the position of the Catholic minority in Ulster, or showed that they believed in a settlement based on radical change in the Northern–Southern relationship.

Robert Nairac was, like Wallace, not very high up in the batting order of the intelligence community. He was important to a particular section of Army operations, and clearly the success or failure of those operations were themselves significant in the overall scheme of things.

If, for example, the killing of Green was, as Raymond Murray, Ken Livingstone and others suggested, an MI5 conspiracy with the Army to end the ceasefire, then clearly the operation had major implications. If the Miami massacre was the tragic consequence of a plan intended to bring about the same result, that too was definitely one for the dirty tricks file. It was certainly not an impossibility, as Anthony Cavendish wrote in his book *Inside Intelligence*: 'I believe that working for a secret intelligence service almost brings about a state of mind which permits anything if it is done for the benefit of the service and hence for the good of one's country.'

Silence, thereafter, is imperative. Cavendish also tells an old intelligence story which was certainly applicable in these times, and which he gave me permission to use here:

> In the bitter cold of the Russian winter in a small village … during a howling gale and darkness falling, a Russian peasant wandering home … sees a small game bird on the ground nearly dead from cold. The peasant picks up the bird and warms it … at that moment a herd of cattle come by and one of them drops a large dollop right in front of him. He puts the bird in the steaming dollop so that it will stay warm and then fly away. But a second peasant comes along and hears the bird chirping happily in the dollop … seizes it, breaks it neck and takes it home for his supper.
>
> This story has three morals: 1) Do not believe everybody who drops you in the shit is your enemy; 2) Do not believe everybody who gets you out of the shit is your friend; and 3) whenever you are in the shit, keep quiet about it.

There is no point in attempting to present a whiter-than-white Robert Nairac. He was at times in collusion with people who had connections with loyalist terrorist organizations; it would be naïve to believe otherwise. But whereas many of these allegations came out as a result of whistle-blowing on the security services, the surrounding murkiness and personal axes to grind must also be taken into account. In spite of loyalists' willingness to embarrass the Westminster government on many occasions in the past, none of the ninety or so sentenced to life for murder in the mid-1970s has seen fit to confirm that Nairac was involved with the UVF in the Miami Showband killings. While many of the claims made by Holroyd and Wallace were patently true, no corroborative evidence whatsoever has emerged to support the theory that Nairac killed Green or organized the Miami Showband massacre. Hard facts are needed. One of the facts about which Fred Holroyd was certainly confused was that neither Nairac and Ball were SAS serving in an SAS unit in 1974–5. Contrary to Holroyd's assertions, Nairac, as I have shown, never was, and Ball did not rejoin the SAS until he completed his tour with 14 Int in mid-1975. But with Nairac and Ball dead, all the elements to forge a conspiracy theory were readily available and Nairac was unjustly accused.

There was, however, to be one other twist in this tale in 1997, when the Republicans recorded the death of a prominent loyalist paramilitary 'for whom we shed no tears'. R. J. Kerr, a leading Portadown loyalist, was found dead in suspicious circumstances. A Republican source said that Kerr had long been implicated in, though never convicted for, a series of murders and paramilitary activities in the Armagh–East Tyrone area. His body was found beside a boat near Newry. He was apparently pouring petrol around it when he accidentally set off the flames prematurely. The report added:

Kerr was one of the ringleaders of a loyalist murder campaign in mid-Ulster during the 1970s. It has long been rumoured that Kerr was in association with a group of renegade police and British soldiers who were known to be in collusion with loyalist murders of Catholics. Capt. Robert Nairac, the undercover SAS officer killed by the IRA, was thought to have been another of Kerr's associates. While Catholics in the North will not be in the least bit sad at Kerr's passing, similar emotions are evident among loyalists in the Portadown area. Kerr was having running disputes with elements of them for the past while, accusing them of extortion and intimidation. The Loyalist Volunteer Force refute these claims, saying that it was Kerr who was the problem, drinking heavily and beating up young lads. Whatever the case, few tears will be shed.

Once again, the tarnish to Nairac's name was applied by association rather than hard facts but there is little doubt that many on both sides of the Northern Ireland divide are convinced that Robert Nairac was not only utilizing loyalist sources, he was quite definitely playing a double game.

The former RUC man, John Weir, gave a long statement to the *Sunday Times* in February 1999, following the publication of this book, admitting that he and other RUC men colluded with loyalist murderers and claiming that he discovered curious links with Nairac. He said the RUC officers feared that the IRA would wipe out Protestants along the border and had established a republican informant in South Armagh in the mid-1970s to help combat this prospect. Relatives of the man, now dead, confirmed that he had associated with the then RUC man.

Weir said he did not entirely trust his informant: 'When I went to him, I would be given a glass of whiskey or he would put a bag of vegetables or potatoes in the car. He was overdoing it a bit, showing that he was my friend.' He was then amazed when the informant told him that a British undercover soldier called Robert Nairac was also a regular visitor and had even stayed overnight.

After Nairac's death, the informant told Weir that the Guardsman died because he had tried to infiltrate the IRA. He had approached members of the republican movement, told them he was a British soldier but offered to work for them. According to Weir, Nairac even got the informant's help to move explosives across the border for the Provisionals. He also told him who had been responsible for recent loyalist attacks and revealed the names of loyalist paramilitaries and members of the Ulster Defence Regiment (UDR) who were helping British Army special forces.

Rumours to that effect had been circulating for some years and Weir's story raised a further issue, as Liam Clarke pointed out in his piece for the *Sunday Times*: that, if true, how did Nairac's information find its way back to the IRA and did it lead to the deaths of part-time members of the UDR, or others involved with the loyalist paramilitaries?

Again, in February 1999 after this book appeared, a group of Armagh Unionists asked Amnesty International to investigate exactly that possibility. Members of Families Acting for Innocent Relatives believe that Nairac did give the names of their loved ones to the IRA. They made their claim independently of Weir. They say, however, that his account confirms their suspicions. Willie Frazer, a spokesman for the group, said: 'It was those who were helping the SAS and special forces who were selected for killing by the IRA. Other members of the UDR weren't assassinated. How did the IRA know? Nairac must have given good information to get himself into the republican pubs where he was drinking. The only way he could do that was to sacrifice somebody.'

Frazer's father, Robert, a UDR soldier who had worked closely with 14 Intelligence, was assassinated by the IRA. 'Those men knew they were going to die,' said Willie Frazer. 'They knew their names were compromised. My father told me I would have to get used to more funerals, that I would have to look after myself. The IRA drove past the homes of other UDR members to get to him.'

Brian McConnell believes that his uncle Robert, a UDR man who liaised between British special forces and the illegal Ulster Volunteer Force, was also set up. He said: 'I have no doubt that my uncle gathered intelligence in South Armagh. He was a dedicated soldier and he would have defended his country at all costs. His information would have led to the deaths of IRA terrorists. The army was prepared to use our relatives for as long as it suited them, but then they were no longer of use and the strategy changed.' A spate of UDR deaths followed. They weren't just random targets; all had been involved in something together.

Meanwhile, on the other side of the fence, a former IRA member who maintained he had been briefed on Nairac, claimed the soldier first made contact with the republican movement in England, in North London. 'Nairac had been mixing with republicans for some time,' he said. 'He had contact with republicans but he had not yet come close to the actual active service unit. He did know the workings of the movement and he would have known some of the actions that individual volunteers had carried out. He was beginning to be trusted but he was not yet trusted as much as he needed to be.'

# 9

## A BRIEF RESPITE

Although the individual outbreaks of terrorism in Northern Ireland were serious and frequent enough to keep up pressure on the military presence, by the summer of 1975 the overall picture painted privately to Harold Wilson and his Northern Ireland ministers by their advisers was one of optimism. There was a belief that, in general, the ceasefire was being observed and the violence in Northern Ireland had been held at what the military termed as an 'acceptable level'. The British Army had taken the opportunity to examine its strengths and weaknesses, and establish other avenues of secret combat against the IRA, such as the extension of training of operatives in the intelligence war.

The IRA, with the benefit of hindsight, considers this period to have been one of its most damaging, both in relation to its ability to carry out operations in response to loyalist attacks or military action and to the morale of its younger members. This was reflected in intelligence reports to Westminster and as a result further concessions to the IRA to keep up the dialogue were considered no longer necessary. In fact, before the summer parliamentary recess of 1975, contact with the IRA was being curtailed to the point of being non-existent, and younger members, such as Gerry Adams and Martin McGuinness in the north, were expressing deep dissatisfaction with the IRA leadership and its ceasefire policy. Others, more powerful, and resident in the Long Kesh prison were even more vociferous. The prisoner-of-war status of terrorists held in Ulster's prisons was being withdrawn and they saw this as the thin end of the wedge. They were already demanding an end to the ceasefire and called upon the IRA's London bombing units to prepare for a new campaign.

For Robert Nairac and Tony Ball, the summer saw the end of their current partnership in their 14 Int unit. They returned for the time being to their regiments on the mainland and, after a long stint in the province, there was an opportunity for some much needed rest and relaxation. Nairac headed north for a fishing holiday in Scotland. It was there that he first met and struck up his friendship with Martin Squires, which was kept up upon their return to London, and thus continued into the period prior to Nairac's death. Squires recalled:

I first met Robert in the Outer Hebrides. We were both at South Uist on a salmon fishing holiday. I was with an actor friend of mine, while Robert was with a fellow officer. They were staying at our hotel. I knew the owners, from the Walker whisky family. We had a roaring good time, with lots of good sport. We all had gillies and so on. It was splendid – fishing by day or tramping over the wonderful countryside if the weather was too bad, then rollicking good evenings in the hotel.

We used to drink with the gillies and Robert and David would get fairly tanked up; in fact we all did. The owner used to scream at us to get through for dinner and then we'd have fishing tales after dinner, and all the entertainment was in the telling. They were marvellous evenings. We were up there for a couple of weeks and I got to know Robert very well indeed.

Fishing was banned on the Sunday between the two weeks. Not for Robert, though – and this will perhaps give an insight into his character. 'We're bloody well going fishing and that's that!' So on the Sunday between the two weeks the four of us went to a secret loch he'd discovered six or seven miles from the hotel. He and Sewell were exceedingly fit, of course, and kept marching on at a pace that I and my chum had difficulty keeping

up with. We were absolutely shattered after the first mile
or so. I knew Robert was a falconer and so every time we
needed a break, I shouted, 'Robert, over here! What's that
bird of prey?' So he'd stop and look around. Couldn't
find one of course, but it was the only way we could get
him to slow down. And he absolutely had to have a look.
He really was Mr Action Man.

Although he was in very good shape, he was I must
say something of a conundrum as a person. I saw him up
there in the wilds of the Outer Hebrides and he was
wonderfully good fun, excellent company, full of charm
and bonhomie, but there was below that something I
could not quite identify. It was as if there was a darkness
beyond the charming exterior that was impenetrable. I
didn't give it a lot of thought at the time and anyhow, the
holiday went marvellously.

It became one of those holiday friendships that actually
did continue after it ended. We exchanged telephone
numbers and sure enough, we had only been back a
couple of days when Robert called. Thereafter we met
often. He was back with his regiment at Wellington
Barracks then, having a respite, I believe, from his service
in Northern Ireland. Our first meeting after we came back
from the Hebrides was at a drinking club in St James's
Place where I was a member. Several chums including
some of his cronies, arranged to meet there, and it was
absolutely wild.

They had a Grenadier Guards game called 'Choose,
Lose and Booze' and Robert was pretty keen on that. You
spun a coin and the first one chose the drink, usually a
lethal combination of crème de menthe, drambuie, gin,
vodka, etc., all in one glass. You could choose six
elements. Sounds pretty daft to talk about it now but we
were all young and fairly hot-headed. If you won the

From Oxford to Sandhurst and directly into the Grenadier Guards ... Robert
Nairac (centre) possessed a determined, if romantic, notion of his future.

*Right and far right:* At Ampleforth. He was a good scholar and excelled in sports, especially in athletics and rugby as seen here in 1996.

*Below and below right:* Robert Nairac's interest in the countryside and field sports led him to Ireland. He shared a love of falconry with a fellow Ampleforth student, the son of one of Ireland's foremost families, and spent holidays there, flying birds over the peat bogs.

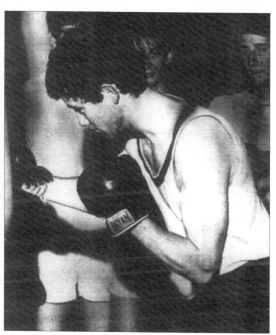

At Oxford his love of sports continued and he led the move to reform the defunct boxing club and won the respect of many of his fellow students. He reputedly later boxed IRA activist Martin Meehan.

*Top:* Belfast 1973: Nairac saw his first posting to Northern Ireland, on patrol with the Grenadiers when scenes like these were commonplace and a source of intelligence.

*Above:* London 1974: An IRA funeral in Kilburn attracted Nairac's interest. He spent many nights in Irish-populated pubs around North London. He grew his hair long, wore a donkey jacket and jeans and led the singing of rousing rebel songs.

*Top:* South Armagh, wild countryside then known as bandit territory, with an easy escape for the IRA across the border. It became the hunting ground of Captain Robert Nairac in his undercover role.

*Above:* The enemy … an IRA publicity picture of their training for ambushing army patrols.

*Above:* Ireland's best-known pop group at the time ... and notoriously at the centre of what became known as the Miami Showband Massacre. Was Nairac involved?

*Right:* Peter Cleary ... shot by the SAS.

*Far right:* John Francis Green, IRA commander, assassinated south of the border.

*Right:* Liam Townson, Nairac's killer in 1977 and in 1990 when he was released from prison (far right).

Scene of the crime: *Top:* The Three Steps pub at Drumintee … *Middle:* the bridge over the river Flurry where Captain Nairac was shot … *Above:* the spot by the bridge parapet where blood was found.

# Provisiona
# killing offic

**From Niall Kiely,**
**in South Armagh**

ALTHOUGH a search continued
last night on both sides of the
Border for the British Army captain
abducted by the Provisional IRA in
South Armagh last Saturday, hopes
of finding him alive faded as the
Provisionals announced that he had
ben killed following interrogation.

Captain Robert Laurence Nairac,
aged 29, was drinking in plain
clothes in the Three Steps Public
House, near Drumintee, just two
miles from the Border, before his
abduction on Saturday night.

Captain Robert Nairac photographed three months ago talking to children in the A. doyne area of Belfast.

The most famous picture of Nairac ... taken in Belfast and, according to the
*Irish Times*, three months prior to his death while he was still working undercover
in South Armagh.

spin, you didn't have to drink it, which you hoped and prayed for, but in the end most of us ended up staggering. I lost my membership of the club because the owner didn't agree with that kind of madness.

We used to meet up several evenings a week if they weren't up to much. Then he began to go away again and our meetings were intermittent over the next year or so. There were a group of six of us in the end who were all rugby fanatics and we used to meet up at the Cross Keys in Chelsea, our main watering hole. Occasionally, Robert would be in full mess kit, and we'd have a formal dinner at St James's Palace. My actor friend and I would be in dinner jackets and all the others in full uniform. There were some dangerously wild evenings. One night at St James's, Robert, after the fifth decanter of port, ran his dress sword through a busby that was perched on a bust and a waiter coming out with the drinks got it in the ribs. It wasn't fatal but I think blood was drawn.

That was Robert, so high-spirited; and, no doubt, that had something to do with his letting off steam after his experiences in Northern Ireland. Mad as a hatter.

The territory Nairac had left behind was about to explode into another crescendo of violence. By the late summer of 1975, the IRA's ceasefire was hanging by a thread that was about to snap. Five Protestants were murdered at the Tullyvallen Orange Hall in South Armagh. Responsibility was claimed by a group calling itself the South Armagh Republican Army, thought to be a cover for hard-line IRA members in the area who had declared their intention to end the ceasefire, as the Real IRA was to in 1998.

They were joined by young bloods of the Provisionals in the north, who were pressing for an end to the truce – which was still officially in force. The IRA command, as a concession to the pressure for a return to the armed struggle, agreed to activate the

London bombers. The team, still *in situ* since earlier in the year, were ordered to prepare for operations.

If there is a parallel to be drawn with events of the 1990s, it is in the fact that at this time the power was, over a period of months, gradually being wrested from the Dublin command of the IRA by the Provisionals in the north. The control of the more senior figures of the IRA had been overestimated and London was once again to become the front line of PIRA attacks.

The IRA bombing cell had been living quietly in north London, changing their addresses occasionally. They had used their period of inactivity since throwing a bomb at Edward Heath's London residence to scout for fresh targets and practise their bomb-making skills. The new campaign was given the go-ahead at the end of August 1975. Between then and the end of September, they had hit half-a-dozen targets around London, including the Hilton Hotel, the Portman Hotel and the Hare and Hounds public house in Maidstone. At least five people, including Army bomb-disposal specialist Captain Roger Goad, were killed and dozens were injured.

Back in Ulster, the loyalist terrorist gang was wreaking revenge for IRA attacks. On 2 October, a wave of killings claimed eleven lives, six of them Catholics. Four of the other casualties were members of a loyalist paramilitary group whose bomb exploded prematurely while they were sitting in their car, bringing the total for 'accidental deaths' of their bombers to six that year.

In London, on 23 October, the IRA team used an anti-handling device that blew up on touch – similar to that which killed Captain Goad – in an attempt to kill Tory MP Sir Hugh Fraser. The bomb was placed under his car and would have exploded when he went to get in. In fact, it killed another famous person, Professor Hamilton Fairley, one of the world's leading cancer specialists, when it went off as he walked past with his dog.

A second attempt was made to kill Edward Heath in early November, when a bomb was placed under his Rover car. It had been set to explode when the car was driven away, but did not go off. When the Rover drove off, a taxi pulled into the space, and the bomb was spotted and defused by a bomb-disposal team. The same month, the IRA bombed a high-class Mayfair restaurant, Scotts, killing two customers and injuring a dozen others. On 27 November, the same team went to the home of Ross McWhirter, editor with his twin brother of *The Guinness Book of Records*, who had offered a £50,000 reward for the capture of the bombers. They shot McWhirter, emptying a Magnum into his body in the hall of his house at close range.

It was, coincidentally, around this time that Nairac began to visit the areas frequented by Irish nationals. Whether or not he was operating officially seems to be in doubt, but his motive appeared to be to gain intelligence around the London area and, perhaps, at the same time, to prepare for a possible return to Northern Ireland. That possibility was nowhere in sight at the time, although he was scheduled to begin more training at Warminster College. Martin Squires recalled:

One night, he called and said, 'C'mon, put your old things on, we're going slumming.' It was then that we started going up to Kilburn, north London, in and out of the pubs largely frequented by the local Irish community. He knew his way around these places, I think from his days when he was working on McAlpine building sites. Quite how an Oxford undergraduate came to be doing that is beyond me. He told me to dress down for the occasion when we went to Kilburn and I had to dig out an old pair of jeans and scuff up my shoes. I asked him why the hell we were going to these places, which were pretty bloody dire compared to our more usual surroundings, when we could choose any one of a dozen places nearer our usual haunts. It was, he said, for a particular reason and I did not press it. It became quite clear to me that he was either undercover or about to go undercover again. I went with him to the Kilburn area on a number of occasions; he apparently went quite often on his own.

He too was dressing quite scruffily and in the previous few weeks had grown his hair longer. He would be in a donkey jacket. He would say to me before we went in, 'Now don't open your bloody mouth.' The way I spoke – all plummy – I didn't plan to. We would be standing at the bars, not saying a lot, just drinking. We stuck to Guinness for the whole evening. When he spoke to order drinks or whatever, he did so loudly in an Irish accent.

He had what I thought was a fantastic mimicry of the Irish accent and after several pints of Guinness he started singing these Republican songs. I felt quite uncomfortable. I mean, what was the man doing? Was he rehearsing for something, or just trying to ingratiate himself? This was at a time when the IRA was bombing London again. I kept saying to him, 'This bloody place must be full of IRA.' I could not fathom it out, exactly. I was frightened out of my life a lot of the time I spent with him, you know, because the places we were visiting were pretty tough.

He just carried on, encouraging others to join in his songs. It was quite an incredible scene. But, for all that, he'd be roaring with laughter on the way home and he was such fun to be with. You never knew what to expect and meeting up with him, you'd think to yourself, What the bloody hell's going to happen tonight?

One night, I was waiting for him in the King's Road and I saw him having a contretemps with a minicab driver. He laid him out flat. He could be pretty aggressive, especially with a few drinks inside him, and could knock anyone's lights out. It was another pretty worrying aspect of his make-up. You never quite knew if you were going to get into a fight. If you were, you'd want to be with him, rather than agin him. We made one or two hasty exits from the pubs in Kilburn, or at least I did, pulling at his arm to follow me out. Sometimes he stayed on for a bit of a knockabout while I was hiding around the corner.

That's what worried me about going up to Kilburn and singing those songs. I said to him time after time, 'Robert, you are going to get rumbled one day, chum.' I thought it only a matter of time before he was in trouble. I talked to him at length about this and suggested that he had this unnerving relationship with Ireland, the history, the accent. He claimed he could tell any accent from any of the different counties. I asked him what accent he used, but he did not answer me. I imagine that if anything undid him in the end, it was probably that: good he may have been but, you know, in any country people can identify regional accents almost instantly, and especially when the personnel under scrutiny may have had a few drinks.

The fisticuffs were generally isolated incidents, of course, not every night we went out, but there was no denying that he had this thuggish side of him that I could not figure, very buoyant. Conversely, there was nothing to compare with the elegance and charm of him in St James's Palace on a regimental dinner. He also was a great sportsman, indoor and outdoor. He did not seem to have much religion then, in spite of Ampleforth and all that, but he had a great respect for his family.

Thereafter, Squires saw Nairac only intermittently, presumably on breaks from service in Northern Ireland and during his return for his attendance for a time at the Junior Division of the Staff College at Warminster. They did not speak often about his work, but when they did Squires found him 'somewhat indiscreet, but on the other hand he knew he could trust me not to breathe a word of what he said'.

Nairac's jaunts to the north London pubs, coincidentally, took him to within a ten-minute drive of the two flats being used as the headquarters of the IRA's London bombers, at Crouch Hill, Hornsey, and Milton Grove, Stoke Newington. There, the IRA team of Tom O'Connell (26), Edward Butler (26), Henry Duggan (23) and Hugh Doherty (25) were preparing for another hit. They had by now accumulated a small arsenal of weapons and sophisticated bomb-making equipment, including Sten guns, Magnums, a .30 carbine and semi-automatic pistols.

Their next target was a return visit to Scotts restaurant in Mayfair. They were getting over-confident and too arrogant, and angry now that Scotts had opened for business again so quickly after their last attack. They would give them another taste of IRA lead. Armed with the Sten guns and Magnums, the four of them drove from the Crouch Hill flat in a stolen Ford Cortina, fitted with false number plates. They reached the restaurant at around 9.15 p.m. and one of them fired from the open passenger window as they drove by. Two plain-clothes policemen on duty at the restaurant saw the shooting, and commandeered a taxi to follow the Cortina as it sped away.

Other police units were immediately alerted by radio and began to converge on the area of the chase. The Cortina sped towards Marylebone station with the taxi still in pursuit. The gang turned into a cul-de-sac, abandoned their car and made a dash for it on foot. Duggan stopped to fire the Sten gun at the advancing policemen but it jammed.

Other police squads had now reached the area, and were exchanging fire with the fleeing IRA gang, who ran on into Balcombe Street, where dozens of police were arriving, blocking both ends. The four ran into a block of flats and forced their way into the home of Mr and Mrs John Matthews, who became their hostages. There began the famous Balcombe Street siege, watched by television viewers around the world as the drama unfolded.

The bombers demanded an aircraft to take them to Dublin. Police negotiators kept them talking on the telephone and dug in for a long game of cat and mouse, with every move being monitored by a bank of television cameras and media camped outside the Balcombe Street property. Northern Ireland specialists from the military, MI5 and the SAS were all rushed to the operations room at Marylebone station and used for advice. The police team were specially trained for such an eventuality and began their softly-softly approach. An SAS team were placed on standby, to storm the flat if necessary, but the Metropolitan Police Assistant Commissioner Ernest Bond, who led the negotiating team, insisted on trying to talk the bombers out. The Met wanted the gang – and the hostages – alive.

The siege went on for six nerve-racking days before the four bombers eventually surrendered. I later met Ernest Bond, who told me that the IRA team on the mainland at the time were credited with forty bombings and fifteen murders. The London police force took credit for a classic operation in ending the siege without loss of life. They earned great praise, also, for capturing the four most dangerous men in Britain, although it was not quite the great intelligence coup it was cracked up to be.

They were lucky, and Bond admitted as much to me. The four bombers had had such a run of good fortune that they began to believe they were invincible. It was fortunate for the police, said Bond, that they had been stupid enough to return to the scene of a previous crime. They made other errors that caused great consternation back at the IRA GHQ.

The four had left enough evidence lying around their flats in north London not merely to connect them with many other crimes but also to compromise IRA operations in Britain for months to come. When police raided the apartments, they found lists and maps of potential targets, along with suggestions from Dublin as to how the gang might attempt attacks on other sites that would produce spectacular results.

Goodge Street underground station had obviously been surveyed, and Dublin suggested that bombs could be placed in the air ducts in the ceiling. There were also detailed instructions for them to carry out a recce of Walthamstow reservoir and Hackney Down pumping station. They were to report back on suggestions for blowing up the pumping station and poisoning the lakes feeding the reservoir.

The police also found details of their courier system from Dublin, photographs of senior police figures for possible assassination and lists of names of public figures who might also be targeted. The Christian names or nicknames of other IRA operatives already in Britain were discovered scribbled on notepaper, and by cross-checking them with their own intelligence, the police, MI5 and Special Branch were able to identify many of them.

Yet, even as the London police basked in the glory of a job well done, the RUC and the military in Northern Ireland were facing another massive onslaught of violence. The Balcombe Street siege seemed to light the touchpaper to an explosion of the most bloody and vicious outbreak of tit-for-tat killings for many months.

A new wave of pure sectarian violence began six days before Christmas 1975. A Catholic bar at Silverbridge in South Armagh was attacked by loyalist gunmen. Three people, including the fourteen-year-old son of the owner, were murdered. On Boxing Day, another attack was launched against a Catholic bar in which one man was fatally wounded; and on New Year's Eve, the inevitable reprisals were launched, with a bomb placed at the Protestant pub in the hitherto peaceful village of Gifford, County Down.

The attack marked a gruesome link between the turn of the old year and the beginning of the new. Two victims were killed instantly, taking the final tally for 1975 to 246 deaths. A third victim did not die until the early hours of New Year's Day, becoming the first fatal victim of violence in 1976.

This single digit would, before the first week of the year was out, be increased to seventeen. On 4 January, five Catholics, all members of the Social Democratic and Labour Party, were murdered in a loyalist attack at Whitecross, South Armagh. Within twenty-four hours, the IRA chose to exact their revenge in the same place, Whitecross, and there to commit one of the most atrocious mass murders since the Troubles began.

Twelve workmen, all from the Quaker village of Bessbrook, boarded a minibus at the textile mill in Glenane where they worked. The mill in their home village had shut down and had been taken over by the Army as a fortified base. Since then, they had travelled daily to their new place of employment.

As the bus reached Kingsmills junction on the homeward journey it was already dark, and the driver saw a red light being waved ahead of him and slowed down. It was normally the signal of an Army checkpoint. As he came to a halt, a gang of men, up to twenty of them, emerged from the ditch by the side of the road. They shouted their orders: Everyone off.

The men were lined up and, with a collection of gun barrels pointing at them, were ordered to call out their names. They were all identified as Protestants, bar one who said he was a Catholic. He was kicked into the ditch and told to make himself scarce. The rest were told to say their prayers and then the IRA gang opened fire with machine guns. Ten of the Protestants fell dead beside the little red bus in a shattered tangle of metal, glass and blood. The bodies were shot to pieces, and dozens of spent cartridges were later found on the ground where the gunmen stood. The eleventh of the workers was severely wounded but alive when the gang took off. The twelfth man, the Catholic, who escaped unharmed, raised the alarm.

Northern Ireland Secretary Merlyn Rees described the murders as Al Capone gangsterism, and the Roman Catholic Primate of All Ireland, Cardinal Conway, said the act was 'spitting in the face of Christ'. That night, Protestant leaders were on the telephone to

Rees and Harold Wilson direct, demanding that they take some form of action to combat the rising violence. They especially wanted something done about South Armagh, which they complained was grossly undermanned by the Army and had been allowed to run out of control since the IRA ceasefire – still supposedly in force – had begun. Hapless troops, it had to be admitted, found themselves once again bemused by the prospect of controlling the maze of country roads and lanes that provided more than fifty border crossings for IRA terrorists to flee from capture into the bleak countryside.

The Protestants demanded that Wilson should send in extra troops immediately. Wilson had his own problems, still, but listened to the demands and agreed. Within twenty-four hours, 600 extra troops were preparing to leave for Ulster, including the first contingent of the SAS. The long-rumoured presence of this most feared of regiments was at last to become a fact.

Not long afterwards, Martin Squires heard from Robert Nairac. There was a note of true seriousness in his voice. He said: 'Martin, please do not attempt to contact me. I'm going back to Northern Ireland. I'm going back undercover.'

# 10

# IN WITH THE SAS

The SAS had completed one previous tour of Northern Ireland in 1969. D Squadron, 22 SAS, was sent in to gather high-grade intelligence which was not forthcoming elsewhere. They patrolled openly in specially adapted Land Rovers, nicknamed Pink Panthers, and spent much of their time on the province's eastern seaboard vainly trying to catch arms' smugglers. Their presence was so open, in fact, that SAS soldiers marched through the market town of Newtownards, County Down, to Movilla Cemetery in full uniform on Remembrance Sunday 1969 to lay a wreath at the grave of Lieutenant-Colonel Blair Mayne, a native of the borough and one of the most highly decorated members of the unit, as well as one of its founders.

But Ulster was not the place for the SAS, and during a lean time for the Special Forces – there were even rumours of possible disbandment – a small group of the regiment's officers looked to more traditional, faraway hunting grounds to provide their men with suitable employment. They found one in Oman, the scene of a wild colonial war that had engaged them in the late 1950s when rebel tribesmen began their guerrilla attacks against the oppressive regime of the country's dictatorial ruler, the Sultan of Muscat and Oman.

The British government supported the Sultan as part of its overall Middle East strategy but had no intention of putting in a large-scale force. Instead, it opted for a low-intensity operation devised by Frank Kitson, who was at the time working in a sensitive role as a Ministry of Defence operations planner. The plan was to insert teams of British soldiers, who would carry large amounts of money to bribe the locals and turn them against the guerrillas, and in consequence capture the relatively small bands of rebel forces. (A decade later, similar tactics were to be employed in Northern Ireland under the guise of the Military Reconnaissance Force.) Kitson's plan for Oman was eventually ditched for a more rapid military solution, a low-key, covert intervention, which, in difficult terrain, required the expertise of the SAS, gained from its classic counter-revolutionary campaigns in colonial outposts since the end of the Second World War.

Twelve years after the successful conclusion of that campaign, in the spring of 1970, the SAS returned to Oman, this time to the hostile terrain around the southern mountains of Dhofar, to fight Communist-backed guerrillas and help train the Omani army. It turned into a long and arduous six-year war, which eventually required the involvement of thousands of Iranian and Jordanian troops supporting Oman's own forces to isolate the guerrillas and cut their supplies coming in from South Yemen.

Incredible stories of SAS activity filtered back through the grapevine, some of which bore remarkable similarities to operations at another time, and in another place. One involved a former officer who was recruited from the original SAS force to the Sultan's fledgling special forces. Under the direction of another SAS officer, then running Military Intelligence, he disguised himself as a native and lived for months in border communities, dressed like a Dhofari and apparently unrecognizable as an Englishman. From this position, he ran agents to and fro across the South Yemeni border and, in 1972, began an operation to blow up a Yemeni army supply depot, eighty miles over the border. The clandestine operation was such that had he been caught, the British would have disowned him because of the sensitivity of border crossing. Using two Bedford trucks loaded with 500 pounds of volatile gelignite, he led a force of eighty Yemeni exiles across the border and under the cover of darkness laid the explosives on each corner of the fort, linked by a time fuse. They retreated and saw the fort explode in spectacular fashion against the night sky. Thereafter, Westminster banned all border crossing by any SAS teams.

The battle was won in the final weeks of 1975, but in January 1976, the SAS were still heavily committed in Dhofar when the announcement was made that the regiment was to be deployed to Northern Ireland. The news was treated with general disdain by the British Army in Northern Ireland, to whom the announcement came as a total surprise – as indeed it did to the SAS. The Army did not want the SAS there, and soon demonstrated that they were not welcome. Some were scared of the hard-line reputation of the regiment and particularly hated the media hysteria that surrounded it. Others felt that the SAS would come wading in and steal their glory.

And so intially the SAS were confined to the southern tip of the Six Counties, working to a specific brief of tackling the lawlessness in South Armagh and the border regions, and opening up the no-go areas – nothing else! In the first six months of their presence in the Six Counties, they could not and would not extend their sphere of operations beyond that area.

Colonel G, who had returned to his regiment after his secondment to the intelligence post with 3 Brigade, Northern Ireland, recalled what happened:

In January 1976, I was back in Hereford. It was at the time of the Kingsmills massacre, when twelve Protestant linen factory workers travelling home in their minibus were ambushed. The following day, Harold Wilson did his wonderful instant cry of 'We'll put the SAS into Northern Ireland.' I was 2IC at 22 SAS then. The CO was away in Dhofar at the time, wrapping up the end of the Dhofar war, which was quite a critical period for us. We had taken a number of casualties and there was still a good deal of work to be done. I and one other in Hereford were the only two people who had been in Northern Ireland before, despite all the cries that the SAS were over there. Were they heck! Up to that point the SAS had not had a presence as such in Northern Ireland, although we had input into the intelligence element, sending people who had previous experience with the SAS, like Tony Ball. But now we were going and it happened almost by accident, and certainly with a good deal of rancour among senior-level Army management.

The story was that following the [linen workers'] massacre, Harold Wilson was faced with a very hard-nosed Protestant demand for a very positive military and political reaction. There was some considerable anguish over the cost, with the Army talking of a brigade of troops. Then one of the Protestant leaders eventually said words to the effect of 'Look, if you put the SAS in, that will meet our demands.'

Wilson – and few people have registered this – said, 'Well yes – why not? They want the SAS instead of a brigade. Send in the SAS.' He never asked the Chief of General Staff, and even before consultations with the Army began, it was announced on the radio that the SAS were going in.

I was in a pub in Chelsea when I saw the news on television and I went straight back to our headquarters. Later, the Director of the SAS phoned me and asked me if I'd seen the television and if I knew anything about it. I did not and nor, apparently, did he. The next thing we heard was that he had been ordered to the office of the Chief of General Staff General Sir Michael Carver, who was not, incidentally, a fan of Special Forces. The SAS Director found himself in a confrontational situation – he was on the mat. Some of the top brass were convinced that the SAS were conniving to get into Northern Ireland, which was simply not the case and certainly not at that point in time. We were heavily committed elsewhere, at home and abroad, at that stage and would be, it seemed, for at least the next year.

At the time Wilson made his arbitrary decision to send in the SAS, there was simply nobody about at Hereford. We still had a heavy presence in Dhofar and had taken casualties, one squadron was on counter-terrorist team duties, another squadron was on a very important NATO exercise, which was a major breakthrough for us as it was the first time we had been assigned to it, and we had one squadron on commitments all over the place, on courses and so on. We were a small and always understrength regiment, nothing like the size of an infantry battalion.

The upshot was that I was sent immediately to Northern Ireland for an initial recce. We were bitterly resented, partly because of the publicity, and I could appreciate that point. Publicity was the last thing we wanted. The Army didn't want us there. That was made abundantly clear when I arrived. I had gone into the intelligence corridor at Lisburn where I had previously worked to meet one of the chaps I knew, and at that moment the Colonel, GS Intelligence, came out of his office, saw me and said: 'Get off this corridor. You're not allowed up here.' Anyway, my friend smoothed that over by explaining we were old friends and that I had just been invited in for coffee. The Colonel grudgingly accepted that.

The principles of SAS commitment to any operation are command at the highest level, intelligence at the highest level and being allowed to plan our own operations. We were to discover that the first two principles were being thrown out of the window straight away – that as a regiment we would come under the command of the South Armagh-based battalion, 1 Royal Scots, down in

Bessbrook Mill and that our intelligence would come from their IO.

This was preposterous. We had been put in by the Prime Minister, but that didn't matter. We were being banished down there to Bessbrook Mill, which was an horrendous place to be based for any sort of covert operations, to do a job in which the Army and Royal Scots had seemingly failed, which was not necessarily their fault. But the message was quite clear: 'You'll do as you're told.'

We should have been going in with much higher backing. Instead we were virtually banned from mainline headquarters and we would not be receiving high-level intelligence. All our intelligence was to come from the Royal Scots Intelligence Officer, which was pretty low-level stuff for a unit like us, seemingly expected to work some kind of miracle. So at this stage, I came to the conclusion that we had to have someone out here with us who could establish access to the RUC and Special Branch and hopefully tap their intelligence. I had the highest regard for them and what we needed was an experienced, credible intelligence officer of our own who could liaise with them.

I knew that Robert Nairac had, in the meantime, gone back to his regiment. When I got back to Hereford after my initial recce I telephoned him, and asked him if he would join us, on attachment. He jumped at the chance. The Grenadiers were very good; the Household Division was always very helpful. Robert was released and came for a briefing with us at Hereford. He was a bit resented by the boys: 'Who is this man?'

We hadn't had any connection with any unit in Northern Ireland, other than a few of our own who had served there after returning to their own regiments, and our soldiers had little connection with the personnel selected for intelligence duties in Northern Ireland. They had their own selection course and did their own training, which originally had quite a heavy SAS input, but thereafter there was not much liaison between the two units and certainly personalities in the middle and lower levels didn't know each other. So Robert, appearing at Hereford, was treated initially with a touch of offhandedness.

Well, Robert charmed his way into most hearts, but being a Grenadier and a Guards officer made him instantly suspect in the minds of some of the more cynical SAS hard-line soldiers.

We actually went across to Northern Ireland with just eleven men, which quite frankly was all we had available at that moment in time – nothing like the '1,000 SAS move into Ulster' which was screamed out in the headlines. Several of those eleven men were at the time on convalescent leave, having been wounded in Dhofar, and were dragged in, along with some instructors from the Regiment's Training Wing. We went across to Bessbrook Mill, where we were greeted by a mixture of curiosity, suspicion and resentment by those British forces already *in situ*. We were expected to fall in with the *modus operandi* of the British Army in Northern Ireland and merge with those present in their infantry role.

The Royal Scots were certainly hospitable but at the same time they were having to work under strict instructions from their Brigade HQ, then HQNI, then the MoD, on curbing our ideas of independent action and activities, and ensuring we 'toed the line'. It seemed that the Army simply did not understand us and had no concept of the way we operated, or needed to operate to 'secure peace in South Armagh'. I recall that when we were discussing accommodation and messing arrangements, and I told them we just wanted one area for all of us, regardless of rank, and that we would remain all together, they said, 'What do you mean "all together" – that does not include officers, surely?'

'Yes,' I said. 'We work together and remain together at all times.'

'Ah ... but you will come into the officers' mess, won't you?'

'No,' I said. 'We eat together, we do everything together as a unit. There is no separation.' We just wanted one area of Bessbrook Mill to be on our own – thus no trouble to anyone, I said, and we'd all be in there.

'Oh ... good God!' came the reply.

They simply could not comprehend SAS methods and ways of living, let alone operating. Robert progressively smoothed our path with the Royal Scots and other units.

Robert Nairac had a fairly precise brief as far as the SAS were concerned. His specific task in the initial stages of the SAS presence was to link up with the RUC and the RUC Special Branch for information. This was necessary for SAS needs. General Army intelligence at the time was very thin on the ground in South Armagh, largely because the Army simply could not establish agents and informers in what were no-go areas for any military personnel. Nairac would meet his contacts at the RUC, who would put up suggestions, ideas and leads. He also had access to a good deal of other intelligence from other sources, which he would then link together. He would often go out into the field, check things on the ground on his own and perhaps follow leads and contacts before presenting the SAS squadron with an intelligence package.

Officially, he should have had back-up on these missions, whether he was on a recce of the ground or meeting contacts or agents, but often, in his rush to get out or, more likely, because of the nature of the contact that demanded his clandestine attention, he did not inform his SAS unit what he was up to. When he had formulated a particular line of investigation or plans for an operation, he would present it to the squadron commander and would sit in on the intelligence briefing, at which the project would be discussed and decisions taken on the plan of action.

Colonel G described his contribution in these initial stages as invaluable. He knew the ground very well and in those early days, if, for instance, it was suggested a surveillance operation was to be set up at a certain point, he might chip in and point out that they would never get away with it because the IRA and friends were heavily represented in the area, with their own patrols who scoured the hedgerows and the local terrain with dogs morning and evening for signs of Army surveillance teams:

> Initially, being such a small unit, we set ourselves what we considered achievable targets in surveillance and ultimately apprehension of known IRA operators. We decided that because we were so small, rather than rush around trying to swat the drones we would go for the queen bees. We drew up a list of leading IRA personalities in South Armagh – the commanders, the organizers as we understood them to be – and we were planning to lift them one way or another. If it came down to shooting them ... well, if the situation demanded it, yes, but perhaps we were naïve about that. Even I, who had been in Northern Ireland for about a year, was too hard-line for what was wanted. We had been put in specifically to clean up South Armagh. Yet we had a situation where we were supposed to obey all the rules that the Army had to obey and which had led to the loose situation down there in the first place.

It was a no-go area in many parts to British Army vehicles … The way we saw it was that we were either in, and playing it our way, or could go home. That first bunch of hard-line SAS – and I include myself – were used to a shoot-on-sight situation in Dhofar. We were very frustrated.

We had to ask for all those specific instructions for opening fire in the province and commence special training for our soldiers. But the truth of it was that we soon realized that the Army simply did not want us at all. They thought it was an insult, which was all down to Harold Wilson and the way he had handled it.

Robert was also invaluable as we began to set up our initial contacts. He knew the head of Special Branch at Newry extremely well, having worked there in the past. He knew the RUC senior-level officers very well, too. He really paved the way for us to get alongside them. Again, Robert Nairac was invaluable to us in knowing his way around and knowing the Army system and routes to Special Branch. South Armagh was no different to anywhere else in that regard. The Army and the RUC had a sometimes difficult, sometimes uneasy relationship, but Robert was able to cut through those concerns and suspicions by way of his personal contacts. I wrote to a very senior RUC officer, explained our position and virtually pleaded for his cooperation. I explained our difficulty, our lack of good intelligence, which was always the key to our most effective use, and asked if we could have the assistance of the RUC. He wrote back with one word: 'Yes!' with his initials. That was the difference. And they gave us the help that did enable us to apprehend five of the eleven top names on our list within two to three months. That was still with our eleven men, and just a few more as numbers slowly began to increase as Hereford was able to release returning soldiers from various jobs abroad.

Meanwhile, the Brigade Commander's rule at Bessbrook Mill initially was that we could go out on patrol with the Royal Scots, provided we had their permission and provided we wore Royal Scots uniform. Now he was a charming man, but ... to see a mixed Royal Scots/SAS patrol out on the streets was a bit of a give-away. Most were smallish Jocks and on the end were a six-foot-two Fijian and a six-foot sun-tanned Londoner in tam-o'-shanters – they stood out a mile. It was ludicrous. Trying to make that point to 'them' was very difficult.

Gradually, they began to give us some space and Nairac paved the way for a great deal of that. He also faced some resentment from the more senior ranks of the SAS. He wasn't one of them, but he had a position of considerable power. People asked me if he had ever done SAS selection. I had to explain that he wasn't with us for any SAS capability. He was not SAS. He was with us because he knew the score; he would make life easier for us, he would get us the vital intelligence we needed because no one else was better equipped for that particular role than Robert Nairac. And he did just that.

It is worth reminding ourselves of his position at that time, because there was a good deal of confusion about his position after his death ... He came out to Northern Ireland at my request, as a liaison officer for the SAS. He did on occasions wear a regimental beret, but he was given the choice to wear what beret seemed most appropriate to the task at hand, such as meeting Army personnel. Again, this also rankled with some of my people: 'Why is he wearing an SAS beret?' I had to explain that I trusted his judgement. He was not always going to be right, but by and large it worked well and I still believe he did us very well.

A few of his old chums, like Tony Ball, who had worked with him in intelligence earlier, came back to Northern Ireland for a tour, this time as SAS. Tony Ball took charge of our first detachment and again established an ideal working relationship with Nairac. They operated in South Armagh in a softly-softly capacity, and when we finally established the need to go looking for key IRA personnel in South Armagh, Robert and Tony Ball between them put together the early successes, which were absolutely critical to establishing more effective control and obtaining high-grade intelligence over that whole region.

The first IRA man that Nairac led them to was Sean McKenna junior, one of a family of six and inheritor of Republican traditions from his father, Sean McKenna senior, who had died the previous year aged forty-two. McKenna senior had been one of those arrested in the early days of the struggle, soon after the beginning of internment, and one of the 'hooded men' in the European Convention of Human Rights' reports who suffered interrogation by way of sensory deprivation torture. His family claimed his early death was due to this treatment by the security forces.

Sean McKenna junior followed his father's allegiance to the PIRA, and at the age of seventeen was arrested and interned for three years, until his release in 1974. Thereafter, he went to live at one of the family's homes south of the border at Edentubber, Dundalk, just across the border in the Republic of Ireland. He was arrested on 12 March 1976.

McKenna himself claimed that he had been in bed asleep at 2.45 a.m. when two men got into his house through a window, kicked open his bedroom door, put a 9mm Browning to his head and told him not to move. They threw his clothes at him and told him to get dressed. He claimed:

One of them said, 'If you put up a struggle or don't want to come with us, say now. I will have no hesitation shooting you.' I said that I would go with them. Outside, another one was standing guard with a Sterling. They took me down to the river, to a point where we could jump across. We walked across another three fields to a point where there were three more of them standing behind a wall. One of them radioed in, 'We have our friend.' The ones who arrested me took off their civilian jackets and put them in a hold-all. The officer told me if I made one wrong move they would shoot me.

At his trial, fourteen months later, several SAS soldiers gave evidence. They said that McKenna was arrested by three soldiers wearing civilian clothes in a field 250 yards on the northern side of the border. He later made a statement confessing a number of crimes. McKenna was sentenced to twenty-five years' imprisonment for what the judge described as a 'catalogue of terrorist offences'. They included two of attempted murder, two of causing bomb explosions, and other charges of kidnapping, possession of firearms and belonging to the IRA. The date of the trial was 14 May 1977, the day Nairac disappeared. In October 1980, McKenna was one of the seven IRA prisoners who went on hunger strike in the H-Block prison. He ended his protest at Christmas.

The second major arrest by the SAS, again with the help of Nairac's initial intelligence input, had a less successful outcome, at least for the alleged offender. Peter Cleary, aged twenty-five, was, according to Republican sources, a staff captain, 1st Battalion, South Armagh IRA, and also its treasurer. He had been on the run from arrest warrants in the north, and while south of the border had picked up one conviction in 1975, appearing at a Special Criminal Court in Dublin charged with the possession of firearms and ammunition. He was given a three-year suspended sentence.

Early in March 1976, a group of men wearing hooded masks arrived at his house in Belleeks. Finding no one present, they inquired of his whereabouts from neighbours. They claimed to be PIRA, but some said they had British accents.

On 31 March three members of the Royal Scots, David Ferguson, Roderick Bannon and John Pearson, were blown up by a landmine in Cleary's home village of Belleeks. Later the same day, a group of Royal Scots and SAS raided Cleary's home. He was not in.

The SAS later established that Cleary made visits to see his fiancée Shirley Hulme at the home of her sister at Tievecrum, a short sprint from the border on the northern side. They were to be married the following month. On 12 April, the SAS team had the property under surveillance with a close-observation team, faces blacked up and dug in just 120 yards from the house, and linked to a communications base 300 yards away. Three nights later, Cleary was seen driving from the house heading for the border, which was just fifty yards away, so the SAS team did not pursue him.

At 7.45 that evening, an Army helicopter coming into land at Crossmaglen came under rocket and machine-gun fire. Cleary arrived back at his girlfriend's house later that night. There were several visitors, apparently inspecting a car that a member of the family was selling under a spotlight attached to the wall of the house. They were being watched by the SAS close-observation team, still positioned in a ditch just 120 yards away. Other SAS soldiers were at the back of the house.

Suddenly, dogs at the house began to bark and two of the men set off with a torch to search the area. They walked straight into the SAS surveillance team and one of the soldiers stood up and fired a shot over their heads. The shot served as a warning to the rest of the SAS unit, and the soldiers moved in and ordered everyone to stand against the wall. According to the witnesses, Cleary was identified from a photograph carried by one of the

SAS men, a civilian in chequered coat and black trousers – Nairac. Cleary was taken into an outhouse for questioning. The family complained later that Cleary was kicked and dragged along, and was beaten up inside the barn.

The SAS officer who was commanding the operation radioed for a helicopter to take Cleary to Bessbrook. It arrived at around 11.00 p.m. and the SAS team went out to meet it. They were all standing by a wall guiding it in, leaving one man alone to watch the prisoner. Cleary, according to SAS evidence at an inquest later, tried to make a run for it by grabbing his guard's weapon. The soldier had the butt of his SLR under his armpit. The rifle was cocked and Cleary 'hurled himself at me' the SAS man said, and in accordance with his training he opened fire and continued to do so until the threat to his own life was over. He fired three shots in all and stopped firing when he realized that Cleary was no longer a danger. The body was taken by helicopter to Bessbrook camp, where a medical officer pronounced him dead. A brief Army statement said that Cleary was shot by the SAS attempting to escape. He was wanted for questioning in connection with a number of offences.

Some of the British tabloid newspapers took the story way beyond the available facts and hung on him the major atrocities of recent times, suggesting that Cleary was wanted for murders the previous September, and was a member of the gang that machine-gunned to death the ten Protestants in January and blew up the three soldiers with a landmine in March – a step too far, but there was little doubt he had been involved in at least one of the incidents.

As Colonel G said, far from having a licence to kill in Ulster, the SAS were under strict orders to follow the code on the yellow card – the rules under which a soldier may open fire. Because they were SAS, they were also under close scrutiny from every quarter – media, politicians, civil rights and the Army itself. He recalled:

When Cleary was arrested, there were a number of articles about the fact that he was shot while resisting arrest. The regiment was hauled over the coals – 'You shot him!' – and that came from the Army, the politicians, the IRA and everyone. In a way, it was because it was what they expected of us, not least from the media hype. But in fact what happened, and again this has never really registered when the story has been repeated down the years, was that a helicopter was coming down to collect. We had a small patrol on the ground and put four men out with lights to guide the pilot down in the darkness, which is what we used to do in Dhofar and elsewhere. But the RAF, operating in a UK environment, needed more lights – six or eight, I can't remember exactly – and the upshot was that we only had one guy guarding Cleary. He took his chance and tried to grab the weapon from our guy and make a run for it. I know it's an old cliché for shooting a prisoner, but that's exactly what happened. He was far too valuable to be needlessly shot and everyone knew this. In a tactical sense, it was our loss too. It was the last thing we wanted.

The IRA vowed to avenge the death of Peter Cleary, and for weeks there was an air of anticipation as to what form it would take. They aimed high – a life for a life; and the victim they chose was of the highest calibre: the British Ambassador to Dublin, Christopher Ewart-Biggs. South Armagh IRA killed him, blowing up his car with a landmine on 21 July 1976.

# 11

## WARNING SIGNS

Throughout his time in South Armagh in 1976, Robert Nairac was digging himself deeper and deeper into a region where the dangers to him personally, and to any operative of his kind, were on every street corner, in every pub and in every one of the myriad of country lanes he drove down in his unmarked, slightly battered 'company' car. Quite clearly, however, he was pushing himself towards some grand effort that took him well beyond the bounds of his duties as a link man for the SAS. There were rumours, even then, that he was working for someone other than Colonel G at the SAS, reporting to a higher level of intelligence, and that that is what pushed him beyond the role of mere liaison officer.

All the SAS officers interviewed for this book said they knew of no such connection and most doubted that he was being used as such by either MI5 or MI6 specifically, although the possibility – as will be seen in their personal testimony in forthcoming chapters – had clearly crossed their minds. His pursuit of intelligence and information led him constantly to the danger zones. Whatever the contacts and leads he pursued outside his SAS brief were, it was suggested to me on numerous occasions, they seemed to have more to do with a personal quest than an official one.

All the officers I spoke to, without exception, expressed the same concerns: that while working alongside the SAS, he consistently flouted their rules, by which he was expected to abide. In theory, he should not have been 'wandering around the countryside looking for the IRA alone at night, or meeting unknown contacts in some godforsaken stretch of terrain, or going into dodgy pubs without back-up, or singing rebel songs at the bar and calling himself Danny, but he was apparently doing it, most of the time without the knowledge of his SAS controllers'.

Hard-liners in the SAS and the NCOs who were sticklers for the rules did not like it, or him. They had to run by the book, which was a control system created for the safety of the men and for the regiment as a whole. Every man in the outfit had to be logged in and out; every one of them going out on operations had to have back-up. Every one of them had to call in their positions at given times; every one of them had to appoint a time when they were expected back, and if that changed they had to call in with an alteration and an explanation. If the men did not call in or return by the appointed time, the company sergeant major or duty officer would have to send out a team to look for them. If the men were on surveillance, it would take the form of drive-bys in unmarked cars. If visual contact was not possible, it might be necessary to put up a helicopter equipped with night sights for a search. 'Never be out of contact' was the number one rule. If they were, or were late, explanations were required when the men returned to base. If the explanation was not considered good enough by the company sergeant major, they would be fined – regardless of rank or position. If officers repeatedly flouted this rule, they were hauled before the commanding officer. Robert Nairac was expected to do the same, and follow SAS guidelines.

When Nairac was in Northern Ireland, those who failed to conform were heavily fined by the company sergeant major; real bad boys had to pay up to £1,000, usually when choppers and ground transport had to be sent out to look for them because they had failed to check in. For undercover soldiers, checking in was not always possible and a certain leeway was given before the search parties went out.

Nairac hated the restrictions the rules placed upon his movements. He had run-ins with several NCOs over his failure to keep in touch and ran up a heavy tab in 'fines'. He had a number of infringements against his name and usually paid up even though – as we now know for certain – he was not a member of the SAS. Fines didn't stop him. Clearly, he did not feel honour bound to be governed by their rules. In any event, according to Captain D, Nairac was by then working very much to his own agenda, or at least that of someone who wasn't SAS. No one seemed to have a full picture of exactly what he was up to or, for that matter, who, if anyone, was controlling him.

A stickler for the rules of the game – 'that way we won't all get killed' – Captain D did not like the way Robert Nairac flouted them. The rules are supposed to be followed rigidly by all members of the SAS, designed for the protection of the soldier himself as well as the wider security of the regiment. Captured men can be made to talk; they might have their equipment examined, their documents copied, their weapons stolen and used against their own side. The purpose of the rules is to avoid such situations and minimize their impact – the implications go much deeper than just being late for a check-in. The basic requirements, such as calling in at a given time, using back-up on a mission, especially for plain-clothed soldiers meeting dodgy people alone in the heart of bandit territory, are plain common-sense issues in SAS management.

There was another aspect of his 'looseness' in following the rules that annoyed some in the SAS operation and it concerned, curiously enough, the reputation of the regiment itself. The SAS had been the subject of huge media hype, both before and after its arrival in Northern Ireland. As they saw it, they were being hit by a double-edged sword. On the one hand, the political hawks of Northern Ireland and Westminster were happy to see the SAS branded the hardmen of the British military, the ogres brought in to teach the terrorists a lesson. They were happy to promote any advancement of the theory that the regiment was there to cut the terrorists to pieces by whatever means – and if that meant shoot to kill, so be it. On the other hand, the IRA propagandists, left-wing politicians and a large coterie of so-called human rights campaigners branded the SAS themselves as terrorists, torturers and killers.

Many unsolved or unclaimed killings were wrongly laid at their door. By their very nature, they have been categorized as legalized killers, cowboys or the out-of-control Mafia of the British military. Whatever roles may be expected of them, the fact remains that they are one of the most disciplined outfits in the Army, whose punishments for breaches of the rules are rigorously self-imposed. They also obey orders, and that means sticking to the constraints imposed by their own procedural manuals, although historically they have pushed themselves to the very brink of those constraints. That is the nature of the beast.

The fact was, they were not there to organize a Sunday school picnic. They were there to confront head on the viciousness and the violence that has been briefly touched upon in these pages and to attempt to call a halt to the lawlessness where others had failed dismally. It would be foolish to expect them to conform to mainstream military practice, because the SAS was and remains outside normal soldiering; otherwise there would be no point in it being there. On the credit side, the regiment undoubtedly made an almost immediate contribution to the fact that, after their arrival in the province, the annual death toll began to fall dramatically – by almost two thirds in the first year of their operations – and has continued to do so.

The truth was that, regardless of the hype and the rumours, the SAS operated under the strict controls that emanated in part from within itself and partly from the close scrutiny of the Directorate of Special Forces on the outside. There were no marauding bands of SAS killers on the loose in Northern Ireland then, or ever. If they shot someone – as with Peter Cleary or in 'Death on the Rock', the Gibraltar ambush of IRA suspects – the world would know about it. If they caused an infraction of their rules, it would be headlines.

Less visible – and deliberately so – was the other Special Forces operation known as 14 Int, in which SAS personnel were used on secondment in the early days, but on a decreasing scale after 1975. His involvement with this outfit had allowed Nairac greater flexibility in his movements around Northern Ireland, and coming into the SAS regime unsettled him, especially as Colonel G and others kept him on a fairly tight rein.

His connections with 14 Int had never deterred him, for example, from nipping across the border in pursuit of intelligence about IRA suspects, or tracking their movements and hideouts, particularly in the region of Dundalk, where the IRA terrorists hopped back and forth with impunity. Nairac even went across for personal reasons – to fish and renew old acquaintances. The SAS, on the other hand, was specifically forbidden to cross the border, an order which was stringently reinforced in May 1976 when eight of their number were discovered in the Republic of Ireland. Their presence caused a diplomatic incident and uproar in the newspapers.

The long-running saga began when two SAS men, Private Illisoni Vanioni Ligari, a Fijian, and Private John Michael Lawson crossed the border at around 10.30 p.m. on the night of 6 May. The purpose of their trip was never made public, but it has been suggested they were searching for two of the nine Irish National Liberation Army (ILNA) prisoners who had just escaped from Long Kesh prison.

They were driving along the Newry to Dundalk Road, which led into the Irish Republic. Both men were in civilian clothes and were driving an unmarked Triumph 2000 with a concealed radio and, in the boot, a Sterling sub-machine gun, with ammunition. Both carried Browning automatic pistols. An Irish police roadcheck had been established about 700 yards inside the border, concealed from approaching vehicles. The SAS car was stopped and the two men explained that they were members of the British Army and had strayed into the Republic because of a map-reading error.

They were arrested under the Offences Against the State Act and taken to a nearby police station. Meanwhile, back at their Bessbrook base, SAS control reported that the two men had failed to report in. Six more SAS men in civilian clothes were sent to find them. They were driving unmarked cars – a white Hillman Avenger and a Vauxhall Victor – and between them carried several Browning automatics, two Sterling sub-machine guns, one pump-action shotgun and a small cache of ammunition. They too crossed the border, and were stopped and arrested at the same checkpoint. All were arrested and charged.

The incident brought hefty criticism from the Irish media and mixed reaction in London. The *Guardian* called it a border pantomime but a *Sunday Times* leader article said the Irish government should have sent the men back with a wigging. They were, after all, in pursuit of terrorists, but went on to accuse the Irish government of pursuing the case and making an example of the SAS personnel as part of its campaign against the British government over the question of the torture of suspects in the early days of the Troubles.

In the end, the eight SAS men were released on bail of £40,000, for which the British Army stood surety, but the Irish judicial system kept the case hanging around for more than a year before they were brought to trial. They were found guilty of taking weapons into the Republic without a licence and fined £100 each.

Nairac was attached to the SAS during several months of fairly intensive operations in South Armagh, and in spite of his own cavalier attitude to the SAS code, he was at the same time protective of his own association with the RUC. Colonel G remembered:

We'd had one or two incidents which had come under close scrutiny and some criticism because the correct procedures had not been strictly followed. The RUC hadn't been properly consulted in some instances and Robert himself had been critical of this. He was a firm believer in the view that you could not do anything out there unless you kept the RUC in the picture. We were on a learning curve, but by and large we always did liaise closely with all echelons of the RUC. I had great respect for them. These guys often had much better intelligence than the British Army; after all they lived there and it was their part of the UK, and sometimes we and/or the Army would blow it for them. There were some Army people who were there for the results in their time and nothing else mattered. Meanwhile, the RUC would be there long after they'd gone home, facing the same situation and having their families at risk. Robert hated those types and he educated the regiment along these lines. I like to think that the SAS, coming from a 'hearts-and-minds' operation in Dhofar, appreciated this aspect better than most at the time.

Throughout 1976, and onwards, the SAS presence was being progressively bolstered by our soldiers coming back from Dhofar. As someone put it, they came from the jebel and wadis of an Arab kingdom where open warfare existed, on to the streets of the United Kingdom, full of political and military restrictions and limitations. They had gone from one extreme to the other, facing new situations and, as is so often overlooked, they were now dealing with their own people, British nationals, notwithstanding the fact that an element was made up of terrorists, bombers and killers.

The whole scenario was fraught with potential problems, with new personnel coming in who were not only totally inexperienced in the situation in Northern Ireland but they themselves had just come through the rigours of many months of hard-fought guerrilla warfare in the mountains of Dhofar. That is not an excuse, it is a fact. They came in, it must be said, with a hard-nosed attitude. Initially, with the speed of our commitment to Northern Ireland by Harold Wilson (i.e. overnight!), they'd had only basic training for their new role on

British soil. So our attitude, as much as anything, was seen as far too hard-line, compounded of course by media hysterics and the extraordinary speculation in newspapers in particular. It wasn't so much what we did as what we said, what we wanted to do and how we saw the answer to the lawlessness in South Armagh. You must remember that at the time we were committed not to countering terrorism in the province as a whole, just to restoring law and order in the no-go area, and particularly the border area of South Armagh.

Looking back, the political aim was just to keep the hard-line Protestant element happy by giving them something they wanted. The Army was 'lumbered' with a military element that they did not want, found difficult to accept with all the media interest and speculation – remember this was before the Iranian Embassy siege when the SAS became public property – and thought it best to keep us in a box with the lid nailed firmly down.

Against this background, there was Robert Nairac, who knew the area well and knew how far he could push something or, at least, thought he did. He was the man in the middle doing his best to ensure that the SAS achieved its aim in a situation which he undertsood better than anyone amongst us. He was the meat in a strange political/military sandwich of contradictions. The fact is, he'd gone through a great deal in fulfilling this role. He didn't see it that way, I'm sure, but there had been enormous pressure on him in that last year or so, when he was working with successive squadron commanders coming to a situation which they knew less about than Robert. There were officers who believed he was pushing it, particularly in the way he ignored some of the standard SAS procedures, such as calling in at a set time or going out without back-up. The fact was, he wasn't a member of the club. He wasn't SAS and occasionally the veneer of the Grenadier and the Ampleforth lad would come through, and some of the hard-nosed regiment people would say, 'We can do without this guy.'

Some officers who were coming back for second tours were critical that he had been allowed to remain for as long as we wanted him. As the months went by, he had started to become a little isolated in his own mind through the actions and outlook of some members of the regiment. It was human nature but in the pressures under which Robert operated it began to become difficult and then, although none of us saw it coming, dangerous.

There were difficult early days, with poor communications all round and barely an embryo of the sophisticated set-up which eventually transpired. A lot of the boys coming in from Dhofar left the regiment and the Army. They said that if this was the future, forget it! Some very key people were leaving, going off into security organizations, working in parts of the world they knew well such as the Far and Middle East and doing the work they did best, not bound by yellow cards, bureaucracy and a real fear of pulling the trigger.

They were very experienced operators, like Tony Ball, who became totally frustrated with the Northern Ireland scene and cleared out. It was never a happy hunting ground for the regiment as such. It wasn't our scene.

Even so, the SAS completed a task in South Armagh in which others had failed. The region was much quieter after that first SAS tour, which took them into the early summer of 1976, and, having done that, the Army decided to continue using their particular skills elsewhere, in spite of the relatively small number of soldiers available under the SAS banner, compared to the thousands already there. Colonel G continued:

Having taken South Armagh, as it were, the Army then said we will use you province-wide, which was not, I think, the most effective way to use Special Forces, scattering them round. Looking back, I sometimes think it would have been better to use the SAS for 'hearts and minds' rather than thrusting them into a hard-line role, hyped up by the IRA and the left-wing activist propaganda in Britain. Curiously enough, Robert, in his early days, was very much into hearts and minds, particularly when he was on his first tour with the Grenadiers. He got involved with local kids and helped youth clubs and boxing groups. He loved people – he was always the great romantic and yet he maintained the differential that among them were the enemy and he would always be against the enemy.

The enemy was still the IRA as far as the SAS were concerned and although they had been nailed down by the Army into the region of South Armagh, it now seemed that the SAS operations had been recognized by the Army as something of a breakthrough in at least establishing a more systematic – and less haphazard – approach to tackling terrorists. They had, in spite of the restrictions placed upon them, set themselves specific targets, set up their own intelligence-gathering system and generally ignored what Colonel G described as the hysteria surrounding their arrival. Colonel G himself returned to Hereford later in the year, as more of his men were freed from their commitments in Dhofar.

In the summer, Nairac also took a break back in England. He went on a training course at Warminister, and renewed some friendships. He turned up at a dinner at Lord's, where he met Julian Malins, his good friend from university days. Malins recalled:

Liddell Hart [the military historian], when asked to explain why England had never experienced a military coup, pointed out that this was because in the peacetime Army no one of any intelligence was ever allowed to rise above the rank of Captain. In Robert's case, only massive incompetence can explain – though it cannot excuse – what followed. Robert came in [to the dinner at Lord's] and walked across to talk to David Badenoch – also Lincoln – and me. I knew that he was serving in Northern Ireland and asked him how he was getting on.

He said he was working undercover, in intelligence. I simply could not believe this. A child could tell from fifty paces that Robert was Ampleforth, Oxford and Guards. There never walked a man less capable of deception, let alone of anything dishonourable. But it was true. Even at the dinner, he had an automatic pistol in a shoulder holster under his jacket. I begged him to give it up and return to proper regimental duties. I reminded him that he was an officer of the line, that he had no obligation to soldier out of uniform, that he was unfit for such work, that he was a leader of men and not a solo artist.

It was no good. He spoke of duty. He spoke of the importance of his work. He said that people depended on him. We mentioned the Secretary of State. I embraced him and said farewell ... and when, six months later, he was abducted, tortured and murdered by the IRA ... we who knew him, loved him. And we wept.

Similar misgivings were to be expressed by Martin Squires. They had met occasionally during Nairac's sorties back to Blighty and again when he was on his summer break after his first tour with the SAS. Squires said:

He told me how vicious and violent it was in Northern Ireland. During our later meetings, he gave me to understand that he had infiltrated the IRA, to such a point that he was a brigade commander. It seemed a preposterous notion, almost unthinkable. Would he really be allowed to undertake such a dangerous mission? Whether that was an exaggeration, I do not know, but quite obviously from what he said, he was very deeply undercover there.

That was the year, also, that Gerald Seymour published his novel *Harry's Game*, which I read. It was so bloody prophetic. The similarities with what Robert was telling me were incredible. Robert was pretty cavalier about the dangers and in fact I said to him, 'Look, Robert, you really can't go on like this.' It's a corny phrase, I know. But that's what I felt. He said, 'It's OK, it's OK.'

He had such a high profile when we were in pubs and clubs or restaurants or whatever. I kept saying, 'Look you really are, quite frankly and in the cold light of day, in a pretty dangerous situation.' I said, 'Robert, you're mad. You'll be recognized somewhere along the line, either here in London or back in South Armagh.'

He said, 'No, no. It's OK. They think I'm Irish. I'm one of the boys.' That was Robert. One of the boys. But eventually he got unstitched … I was terribly sorry about it and I felt honoured to have known him; he was that kind of character. But I have to say it did not come as a great surprise when I saw the front pages relating his death.

It seemed to fit in with what he had been telling me. When we spoke late at night about his work, he was quite frankly boasting about his contacts with the IRA. He talked about how far he'd got inside that whole community and the only thing I can say is that if half he told me was true, I'm just amazed he wasn't bumped off before.

# 12

## My Destiny

Robert Nairac arrived back in Northern Ireland after his break back on the mainland in September 1976. He was designated to the same role once again – intelligence liaison officer to the SAS, based at Bessbrook Mill. By then, there were many new faces in the unit and he found himself having to make a case for his own way of working, which he had set up in his earlier tours. It was a difficult time.

'Who is this guy?'

The phrase was to be repeated again and again. Many of the fresh people had no idea who he was, nor the extent of his experience. As in his previous tour, NCOs and junior officers who marshalled the troops and saw to it that they all kept within the framework of SAS operational guidelines were soon up in arms over his indifference to the rules.

Nairac, to some extent, interpreted the strict adherence to SAS conventions as a slight against himself and privately protested that he was being kept on too tight a rein. These feelings were related to one SAS officer who befriended him. Major B, whose identity remains anonymous because he is still in a sensitive security occupation, recalled his conversations with Nairac:

> I first met Robert when he literally flew into Northern Ireland that September. He was returning to his old job as liaison officer between Special Branch and what was then a squadron of the SAS. I picked him up at the airport because I was also a misplaced Guardsman in amongst a bunch of heathens in an SAS squadron. My then troop

sergeant drove us back down to Bessbrook barracks, which is where Robert was going to be based ...

The most striking thing about that journey down to Bessbrook was the fact that, on the way, Robert predicted his own death. As we were driving along through the country lanes going down towards the base, he looked out of the window and said, 'I have a horrible feeling that this place is going to be my destiny.'

We continued on and he chatted about his experiences, and I began to bring him up to date with what had been happening. He was to be in the next-door cubicle to myself. I handed over to him a great portion of the contacts and the work we had done during our period of time. A lot of it was very embryonic, although one of the individuals was the same man he was with at the Three Steps Inn, Drumintee [on the night he was kidnapped], with whom, by then, he had already started to have discussions.

We were attempting to focus on a particular area. Robert had not covered it to any great extent when he was there before; in fact the area, south of Newry, was one that had not been well covered in earlier times. It was not the easiest of places for such operations. We showed him around and off he went, doing what Robert always did in his own way. He intrigued me to some extent, being a Guardsman myself, and my personal knowledge of him was drawn more from the social side, and listening to him singing those wacky-do wild Irish songs.

In the more serious moments, I was able to discover and understand to a degree some of his weaknesses in the strong Catholic belief he held. He had a very strong and curious affinity, in the strangest possible way, towards the IRA. This was built, apparently, out of his time at Oxford. He told me that during his college days he had boxed Martin Meehan, later to become an IRA leader of some considerable notoriety and who spent many years in the H-Blocks. I think he felt that because he had gone three rounds with Meehan, the IRA would love him and deal with him.

He also had a great feeling for the whole of Ireland and the belief that he could master the dialect and speak like a native. His interest went much deeper, and in more diverse fashion, than most soldiers posted to their tours of duty in Ireland ever had. He stood out in that respect. He was an interesting character and there was no doubt about it, he was not at all in the usual mode of a Guards officer.

At the same time, he wasn't in the style of an SAS officer either. In that way, he was stuck between the devil and the deep blue sea. As a person and at the level of fellow officer, he was a great and entertaining character and an interesting individual in every single way. A fair old friendship developed between us during that particular time. And indeed, that was his style. He created a good many personal friendships with senior RUC officers, who moved up through the system long after his death. One in particular who went to high office was very much his early link with the Special Branch.

At the time I was there, he was under tremendous restrictions from the SAS side of his activities. The people who were around him at the time, our own sergeant major for example, were not giving him any leeway ... That was not the way he liked to go about his business, but it was felt we could not change the rules just for him ... I think he probably felt more restricted in those early stages with D Squadron than at any other time.

Even so, we had handed him a great deal of material that we had developed while he was away, which he had to sort out. Some of it was undoubtedly dross, but there were some good names and situations which he developed and moved on into very useful leads.

Although I was working with him for only a month, I kept up contact with him afterwards. He used to come to stay with me and my then wife. The most memorable time of seeing him again was when he came to stay towards the end of April 1977, about three or four weeks before he died. We had a very pleasant time socially, a good drink and so on, and he appeared in very high spirits. I asked him how things were going and his words were somewhat fateful. He told me he had been given total freedom of movement and he could get around and everything was going incredibly well. I said to him, 'Robert, that must be the worst thing ever, that you are totally and utterly uncontrolled.' In fact, I said it must be dynamite. He said, 'No, no. It's really good. It's just how it should be.'

I'd already heard stories about him one minute going down as a soldier on patrol, walking around Crossmaglen, and the next going off in his undercover gear. It did seem particularly foolhardy, given the nature of his work. His hair was curly and unruly, although he did not look too out of place in a beret and could probably have got away with the adjutant's nightmare of a young officer not being particularly smart on patrol.

I don't think, however, that put him at risk so much as the level of continued exposure in a relatively small area. Personally, I do not think that the action of going on patrol placed him at too great a risk. The situation he was in overall was a greater jeopardy. Some of things he did, such as going out without back-up, were a little stupid and a little bit – shall I say – Boys' Own, but actually they were admirable in their own way ...

There have been the cynics who have ridiculed his

work and his methods to some degree. I know that there would never have been any question, from a personal standpoint, of my doing it the way he did it – any of it. And perhaps it was for that reason I wasn't surprised by his death, plus the fact that he had told me himself not very long before that he had more or less total autonomy. Anyone who operates in those circumstances, whether he be the best in the world, is putting himself into unnecessary risks. Put another way, he was out of control. Anyone who was allowed to operate in that way was out of control – or people were being naïve about the risks that were potentially there.

I think the longer you are in a situation like that – and he'd been on that particular job for sixteen months or so and in Northern Ireland much longer – the more blasé you become. I have no doubt that in his own way, Robert thought he was safe. But he was of that age when you push the fringes, like driving a fast car to its limits. You take the risks. You're looking for the excitement. So, as in his case, if you are allowed to go and do what you think is right you go and do it.

The risks must have been clear; the ground rules had long been drummed in to all of us. If you're going into a situation like that, you go with back-up. That's the way a coward like myself would have done it. Two men, four men. You would have tried to have got them around you somehow. It would have been easy. Drop off some men close by or put them in a Volkswagen van for close surveillance, listening in if necessary. I've sat for many hours in my time in a Volkswagen outside a pub, just listening to whatever conversation was going on in various ways. One particular time in Camlough, we targeted a couple of pubs where a lot of boyos were hanging out. A couple of my guys, very well trained, were to go in and hover and put some faces to the conversations. In those days, covert communications were, shall we say, underdeveloped. The smaller of the two pubs was OK. It went like clockwork. In the second one, a much larger pub, the communications didn't work very well. In fact, there was nothing but a stony silence. It had been arranged that if we hadn't heard anything for a pre-arranged timespan, we'd go in mob-handed.

Well, we heard nothing and there was also a bit of a raucous noise coming from inside. So I said 'OK boys ... GO!' One of our larger chaps hit the door and we burst in. The whole placed cleared within seconds – 180 people ran to hide in the ladies' and gents' loos while our two fellows were still sitting at the bar sipping their Guinness. Now that operation turned into a fiasco because of unreliable communications – a job rigged up for sound which failed.

But none the less, it was one example. We could put back-up into any situation very, very quickly. There were often certain obstacles to doing it – such as location, communication or visual difficulties – as opposed to the ease with which a one-man band can operate, and I can see why Robert preferred to operate the way he did. Someone rings you up offering some information and a meeting is set. A gang of us might queer his pitch. I don't know what he was meeting the individual for at the pub on the night he disappeared; I don't think any of us knew that. It is very easy, if you haven't got any controls and don't need to get any clearances, to get into the car and drive to the place of a meeting, for whatever purpose. It is a little more complex to say to colleagues follow me, I'm going off to a meeting, clock the area and keep me in communication. But neither of those options would have been difficult.

The difficulties were really those he would meet on a

personal level, such as, for example, being a stranger in the small and close communities in which he operated. I know he worked on his accent, so that he could ostensibly pass himself off as a native Irishman. Even so, strangers were automatically treated with suspicion. If you are in that kind of environment for any length of time, you can be pretty damn sure someone will want to know who you are and what you're doing. They are naturally inquisitive, as well as being suspicious, and the area Robert was working in was swarming with the IRA's own intelligence people.

I know at one time he tried to use a Belfast accent, which was a little more cosmopolitan than a local one. He would say that he had been living away and was visiting the area. Personally, having worked there for a long time I would not think it would be at all an easy thing for anyone to pass off as an Ulsterman who was not. The awful thing about it also is that when you're feeling under pressure, it is very difficult to keep up the charade. It is true that he did not look like someone from the military. His hair, when I knew him, was not particularly short - it was very curly and very black. But that is not to say he would not have been recognized as a soldier.

My own hair was long and shoulder length, dirty and filthy. Even so, I wouldn't fool myself into thinking that I would not be recognized instantly [as] a former member of the Guards, and (at the time) SAS. Robert tried exceptionally hard to carry it off, often using tactics which were the reverse of staying low and out of sight. He would stand up – as he did on the night he was taken – and sing Republican songs with considerable gusto.

The fact is that as far as we were concerned he was not an undercover operator, even when he was in the Detachment. He was a liaison man. That did, of course, include meeting local people. But as regards walking the streets, as regards what I would call genuine surveillance, he was not an operator as such.

The Detachment had three functions at officer level: a commander, 2IC who was also the operations officer, and the liaison officer. The latter was the one who went out and talked to the people, linked up with Special Branch, got the business, briefed the commander and the commander then used the operators. Occasionally, a liaison man who had been specifically trained in the work might be used for operations or other tasks, because there were never enough people, but it was not a day-to-day thing whereby he would be going out following an individual and conducting surveillance or working as a team.

So Robert was not in the classic mould of surveillance operations, nor I hasten to add were our [SAS] people in those early days. We did not know the full techniques and possibilities; these were honed as we worked ourselves into the tasks at hand, which were entirely new to us. The majority of the work I did on that first tour was plain-clothes work, drop-offs or pick-ups; the rest was heavy OPs [observation posts] with uniform on or off as demanded by the circumstances, or combinations of both. That was very much the standard procedure until around the early spring of 1977, when the SAS began to increase their own covert and clandestine operations. Those who arrived at that point had the much greater advantage of having just passed through a training course aimed specifically at dealing with the problems of Northern Ireland and its inherent specialities.

Looking back, my assessment of Robert Nairac was that he was an out-of-the-ordinary character who had a good zest for life but also probably pushed himself to the limit, perhaps because he genuinely had a fatalistic view of it. Those words as we were driving along reverberate: 'I have a horrible feeling that this place is going to be my destiny.' Robert had that very interesting belief in his own destiny. It was not a death wish. He enjoyed life too much for that. It was more of a challenge to leave his mark on life one way or another. He was always a character who was going to be larger than the script that was written in most people's books. He was the epitome of the eccentric Englishman who will go to the fringes just to challenge the situation. It is entirely right to describe him as a hero, regardless of those particular traits that others may consider foolhardy, or even a weakness. I have nothing but good feelings for him.

In the weeks and months after Nairac's return to Northern Ireland in September 1976, the intelligence gathering focused more intensively on the border regions. There had been many discussions about the area, where it was known that leading IRA men were in fairly constant attendance. Key figures were known to come in from the south for meetings and get-togethers with their commanders in the north, and then vanish back across the border.

Nairac's intelligence at the time, it was said, tended to be of good useful local material and colour about who was who in the locality, but the SAS was short of high-grade intelligence that reached into the thinking and the plans of the senior IRA operational figures. Nairac's theory, and he voiced it at intelligence briefings, was that only by going out and about in the communities could they 'spot' who the local supporters and helpers were. Picking away at the bottom level in the chain of IRA people would eventually lead to the big fish who were coming over the border.

This, to some, seemed an impracticable solution because it was labour intensive and very difficult to set up. It would be impossible to have people out 'spotting' at all hours of the day and night, hoping for a chance visual contact with IRA top brass. Spotters would also need back-up and in any event, the likelihood of heavy-duty soldiers sitting around the pubs of South Armagh remaining unobserved for longer than about five minutes was virtually nil. They themselves would be 'spotted' a mile off.

That didn't stop Nairac trying. Another of his brother officers – again new to the experience of dealing with him at the time – told me: 'I don't think any of us realized that he was doing just that – going to pubs and other places, sitting about watching people and basically just chatting to whoever he could engage in conversation. As we all now know, he took it to dangerous levels … It was not part of his job, and being new to this scenario, we did not expect it of him. I don't think any of us at Bessbrook at that time were aware of the extent of these personal expeditions he was making.'

Nairac persevered, of that there is no doubt. One of the names he offered up for surveillance was Seamus Harvey, a member of the South Armagh Provisional IRA. In 1976, Harvey was a staff officer in the Crossmaglen Battalion, whose comings and goings had been of particular interest to the security forces since 22 November 1975. On that day, four soldiers in a surveillance hide on the side of a hill at Drummuckavall, near Crossmaglen, were ambushed by the IRA. Three of them, Peter McDonald, James Duncan and Michael Sampson, were killed.

Seamus Harvey was born and bred in the locality, and at various times, his family's home near Drummuckavall and others in the village were visited regularly by security forces. Many complained about the heavy hand and boot of a Royal Marines SBS patrol that conducted a search of the area in October 1976, causing the human rights campaigners Fathers Raymond Murray and Denis Faul to dash off another of their pamphlets, entitled *Terror Tactics of the British Army: Royal Marines Commandos at Crossmaglen*.

At the turn of the year, Nairac brought in information which, put with other material on South Armagh PIRA, was sufficient for the SAS to plan a work-up for an ambush at a place carefully selected, close to the border where IRA men were known to be coming into the north and retreating later.

It was eventually put into operation on 16 January 1977. That night, SAS soldiers took up their surveillance positions three miles or so outside Crossmaglen, virtually on the border with County Louth, hiding on a hillside among the bracken. An hour and a half later, several members of the South Armagh PIRA came to examine what was supposedly an abandoned car in the middle of the road. They were led by staff officer Seamus Harvey, who wore a mask and a combat jacket, and had an ammunition belt slung around his shoulder containing cartridges for the sawn-off pump-action shotgun he carried.

While his IRA colleagues covered him, Harvey crept forward to look over the car. As he reached it, there was a shout and a gun battle opened up between the SAS and the IRA, and fifty or so rounds were exchanged. Harvey was shot dead. The IRA issued a statement saying that the soldiers – whom they curiously identified as Royal Highland Fusiliers – shot Harvey without warning. The Army admitted that the SAS had shot him and said the soldiers, on surveillance duty at the time, had been fired on first.

Harvey's family declined the IRA's offer of a military funeral and instead members of the local football team of which he had been a member formed the guard of honour.

The day after the shooting, and in the wake of government approval for SAS operations to be extended to other parts of the Six Counties, Conservative MP Airey Neave gave wholehearted support to the SAS. He also applauded Secretary of State Roy Mason's announcement that new measures to tackle terrorism were to be employed. Mr Neave gave a particular welcome to the news of the greater use of the SAS which, he said, should be given priority as the security forces stepped up its efforts to curb the activities of the IRA.

At that moment, Neave, whose association with SAS territorials from 1949 to 1951 was revealed in newspaper reports, became a marked man. On 30 March 1979, by then one of Prime Minister Margaret Thatcher's most trusted aides, he was assassinated by the INLA as he drove out of the car park at the House of Commons.

The IRA also took more instant revenge and once again stepped up the ante, which in turn placed increased pressure on the intelligence operatives. In the early hours of 29 January 1977, a new bomb offensive was launched in London. At least seven bombs were detonated within a two-mile radius of central London, exploding within a timespan of fifty minutes. The bombs wrecked buildings in Oxford Street, Regent Street and Wardour Street, and set Selfridges department store ablaze. The bombs, which included incendiary devices, were left in the doorways of shops and offices. A few days later, police uncovered an IRA bomb-making factory in Liverpool, and the pressure was on again.

# 13

## DANNY BOY

Major Clive Fairweather arrived in Northern Ireland at the end of 1976 for yet another tour of duty, fresh from the Army Staff College, the place the Army sends its brightest up-and-coming officers. He was no stranger to the Six Counties and, as a Scot, he had a much deeper insight into the problems and realities of the situation than some of his English counterparts. The Scots know and understand the religious tribalism of Ulster: there are pockets of it all over Scotland, too.

Fairweather's job this time was based at the Northern Ireland Army headquarters at Lisburn, County Antrim. He was moving into the post of G2/Int, previously held by his brother officer in the SAS, Colonel G, back in 1974. Like G, Fairweather was a seasoned officer who had served in many places both with his own regiment, the King's Own Scottish Borderers, and with the SAS. His first Northern Ireland tour of duty had been with the SAS in 1969 as an officer in the regiment's D Squadron.

Fairweather, like most other SAS officers, rotated between tours of duty with the special forces and his parent unit, with which he again served on the streets of Belfast. He knew the dangers facing soldiers in the IRA-dominated Republican heartlands and he also had experience of the sickening feeling of loss mixed with anger that sweeps through a battalion when a comrade is killed. He had helped quell fearsome street riots in West Belfast, survived shoot-outs – some of them major – and survived a booby-trap bomb that had been smuggled into his regiment's headquarters, killing a soldier.

In the SAS and on its periphery at the time were several veteran anti-terrorist campaigners, old officers and NCOs who had made it their business to study terrorist organizations and their operations all over the world. Over the years these wise old heads had turned their attention to the 'Irish problem'. Fairweather had spent many hours with them, drinking long into the night and absorbing their every word. He was acutely aware that terrorism is not defeated through the barrel of a gun. High-grade intelligence, enabling the police, special forces and Army acting in unison to strike deep into the terrorist underbelly, was the way ahead.

Like them, Fairweather did not look upon his new appointment as a tick-in-the-box job, in other words another rung on the ladder to promotion and better things. To him it was all part of the great learning experience required on the way to being a proper Special Forces officer. Getting it right, in the SAS world, did not mean winning medals and fast-track promotion – it meant hitting the enemy where it hurt most. Professionalism and job satisfaction were the motivating forces, not personal glory:

> I arrived back in Northern Ireland in December 1976 for a two-year intelligence staff job. It was a straightforward military appointment, although, for some reason, the powers that be preferred it to be filled by someone with Special Forces background. I was there to liaise with all intelligence agencies, both at a brigade level and a much higher level.
>
> I first came across Robert Nairac in the January of 1977 when I went to Bessbrook Mill, in County Armagh, the base the SAS were operating from. He was the intelligence liaison officer working with various other intelligence organizations at that local brigade level ... My job was to go round all the intelligence officers in Northern Ireland plus the Special Branch and anyone else helping coordinate the intelligence effort.
>
> When I first clapped eyes on him he was in civilian clothes in his little office in the mill and looked pretty

scruffy, with long black tousled curly hair hanging in ringlets. I think he enjoyed being scruffy. He frequently wasn't that well shaved and I remember the first time we met he had quite a stubble. His hair was on his collar, but he still talked like a Guards officer, albeit one with long hair.

He was wearing a fairly grubby old polo-neck sweater and jeans, and he was obviously trying to look like one of the locals. Hanging on the door he had a donkey jacket, a sort of Wimpey-type donkey jacket without the Wimpey written on it. He was quite wiry and strong-looking. He was a physical individual. He was powerfully built and came over as powerful. He had a powerful face and he was obviously quite a deep, introverted sort of person. He clearly came from quite a good public-school background. He had a funny little sense of humour. He talked in colloquialisms and he quite clearly wanted to be one of the boys. Despite the scruffy clothes, he still looked like a Guards officer.

His office was a simple little office, like a cell, with maps on the wall, pictures of some of the local bad guys and the normal Army sort of stuff. There wasn't any sign of his uniform, but there was nothing unusual about that. Even the intelligence officers of the local infantry regiments wore civvies, because they were always in and out of the camp and in and out of RUC stations and places like that.

Robert very quickly tried to impress me, because he knew I had been an SAS officer, by telling me he had worked with the surveillance unit in Northern Ireland and that he had been trained in undercover work, so wearing this sort of gear was all part of the deal. He was trying to make the point to me from very early on that he had a wealth of experience of working undercover in Northern Ireland.

There was a side to him, almost like a withdrawn side, that I couldn't really touch. I have to say that I didn't particularly like him. I didn't feel I could trust him. I don't know why – it was just something. I felt that almost from the moment I met him he had his own agenda and in a way I felt that behind it all he was laughing at us. I think he thought we were all a bit clodhopperish and he had a bit more experience because he had been there before, working with an intelligence organization in civilian clothes on surveillance duties, and I think he felt that while on the one hand someone like me had quite a lot of SAS experience, he had done more on the ground in South Armagh and probably felt he knew the ground better.

He had also served in the Ardoyne area of Belfast with the Guards. I felt a bit uneasy when I left Bessbrook because I just didn't know where he was going to fit in. On the other hand, he spoke well, quite knowledgeably, and I couldn't fault him on any of that. But there was just a little something ...

Bessbrook at that stage was said to be the busiest helicopter port in the world. There was also an infantry battalion based there, and the SAS lived and operated out of a corner of the base. At that time in Northern Ireland the SAS squadron were operating at brigade level in South Armagh and nowhere else. They answered directly to the brigadier in charge of 3 Brigade, which was the one responsible for operations in South Armagh. Robert's job was to work between the local brigade headquarters, RUC and the RUC Special Branch, the local battalions and any other uniformed intelligence agencies operating in that area ...

On my travels round Northern Ireland I would visit the local units, local RUC men, to find out what sort of people they were, to prime the intelligence mechanisms at their level and to smooth the path for information being passed on up to me at headquarters.

I would then take all the various pieces of information coming in and would pass them upwards for briefing senior officers; sideways to Operations, who might then decide to mount operations; or, depending on where the intelligence came from, back down to brigade level or even further on down to the level where Robert Nairac was operating.

Despite all that has been written, he was not very high up the pecking order in intelligence terms. He was simply the liaison officer for the SAS, working at brigade level. There were two other brigades in Northern Ireland and there was headquarters. He didn't operate with any of those. He was operating with 3 Brigade and, in particular, operating on a fairly narrow front round the border, starting from Bessbrook and around Crossmaglen. The SAS were mainly operating around there because until the previous year when Peter Cleary had been captured and accidentally shot, all the killings in that area had either been of soldiers or RUC men. There had been no fatalities among the IRA. Cleary had been captured by D Squadron, the squadron which I had commanded in Dhofar. His capture had been the only real success against the IRA. The next success was when Seamus Harvey was shot in an ambush by G Squadron.

Robert liked to cosy up to the SAS soldiers. He tended to be quite familiar with them, using their first names or their nicknames. He also liked swearing quite a lot. I got the feeling that when he was around the Special Forces soldiers they felt uneasy about him in the same way as I did.

As a former SAS officer, those who knew me either called me 'Boss' in the usual way or 'Sir'. SAS soldiers who did not know me called me 'Sir'. I cannot remember how they addressed Robert, but I got the impression that they didn't particularly respect him.

The squadron in Bessbrook at the time was G Squadron, commanded by Major Mike Rose.* Mike was also a Guardsman and they used to go around quite a bit together. They would occasionally go duck shooting early in the morning.

Sometimes he accompanied Mike Rose to a few higher-level conferences than there were at 3 Brigade. I can remember them occasionally coming through Headquarters, Northern Ireland. At that level of conference Robert would be in tow with Mike Rose.

I always knew when Robert had been in the mess in Lisburn. He wouldn't necessarily ring me up but he would leave his calling card: I would find he had put either a bottle of gin or a bottle of whisky on my mess bill. Quite early on he had learned my mess bill number and this was his little joke. He liked to play little games with people. He just wanted me to know he had been through Lisburn.

During the first three months of 1977 I was preoccupied with 'Guys Across the Border' – the SAS patrol that had strayed into the Republic armed to the teeth and been arrested and charged, who were due to appear in court in Dublin. I had a lot of involvement in this one, so I was not able to have as much contact with Robert as I should have liked.

---

*Major Michael Rose went on to command the SAS. He was the man in charge of storming the Iranian Embassy in London in 1980, and the unit's CO during the Falklands conflict, where he persuaded the Argentines to surrender. He went on to become a general commanding United Nations forces in former Yugoslavia, before finishing his career as Adjutant General, No. 2, in the British Army.

Three things started to happen. When I was talking to G Squadron I began to get the impression they were a little bit uneasy about him and felt he needed reining in a bit. Mike Rose very much kept him on a tight leash, but I began to get the impression that although he was there to collect intelligence from both the Army and the Special Branch, he might be out trying to develop his own intelligence.

There was also a certain amount of the usual antagonism from the boys towards a public-school-accented Guards officer who was trying to put over to them how much he knew – and, in fact, he probably knew more about operating in that part of the world than the SAS – and yet he hadn't been through the training.

They felt that on the one hand he was trying to show how much he knew and on the other hand was trying to learn from them the other skills he knew they had which he didn't have. There was just a feeling that he didn't know how the SAS operated, that he didn't know what the rules were, and there was this impression that he was beginning to break the rules – instead of just going and collecting the information, he was going out himself and somehow acting on his own and beginning to develop his own intelligence.

At first strands began coming back, and then we began to get information from sources that said there was an SAS man operating in South Armagh and that they were going to get him. The sources were people like Special Branch agents and one, in particular, came saying that the Cullyhanna IRA unit was going to get the curly-headed little SAS man called Danny. Piecing this together it pointed to Robert. He appeared to be using a cover name, had curly hair and was going out on patrol in uniform – there was no reason why he shouldn't go out on patrol – and was then beginning to appear in pubs and other places around the area, driving himself and wearing civilian clothes and so on.

I actually showed him the intelligence report and he laughed at it. I remember showing him the report and saying: 'Robert, there it is ... that is the clearest warning. You want to be damned careful about what you are doing.' He just laughed.

He then approached me in about March or April because he knew I controlled some of the funds used for intelligence gathering and asked me to sponsor him learning the Irish language.

I laughed at him, I'm afraid, and said he really needed to go and have his head examined. I told him that no matter how much he learned about the Irish language he was never going to convince anyone that he was an Irishman because as a Scot, and I speak with a native tongue, I can spot anyone pretending to be a Scot within a couple of minutes.

He didn't just want to learn Gaelic – he also wanted dialect tapes so he could change his accent while speaking English. He still insisted he wanted to learn Irish and I began to realize there was another side to his nature which was a sort of a romantic, fantasy side.

I was really quite alarmed at that. That was the first thing he asked for. He then approached me asking for money to buy an old car. At that stage he was provided with military transport to drive from A to B, as everyone else was in Northern Ireland. These were civilian cars, but he wanted to buy an old banger. I couldn't be bothered to dig out money for that or with all the complications that would go with it. It just wasn't the way we operated. I also pointed out to him that driving round in an old banger he was going to stand out even more like a sore thumb.

I also had a word with him about his donkey jacket and told him that as far as I was aware people didn't drive around in bloody donkey jackets. I told him people wear what they wear here and you will never ever look like them. He again laughed at me because he reckoned he had done a bit more than me.

I think he began to see a different role for himself, doing the SAS liaison officer's job and also going out and doing his own thing. It would appear that he felt there wasn't enough information down there in his area and that he could develop – because of his experience in 3 Brigade before the SAS ever got there – information for them.

By the way, although people were feeling uneasy, he was producing good information; he was tying all that together. He produced some quite good reports, he produced some quite good information as far as I remember, developed some of it. He was doing quite a good job. However, by going out and doing his own thing and operating round the place he was making the soldiers of G Squadron uneasy and, increasingly, making me uneasy. I did talk to him about it several times and said to him: 'Robert, you do need to think again about what you are doing.'

Now, on one occasion, I really did bollock him. He said he was going to reverse the situation in that area, that he was really going to build up a lot of information and instead of soldiers being killed there was going to be more IRA being killed.

I'll never forget this ... he then pulled out one of the files in his filing cabinet, which had details of all the soldiers and people who had been killed in South Armagh. I suddenly realized that probably, in addition to having a slightly sort of romantic view, he had a slightly morbid view of things as well, which, coupled with wanting to learn the Irish language and all the rest, made me realize that on the one hand he was quite an experienced officer – he was obviously quite a brave officer, quite a talented officer, willing to go out and take risks – but there was a side to his nature which I could never put a finger on, and that he was a law unto himself. All that left me uneasy about him.

People in brigade looking at him would probably just have thought that this was the way the SAS and people like that operated. I don't think that Robert realized that in that area one slip could be enough. He was careless, but thought that 'Who Dares Wins' was the ethos of the SAS – you know, take the risks – whereas the SAS very rarely operate that way. There is a strict code and, actually, you only take limited risks. Despite everything you read, the SAS is a very careful organization, not foolhardy at all. A lot of SAS rules are set in concrete – you just do not break them. Robert didn't know about them because he had never been through an SAS training. He was tending to think that how he was operating was the way the SAS either were operating or should be operating. He was trying to blaze his own trail, if you like.

In retrospect he was operating between all sorts of people – me, G Squadron and others – and we were all seeing little bits of the picture, but if we had all seen the whole picture together I think the alarm bells would have rung. I think if we had sat down and discussed the whole picture regarding him he would probably not have been posted away, and his wings would most certainly have been clipped.

## 14

## SPECIAL AGENT?

The moment that Robert Nairac seemed to secure for himself the greater freedom of movement he craved in the badlands of South Armagh, which he described to Major B, came in April 1977 during a changeover of SAS personnel at Bessbrook. He timed his move well, and when A Squadron came in to replace G Squadron, he more or less wrote his own rules of engagement.

According to Clive Fairweather, Nairac began to go out far more often, and as good as told the new squadron commander that he was the experienced guy and that this was the way it was done, the way he operated. He told him that he worked not only to them, the SAS, but to the RUC as well and that he had his own sources out there. Fairweather said:

> I suspect he was trying to make out that his links – to the intelligence services and others – were more important than they really were. He never boasted to me about links with MI5 or MI6. In reality, he would not have had any links to them. As far as I am aware, they did not deal with people in positions as lowly as his. People like that would deal at a higher level. Robert might have liked to imply he had links, but they wouldn't have come out to see a lowly captain in the Guards.
>
> In truth I do not think any of us knew what he was doing ... what he was up to ... how often he was going out.

It was shortly before the changeover of squadrons that Colonel G, on one of his visits to Northern Ireland, ran into Nairac. At that time it occurred to him that Nairac had now been in the place for months, aiding successive SAS squadrons, and expected to be there for the new one coming in. G no doubt picked up some of the gossip around the place about Nairac's increasing lack of respect for the rules. Perhaps he even recognized a touch of resentment that existed about Nairac among SAS people and most notably the ops officer who checked everybody in and out. Nairac, in whom he had himself demonstrated a good deal of faith on two previous occasions, was clearly under some pressure. The warning signs were evident and G flew back to Hereford pretty well determined to get Nairac out of Northern Ireland altogether:

When I got back I said to the then commanding officer, 'We've got to pull Robert out. He's a tired man. He's done the business, he's been effective. In my opinion he's going out on a limb these days and that's always a sign that you think you are untouchable.' The CO told me Robert was needed for one more tour. The squadrons were changing over, and it was vital that they had his input. The squadron commanders were totally different. One was a quiet intellectual and the other was a hard man and going for it, and Robert was needed to be alongside the smooth changeover and 'bed-in' the new squadron and its commander. After that, they would pull him out.

I sucked my teeth and it is a cross I shall bear to my grave: I should have insisted. But that is being wise in retrospect. Robert had done more, much more, than we wanted. He'd stayed longer than he should, and the risks were getting greater by the minute. I must say, though, Robert wanted to stay. He would have been thoroughly disappointed if we had brought him back. He was totally wrapped up in the work. And going through the doors of the pubs in Crossmaglen, as I can well imagine, Robert, standing up there singing rebel songs – without the back-up that he ought to have had but rejected – was asking for trouble. I knew that was the sort of risk he loved and would ultimately take, and as a result he would be caught out.

The mistake of leaving him there was only compounded by the fact that, as I understand it – and I could never fathom how this could have been allowed to happen – during his time with us and unbeknown to me, he had been asked to appear in uniform in the north by the Army for some previous problem about which he had knowledge. This opened up the possibility of recognition, regardless of whether he was miles from his normal patch. Those communities are very close knit. That was an extreme risk and one that, in my judgement, should not have been taken, because it was suggested that on the night [when he was abducted] suspicion had begun with someone saying they had seen him in Army uniform. I don't know the detail and don't want to know now. It's too late …

So the new squadron came in, and Nairac once again went through the procedures of introducing himself and making it known that he was the guy with all the contacts and the knowledge, and they could rely on him. The squadron had already been warned of the difficulties and dangers of South Armagh, and they were under no illusions about the place. A friendly face, like Nairac, who knew his way around was welcome indeed. Nairac himself stiffened up the warnings about the bandit territory, and, according to Clive Fairweather, proceeded at that point to overstate his own importance in the system and the chain of intelligence gathering on which the squadron had to rely.

Captain D, who had not long ago returned with SAS from Dhofar, met Nairac at Bessbrook Mill in April 1977. Mike Rose was still the boss and Nairac was answerable to the squadron commander, as before.

Captain D described his association with Nairac in a taped interview for this book. He said the general feeling among the soldiers in the squadron was that Nairac seemed a pretty stand-up guy – initially. After a very short time, they changed their minds, or at least those like Captain D and the company sergeant major who were directly concerned with his day-to-day activities.

In fact, they discussed Nairac often and usually the cause was his flouting of the SAS rules, which began virtually from the moment A Squadron moved in:

> We had begun to get worried about him and between us, the sergeant major and myself, decided that he was a danger, mainly to himself but possibly to others in the unit. He possessed a great deal of information, much of it in his head. He was, as someone put it, a walking encyclopedia on the region in which we were operating. He also kept a good deal in his Filofax-type notebook – a lot of notes, names and addresses of people in all areas of intelligence and security, as well as his contacts and informants and suspects.

Captain D was also concerned to discover that Nairac appeared to be doing 'some part-time source handling which no one seemed to know about.' It quite quickly became apparent to Captain D and others down the line who were closer in touch with him that the information he possessed was lethal in the wrong hands. Captain D and the sergeant major agreed between themselves that it could be a very dangerous situation for all concerned and decided to approach their commanding officer – 'a sort of deputation' – to suggest he got rid of Nairac, pronto.

The reply was that Nairac was a good guy, he was doing an excellent job and his removal from our unit was out of the question. I think that view was also the one that came down from on high. It must have been, or he would have been moved out earlier. He was a loner; others must have told you that. He often went out in the field without back-up. That was his choice and our main gripe. Whatever he was doing, he wanted to do it alone.

It was understandable in a way. South Armagh wasn't the sort of area where you could put down a back-up that easily, and especially in the tiny remote places. It could be done, of course. But there was always the chance of us being rumbled. So there were two ways of looking at it – Robert Nairac was either incredibly brave or bloody stupid. Quite frankly, I chose the second option. He did a lot of silly things. He was often out of radio contact and regularly failed to call in at the given time.

Half the time, the ops officer didn't know where the fuck he was. The day before he died, for example, he went across the border into Southern Ireland fishing, which he shouldn't have done. At least, that's what he told us he was doing. Perhaps he was; I know he liked fishing. But he was out of touch and out of contact. We really had no idea what he was up to ... only he knew. That was the nature of the man and we didn't like it.

It appeared to me that he was trying to prove something – to himself mostly. The SAS doesn't operate like that. Quite frankly, we did not want him around us. One of the reasons – and one that I mentioned to our boss – was that we found it a bit hard to accept his behaviour. It worried us that he would also come into us as a liaison man dressed as he did in scruff order and then go down the road to Crossmaglen and patrol with soldiers – in uniform.

He stood out, with his long hair, and wearing jump boots and carrying a shotgun – which only the SAS carried. A half-pissed roadsweeper could have spotted the difference. The reason he went with the patrols was, I presume, so that he could get involved in the kind of activity that helped him get close to the area or person he was interested in. An intelligence officer could attach himself to a patrol to go out in the field and have a look-see, and, perhaps more importantly to him, overtly rather than undercover. If they pulled guys out of a bar or whatever they were doing that night, he was there and able to get a close view of anyone he might want to make contact with, or develop. He could direct the patrol to take a look at any particular place or group. He could take a look at a bar and get the male population lined up outside.

Crossmaglen was not far from the border and generally very hostile to British forces. The communities in that area are small and close. It seemed to us an enormous risk to go out in both his undercover clothes and then in uniform – an unacceptable risk. He had quite obviously a good deal of confidence in his own ability to stay alive, though many of us suspected that he knew he was a prime target – almost setting himself up as one for whatever reason. That's what put the shits up us. He was playing two games – a secret agent one minute and a soldier the next.

Although Major Fairweather had turned down Nairac's request to buy tapes to learn the Irish language and to improve his dialect, he had obviously found the money from his own resources – or from another Army fund perhaps – to go out and buy the tapes for himself. Captain D discovered them.

He had cultivated his Irish accent and I found a set of Irish Linguaphone tapes in his room after his death. The reasons were a mystery. It wasn't his job – or at least, that was not the job we understood him to have. And this was the whole point – he was working outside his remit, wandering between Bessbrook and the intelligence HQ at Lisburn, where he also had office space. Like the old adage in the military, you go from place to place carrying a piece of paper and no one stops you. It wasn't quite as basic as that, but no more devious. I don't think he was working for anyone else. Maybe MI5, but I doubt it. MI6 operated in the south and were concerned with cross-border activity. I don't think Nairac was involved. I would find it hard to believe.

I think it comes down to this: because the guy had been there so long, he knew a lot of people, and had excellent contacts in the Special Branch, who also trusted him, and that was important. He was part of the furniture. He was also, incidentally, personally desperate for success. He had downers if he didn't get it; he pushed himself hard and pushed the boundaries of safety to the limit ... If he had remained within the parameters of his job description he would be alive today.

Working out of Bessbrook Mill and linking up with the Special Branch it wasn't a very good idea to go off into the field – with or without uniform. There were too many prying eyes about. At the time, our squadron wasn't that close to the RUC or the Special Branch, probably because we were new to it. The relationship between the two groups was still a bit chary; it was early days. We were still finding our way and not unnaturally there was a good deal of local suspicion about us. We were so naïve, there is no doubt about that. You've also got to bear in mind that most of the SAS who were there then had just come back from Dhofar; they'd just come down out of the trees, so to speak. Northern Ireland was totally alien to them.

A lot of them were also very pissed off, and that had nothing whatsoever to do with Nairac. It was Northern Ireland and it was the situation as a whole. In a way, we had just witnessed the end of an era for the Special Forces and the British military in general. The SAS, more than any other regiment, felt the effects of the shut-down in our Armed forces overseas that had just happened ... There was considerable unease among the British military and especially the SAS, who were being assigned in ever increasing numbers to help police the province of Northern Ireland, which we didn't like.

The general political situation was also explosive, a fact which we tend to overlook when we look back. The industrial unrest of the early 1970s, the three-day week, etc. – there had even been talk of a coup against the British government at the time. I can remember us discussing it in the mess. What would we do if ...? It came to naught, and probably never would have come to anything, but at the time there were enough people talking about it to make it seem a real possibility. There had been an article in one of the colour supplements on 'How to Take Over Britain', which caused a bit of discussion among us in the bars. But the very fact that there were supposedly people in high office or former high rank who were discussing it demonstrated the unrest, especially among some of the retired old buggers, who hated Wilson and the Labour government and thought the country was going to the dogs.

As far as we were concerned it never got beyond light-hearted banter. On one occasion, we were discussing it rather loudly in the bar in Aldershot, not noticing a large

African gentleman sitting close by, sipping whisky. As the discussion became louder, he came over and said, 'Gentlemen, if you require any advice on staging a coup, I'm your man. I have just taken over my country.' [President Nimeiry had recently staged a coup and was the new leader of the government of Sudan.] What he was doing in the bar at Aldershot, I have no idea ... but that's another story ...

The point I'm making is that Northern Ireland wasn't just about the Troubles. This was a coming-together of military people whose alternatives were Germany or exotica like Hong Kong or Belize, short-term postings where there was not the slightest chance of winning a medal or showing themselves off for rapid promotion. There was nowhere left, and that wasn't just SAS – that's everybody. There was nothing for our vast army of impatient troops to do and, to a certain extent, Northern Ireland had become good value for the military. The Troubles began in 1969, right on cue.

In a curious, unhappy and completely unsatisfactory way, Northern Ireland provided the answer – albeit on British soil. It was as simple as that really, and certainly in the case of the SAS. But I can tell you this, we didn't want to be there.

I don't know where Nairac fitted into that picture. We never had a great deal of time for talk. He was without doubt a 'Queen and country' man but definitely not one who was motivated by the thought of a gong at the end of it; no way. If there was a hidden agenda, it was one he established for himself. He was a romantic – one of those guys who, if it had been the late 1800s, you could imagine wandering about on his own on the North-West Frontier during the Afghan wars, face blacked up, dressed as a native, gathering intelligence ... the only frontier left in the Empire in the 1970s was Northern Ireland and it was just as dangerous, if not more so, and that suited Robert Nairac. He loved Ireland, was fascinated by its history, adored the people ... and he was prepared to take the risks.

I attach no greater mystery to his situation than that.

His usefulness to us was in his role as the go-between and the charmer, and we needed one. I think a lot of people imagined we were going in there for the specific purpose of taking people out – identifying and killing terrorists. Who would ever know in that mêlée of death and destruction? It was even suggested that Nairac was picking them out and we were bumping them off, like a fairground shoot. It wasn't that way at all, of course, despite the IRA propaganda and the fanciful stories of a few loonies. We killed people, but in specific situations where we were engaged in an exchange of fire, or where individuals had failed to stop at checkpoints or whatever. Up to the time of his death, there had been only two shooting deaths from the SAS. I admit that in the early days, the SAS were heavy-handed; but the place was like that. We were dealing with terrorists who would do the same to us and worse if they had the chance, as was eventually proved with Nairac.

The year we went in in force was among the worst ever for atrocities. Something had to be done and Wilson hit them with the SAS, which was as much about propaganda as anything. In comparison to other Army units, the SAS was very inexperienced in Northern Ireland-type operations and needed all the help we could get. The Paras, for example, had already spent five years in the province when we arrived. In the early days, we instituted pretty strong tactics: instant return fire if patrols were fired upon and suspects could expect a good hiding if they fucked us about. But there was no shoot-to-kill policy. There never had been and never would be. If you're fired at, then you can fire back; if your life is threatened, you take action, and if somebody gets in the way, tough shit. That was the rule of thumb then.

The rules were very quickly battened down and eventually it became wholly more sophisticated as a military and police operation, yet the situation itself had never changed until the peace accord in 1998. It was as disappointing for the military as it was for the people of Northern Ireland. So many lives lost for what? Nothing. Not an inch of ground won or lost in thirty years of Troubles.

I reckon Robert Nairac truly believed he could make a difference. There was a developing situation in the days prior to his death that worried us. He had made contact with a source in Newry. He'd met him a couple of a times on the steps of the courthouse there. According to Nairac, this source was apparently going to bring him some of the best intelligence on the IRA ever to come out of Northern Ireland. He was really hyped up about it. We talked about it afterwards. Was it a two-bit hood trying to get money from him? Was he really on to the biggest bust in the area we had ever seen? Or was he being set up?

The other curious thing was that he kept getting telephone calls from someone in the two or three days before his death. The caller was always anonymous and we never managed to get a line on him. Whether it was something to do with his going to the Three Steps pub at Drumintee where he was last seen, I don't know. We talked to him about it. He just shrugged it off ... and now there is no way of knowing.

After he went missing our first thought was that he had walked into a trap. In the light of what transpired, the details did not match that kind of situation and it seems unlikely. But, either way, he was putting himself in big danger in an area like that and that really goes back to the way he operated.

He had a room at Lisburn and a place at Bessbrook. No one knew where he was at one given time unless he had set up a procedure for calling in. It seemed a ridiculous situation. It was very frustrating as far as we were concerned. It was totally alien to the way the SAS operated, even for Military Intelligence. Looking back, it was possible to see how that situation evolved. He had been there so long, knew his way around and had such good contacts that people thought he was doing a wonderful job.

The night he went missing, his room was searched. It was a tip, very untidy, a real mess. The immaculate procedures of Guards discipline had clearly waned considerably. This place had the appearance of a man under pressure. It was full of all kinds of stuff, including documents that frankly I felt should not have been there. I have no idea whether he had the authority to keep them there. It was another of the mysteries, but then Ireland was a twilight world. The intelligence people felt it most. They immersed themselves in this kind of semi-darkness – murky is the best description that there ever has been of their situation. The pressures upon individuals were immense, particuarly those who were new to it, and those who had families. The SAS and most of the Army were on tours of less than six months, largely because of the pressures. Nairac had been there for ever.

That's why, in the end, you can't help have great admiration for the guy. Who are we to judge?

# 15

# MISSING!

In the pubs of Crossmaglen, Nairac had started to call himself Danny McAlevey, from Ardoyne, and apparently had a fake driving licence with that name on it. He was moving deeper and deeper into the realms of some sort of personal quest, of being a true undercover agent who could shake off his true identity and become one of 'them'. To some, he confided he was a Sticky – the nickname for members of the Official IRA – and was now, it seemed, attempting to live the lie he had told Martin Squires, that he had infiltrated the IRA. There is no evidence to suggest that he had and none to disprove it either. The SAS deny it and the IRA certainly would not admit it. The probability – a racing certainty in fact – was that he was nowhere near achieving that goal.

The only other likely possibility was that he was working to instructions from another agency beyond the SAS and the military. As one Northern Ireland source suggested to me, 'It had an MI5 ring to it.' I found no support for that theory among the SAS officers interviewed for this book but, while not wishing to exhume unprovable tales of MI5/MI6 involvements, the questions can be fairly asked at this stage, as we probe further into the recollections of those senior officers directly around him at the time: was Robert Nairac really operating on his own without the knowledge or approval of the SAS or any other arm of military intelligence? – or, as some suggested, was he reporting back to someone (MI5 or MI6?) whom the SAS knew nothing about?

He was seen in numerous places in South Armagh, from tiny hamlets just north of the border to other troubled places like Jonesboro, Forkhill and Crossmaglen. These, without doubt, were the most dangerous areas for troops, and especially so for a soldier who was pretending not to be one and who might be recognized at any moment. It was and is, even in the late 1990s, a region where strangers are not welcome.

The South Armagh Provisionals were the toughest of their breed. They did not consider it necessary to confirm their intended operations to the IRA Army Council. Among their numbers were some of the most deadly of all the IRA active service units and bombers. Within their region, some of the worst atrocities of modern times had been committed in their battles with the loyalists and the British Army.

Robert Nairac well knew all of this from past experience. He had been through the place a thousand times and from his intelligence briefings with the Special Branch, he had a list of pubs that were regular meeting places for IRA people and their supporters. According to another Northern Ireland source, Nairac was specifically tasked by 'senior people in British intelligence' to get into these places, turn up regularly as a customer so that his face would become known, chat with the locals, identify IRA people in the area and, if possible, develop contacts. If that was the case, it was not so much the fantasy it appeared – he was merely carrying out orders to try to fill in the vast gaps in intelligence in the region.

But for Nairac, alone and without back-up, to set about 'developing contacts' was not only exceedingly dangerous, it was ridiculously irresponsible, given all the circumstances (such as going out in the same area in his uniform). Recent history was littered with the bodies of informers, and anyone even talking to a soldier would be classed as such and, regardless of what passed between them, would be ostracized, interrogated, knee-capped or executed.

Even so, as we have seen, in the hostelries of Crossmaglen, Nairac appeared to have established himself as a regular in several pubs. But reports of this guy who was 'probably a soldier' were already filtering through Military Intelligence and landing on the desk of Clive Fairweather who, as we have also seen, discounted the theory that Nairac was working for either of the main agencies of British intelligence. He explained it thus:

He felt he had to try to spot far more of the local supporters and to see who they were meeting with, in the hope that this would lead him to people who were coming over the border. That would appear to be why he took to going out on his own to pubs ... I don't think any of us realized he was going to places like that to chat people up. It was not part of his job. Surveillance was not part of his job either, but I think he was doing that, too, sitting about trying to watch people. Surveillance is a job for specially trained people including the SAS and other organizations.

We later found out he was using the name Danny McAlevey. If he was carrying documents supporting that identification they were not official issue: they would have been of his own making. There was never anything like that officially sanctioned. If he did it he was acting out to a degree his feeling that there was not enough information down there and that with his experience he could develop more information.

I imagine Robert was doing up to two thirds of his staff job as required and then maybe a third on his own not agreed by anyone or tasked by anyone, just going out and doing his own thing. He was doing a staff job which was important for his career, but he wasn't required to carry a rifle and patrol the streets in uniform. However, there was nothing to stop him going and doing that if he wanted to get a feel for the area. But it is kind of unhealthy to walk through somewhere like Crossmaglen and places like that in uniform one day and be talking to local people, and then be in the pubs wearing the donkey jacket or whatever else come nighttime, talking in an Irish accent and pretending to be Danny McAlevey, a Sticky from Ardoyne.

This is what all these intelligence reports reaching me were about. There were quite a lot of them. They were source reports – information from informants, and the local people and the local IRA were beginning to spot what he was doing. For the reports to say they were going to get the curly-headed SAS man, he might even have been whispering in places that he was in the SAS. He must have been – he must have been saying something like that – for them to come back with the information.

I think that behind it all he was creating an aura for himself and what none of us actually realized was that he was leaving quite a big footprint, quite a big signature, of Robert operating on his own down on the border area. This was beginning to stand out in that area like a sore thumb. That's why he wanted to learn the Irish language, the Irish dialect; that is why he wanted the car – to develop things and become some sort of agent handler, which is what he wasn't.

There were agent handlers in Northern Ireland, but he was not one. They operate under very, very specialized rules. Not everybody can be one, but he had decided that he was his own agent handler. To be fair to him, he knowingly decided to take on the risks to try to better develop sources of information so that the SAS would be more successful in South Armagh, which they had started to be with the Cleary incident, the Harvey incident and so on.

Nobody else was doing it except, perhaps, the RUC Special Branch. But, really, only an Irishman could operate in that area, talking to people or going into pubs. That area down there is real bandit country.

Soldiering in South Armagh was different to soldiering in Belfast. You operated mainly at night and when you did go out in uniform during the day people were nowhere near as friendly. The IRA had a much firmer grip down there. The first thing which struck soldiers was that they couldn't strike up that much of a rapport with people. They were patrolling without a lot of intelligence, patrolling against an enemy that by and large melted back over the border and an enemy that had been extremely successful, probably one of the most successful ASUs [active service units] down there using landmines mainly against vehicles and quite a few successful shoots.

At that point there must have been about twenty-five or thirty deaths in that area. It really was a very dangerous place for a soldier to be, either in or out of uniform. That is one of the reasons why they operated in and out of bases so much by helicopter. The deaths among soldiers at that time were mainly in ones and twos of men caught in vehicles by landmines and, occasionally, rocket attacks.

The RUC suffered in the same way, mainly twos and threes caught in cars by culvert mines. The enemy in that area were extremely careful about their operations: they used to take months to plan them and when they finally struck they were normally very successful.

Getting intelligence in South Armagh was harder than getting it in any other area. In other areas of Northern Ireland your problem is too much information – it is stopping people coming up to you all the time in the street and chatting. But this area around Bessbrook and Crossmaglen was a part of the United Kingdom that was almost a no-go area. It was a rural area where everyone knew everyone else and strangers like soldiers and policemen stood out like the dog's balls. That is why there had been no major successes for the security forces down there until the SAS incidents with Cleary and Harvey. There were one or two low-level successes, but no major arms' finds or anything like that. The information was not coming in. Only Irishmen could operate properly as intelligence gatherers there and there were none around. The IRA were very stealthy, operated mainly from south of the border and knew all the people they needed to know.

Whether he had been going to places like the Three Steps Inn at Drumintee for a long time – he had certainly been there before – or whether he saw his opportunity when the two squadrons changed over we do not know. But I got the impression, from talking to eye-witnesses and all the rest, that he had been in there within the two or three weeks before he was killed. He had been seen in there. Maybe he had just started to do that during that period – it was at about the same time that he started asking me for the Irish lessons, the car and all the rest.

But certainly if he was going to places like that it was absolutely mandatory that the ops officer in the SAS or whichever base he was going out from would know where he was going, why he was going, when he was coming back and what the back-up was if something happened to him. There would also have been a procedure whereby he would have had to check in at regular intervals by telephone or radio saying he was OK and if he did not do so within a certain time something would have to be done etc.

When he went out he should have been in a car fitted with a radio – a covert radio, the sort of thing where he would have been able to speak up into the sun visor or towards the windscreen. The microphone would have been up in the roof lining or the sun visor so that he didn't have to use a handset and draw attention to himself. He would have been armed, as I and any other officer going out would have been, with a pistol, a 9mm Browning and two or three spare magazines. He would have had an ID card which said he was a British Army officer. After he went missing we never did find his ID card. There weren't any funny ID cards saying he was something else. If you are stopped by the Army, or stopped by the RUC, you are who you are. As far as I am aware he would not have had any false papers.

He would also have been trained in counter-surveillance techniques which would tell him if he was being followed or watched. All of us had that. But the basic rule always was: don't set up a routine – vary your times and routes. Don't do the same thing today as you did yesterday. What you are trying to avoid above all is people knowing that you are going to do something, because any operation mounted against you takes days to organize. They have to get weapons and they have to get people there to do it, so you don't set up a pattern. And another key principle is that you are always looking to see if you can see anyone watching you. If you have any idea that you are being watched, like seeing people on motorbikes, or standing at the same bus stop, at the same street corner, or in the same car, that is when the alarm bells should ring.

As soon as you realize it you go back and report it, discuss it and you would either mount an operation – it might be a fairly elaborate process – to deal with those people or you might have to change your entire routine, or you might even have to be taken out of the job.

In that area by day strangers would tend to stick out either when they were on foot or if they tended to use the same car with the same number plates all the time, and you are certainly going to stick out if you are walking around with soldiers during the day and later going to somewhere like a pub at night. The same people in that pub could well have seen you in the town during the day.

Once you are out of your car in Northern Ireland you have about a minute – it is something like a diving bell giving you a minute's air – because once you start talking to people you might get away with a few phrases, but once you start talking in any detail people's ears are right up – and I base this on being a Scot – and they know there is something that is not right – people are naturally suspicious in those sort of areas. So I would imagine – and I'm guessing here – that his activities had been going on for some time and the local population and the local terrorists began to notice Robert, and then we started to get the reports saying they were going to get him. The SAS soldiers were also uneasy about him.

I don't think, on the other hand, that they had the first clue on the terrorist side of how to deal with it. From the events that happened in the Three Steps Inn that night it would appear they were gobsmacked when Robert turned up there and it took them some time even that night to get their act together. They weren't waiting for him that night. I don't think so, anyway. I think he just popped up in their midst. I think what was done to him that night was done on the spur of the moment. They even had to go to get someone to come and do it.

In the previous couple of weeks, I began to hear that he was interested in a group of people and that he was going out to meet people. I did not know where. I imagine he did not tell the ops officer exactly where he was going or why, or he might have said where he was going but not why. There was every indication he had been out a number of times and that he had not come back on time. This became apparent when he went missing. But that night, when he went missing, the ops officer certainly knew he was going to the Three Steps Inn, but I don't know if he knew why he was going there. There was an agreed set of timings that night as well – I investigated it afterwards.

Saturday 14 May 1977: Robert Nairac spent the early evening in his room at Bessbrook preparing to go out once more as Danny McAlevey, the Sticky from Ardoyne. By all accounts he planned to meet a contact at the Three Steps Inn at Drumintee, possibly the one – or several – who he believed would help him secure the biggest intelligence breakthrough in years, about which he had boasted to Captain D.

Then he informed SAS Captain David Allan Collett, the duty officer, that he was leaving, and that he was heading for Drumintee. Collett, when he was later called to give evidence at the Special Criminal Court in Dublin, said that Nairac wore his usual civilian attire – black donkey jacket, a pullover, flared grey trousers and scuffed brown suede shoes. Before he left the office, Collett checked out his 9mm Browning pistol, patent number IT774, and two magazines. The gun had modifications: the standard safety catch had been replaced by a larger one and the handgrip had been filed. Nairac loaded the pistol and slotted it under his arm in a special holster he had bought himself. Nairac also had 80 rounds of 8.82 ammunition for his SLR rifle, but did not take that weapon from the Bessbrook armoury that night.

Nairac told him he was going to the Three Steps Inn, but gave no reason for his visit and for Collett, who was one of the latest batch of SAS beginning their tour of duty, this was already an accepted practice. Even so, Collett questioned him about back-up, and said a team could be ready in minutes. Nairac refused and said it was not that kind of a job. He said he was only going out for a couple of hours and gave his return-to-base time as 11.30 p.m.

He drove out of Bessbrook Mill in a red Triumph Toledo car shortly before 9.30 p.m. His radio was hidden behind the car radio and the microphone was under the seat. He used his radio with his call-sign '48 Oscar' to report his position some twenty minutes or so later, informing the operations room at Bessbrook base that he was travelling towards Drumintee. At 9.58 p.m., he reported that he had reached the pub and was closing down his radio contact.

His colleagues at Bessbrook were unaware that he had been in and out of the pub several times in the previous two weeks, and that it was Nairac's second visit within two days; he had been there around the same time the previous night. A local woman who had been at the pub with her husband later saw his photograph and identified him, having seen him sitting near her table. He had smiled at her. She remembered specifically that he had been looking around as if he had lost something. He went to the bar and came back again, and told her he had mislaid his cigarettes. When she left the pub at around 10.00 p.m., he was also preparing to leave. She saw him again the following night, when she was surprised to see him singing with the band.

Saturday night was always a busy one at the Three Steps. It was one of the liveliest pubs around, with live music provided by a popular local band which attracted customers from a wide area. There were about 150 people there. It was so busy that the landlord Desmond McCreesh spent some time sitting outside in his white Mercedes, keeping a check on customers arriving and making sure cars were correctly parked. It was also a security operation – he was fearful of the possibility of car bombs – and as a matter of course, McCreesh checked the cars of anyone who might be suspect.

He saw Nairac's red Triumph Toledo drive in from the Jonesboro Road. The driver parked it at the top end of the car park, well away from the pub, and walked into the bar. He was wearing dark clothes and had bushy, curly hair. McCreesh decided to check out the red Triumph because he noticed something unusual about the number plates. Closer inspection revealed that some of the figures were blurred by cement. He looked inside and saw only cigarette packets strewn across the back seat. Later that night, when he was watching over the car park again as customers departed, he saw the same man leaving the pub in the company of other men, two strangers, but saw and heard nothing suspicious.

Nairac went inside, pushed his way to the bar and ordered a pint of Guinness. In the crowded pub his movements went unnoticed for most of the evening. One of the barmen, Malachy Locke, remembered serving him. He was standing at the bar, apparently talking to two other men whom the barman had never seen before. According to a Northern Ireland source, there were already a number of IRA men in the bar that evening who showed an interest in the man, who was talking away to people.

More positive recollections of his movements came from members of the John Murphy Band from Creggan, Crossmaglen, which was playing that night at the pub. One of them, Edmund Murphy, was able to recall Nairac with a group of people, perhaps four or six men, late in the evening. He remembered especially that Nairac went to the toilet about three times within quite a short space of time. There was speculation among investigators later that Nairac had already realized he was in trouble and made the visits to the toilet to dispose of any documents or other material from his pockets.

On his way back from his last visit to the toilet at around 11.15 p.m. Nairac went up to Eddie Murphy and asked him 'if a Belfast man can sing a song'. Murphy told him to write down his name down on a piece of paper. Nairac said no, but asked them just to call his out name – Danny McAlevey – when they were ready for him.

About ten minutes later, band member Charlie Quinn made the announcement that there was a special request from 'Danny – all the way from Belfast' to sing a song. There was a round of applause and 'Danny' made his way to the microphone. He sang a well-known song popular in Republican pubs, 'The Broad Black Brimmer', loud and clear, and got the audience to join him. Murphy was impressed by 'Danny's' singing voice and so were his audience. The applause was such that the band invited him to stay. He sang another three songs, and afterwards Nairac went back to the bar and rejoined the men who he was with earlier.

Nairac had a further chat with the band at the end of their session. As they were packing up to leave, Eddie Murphy accidentally struck Nairac on the head with his guitar. The band were loading their gear into their van outside when Murphy noticed two men at the door who appeared to be waiting for someone. At that moment, unbeknown to any of them, an IRA man sent one of their number to scout for possible Army vehicles around the roads leading from the Three Steps to the border pub not far away. He left with another man, saw nothing and came back to report.

Nairac appeared agitated and one member of the band, clearly noticing that a fight was possibly about to break out, asked Nairac if he wanted to go with them. He declined. They did not see him again, but around 11.45 p.m., as they were about to drive away from the Three Steps, Murphy saw what appeared to be a fight at the top of the car park. About five people were involved. Since it was not particularly unusual to witness a brawl at the end of a night's work, they drove away without paying much heed.

Back at Bessbrook Mill, the operations officer checked the clock again at midnight. Nairac was now thirty minutes overdue and he was cursing the man who once again, had ignored his check-in time. It had happened so often in the past, but none the less Captain David Collett knew he would have to go through all the procedures and report that Nairac had failed to make contact.

He telephoned his commanding officer and it was agreed that they should give him a few more minutes. By 12.15 a.m. there was still no word.

The commanding officer then rang Major Clive Fairweather and relayed the news: Robert Nairac is missing.

# 16

## EXECUTION

As Robert Nairac headed towards the Three Steps Inn that night, Major Clive Fairweather had gone out with a friend to dinner, at a restaurant in Saintfield, near Belfast. He did not live in the camp at Lisburn but had a small cottage a short drive away, attempting to live as near normal a life as possible under the circumstances in which he found himself. It was a fairly warm, almost summery evening, one of the first summery nights for a while. It was light until quite late. He returned to his cottage at around 11.00 p.m. The first he knew of Robert Nairac's disappearance – or indeed that he had gone out at all that evening alone – was sometime after midnight, when he received a phone call from the SAS informing him that Nairac had failed to come back from a meet.

The call came from an officer in his area who told Fairweather that Nairac was more than half an hour overdue. They discussed what they should do about it. They spoke about the fact that he had been late before when checking in, either when he had been out for social occasions or on meets with contacts. Fairweather enquired about the back-up team and was told there was none. Nairac had gone out alone. In fact, had he had back-up somewhere in the vicinity, they would have been SAS soldiers and they would have been able to dig him out of anything that happened to him.

Fairweather's frank recollections of that night point up the dilemma that now confronted him and Nairac's SAS colleagues:

> We discussed at that point what we were going to do about it and we decided to leave it for the time being, because it meant I would have to alert very senior officers

that someone was missing and, of course, if he then turned up we were going to end up getting an awful lot of people out of bed for nothing.

It was a question of saying it had happened quite a few times before, so we waited longer to see if he would turn up. Had I been aware that he had been late on the number of occasions that he had then, I think, we would probably have banned him from going out. If that had not worked then removing him from his post would have been the next step.

When I realized he was missing I was more worried about where he was than thinking about disciplining him. After about two hours had gone by we decided to put a helicopter up to look for him at first light. We just didn't know what the hell had happened to him. I spent most of the night making phone calls from home and taking calls. I was in contact with the SAS squadron on the ground, and then I went to my office and started talking to people at a higher level.

As soon as the helicopter got up it went straight to the Three Steps Inn and saw his car outside in the car park. From what I can remember their first report said they could see the car and that there were no other cars in the car park. They said they could see some damage to the windows.

At that point it really became a search for his body, although we could not be sure he was dead. We realized that he had been captured and was probably south of the border. The whole thing then became a very big operation, which passed out of my hands very quickly. I did a quick brief for the general and the ops officer at HQ Northern Ireland. The general had been alerted very early that morning. It then became a joint RUC–Army operation to try to locate where he was.

Later that morning, I went home and one of the source handlers – an ex-SAS guy who had contacts on the ground – came to me, and we had a long discussion about what the hell could have happened to Robert. He said he was worried about how much Robert knew, how many names he knew of locals. At that point I began to worry, because he knew where my house was – and did he have my address and the addresses of the others who lived outside? We were trying to work out if he was alive or dead, if he was alive where he was going to turn up, what he knew, etc.

We even briefly discussed the possibility of him having some romantic notion of going to talk to the other side. We weren't at all sure. We did a full risk analysis, running through who he knew, what he knew, who else could be at risk from the information he carried, whether he had been deliberately targeted, whether it was a chance occurrence, all of those things. That Sunday was a very, very busy day.

We didn't run around changing all the procedures because the rules were already in place, but by the Monday, people were being reminded that those rules must be absolutely obeyed. The SAS squadron were very alarmed and angry about him going missing. From very early on they had been very critical about the fact that someone had gone alone into that area without back-up and had really gone there like a lamb to the slaughter.

We were involved in a lot of contingency planning about what might have happened, because at that stage it wasn't known if he was dead. What if he turned up at a press conference in the south, if the IRA had captured him? If he had been captured how did we try to stop it happening again?

We were waiting, most of all, for news of what had happened to him. It was only later on that Sunday morning, once the ground party got to the car and found bloodstains and the damage to the car, that we began to realize there had been a struggle. All that took some time to come out. At local level they might have been a bit more aware.

Also during the morning I alerted the SAS at Hereford to the fact that the liaison officer had gone. I know that later that day Captain Tony Ball became very agitated about the whole thing, because he had a very good idea who might be involved in lifting Robert. He had a very good knowledge of the local terrorists. He was back in Hereford at the time and he had to be persuaded not to go to Northern Ireland. He felt he knew who was involved and what we should be doing. He knew who the players were.

He had been an intelligence officer down there before I arrived ... I think Robert had actually worked with him at some stage and was trying to copy some of the methods of operating he had seen Captain Ball involved in. His parent regiment was the same as mine, the King's Own Scottish Borderers, and he was an extremely professional, extremely capable, very cool individual, probably one of the coolest I have ever come across. He had developed his own unique style of operating both in uniform and out of uniform.

As the day unfolded it became apparent that Robert had been kidnapped or killed, but there was no body.

The conferences and meetings went on all day at Army headquarters in Lisburn and at Bessbrook. Nairac's room was searched immediately for any clues as to who he might have been meeting. None was found. Nor was there any trace of the Filofax-type book that he often carried around with him. The RUC, meanwhile, was holding its own briefings, which included input from local Special Branch men who had worked with Nairac in his liaison work for the SAS. They were furious that Nairac had gone out without back-up, that he was in that area alone at all and that the SAS had not informed them immediately he was assumed to have gone missing.

The RUC's own damage limitation had to be put into place immediately. They were already aware from their own knowledge that Nairac carried much information around with him, stored both in his head and in paper form. If his notebook alone was found it could have damaging results. If he was tortured or drugged and forced to reveal other details, then the whole security operation of that region, and perhaps beyond, could be compromised. The RUC chief who led the meeting concluded he had been snatched, and as the meeting closed with speculation as to who had picked him up, the officer insisted, 'We've got to get these fuckers – fast.'

Meanwhile, more than 300 troops and 100 extra police were drafted into the area to search for Nairac. Heavily armed foot patrols, nervous that they would be ambushed by the IRA, taking advantage of the vast numbers of soldiers suddenly appearing within their gun sight, scoured hedgerows and ditches and the terrain leading towards Drumintee. Mobile patrols searched remote farms and the many derelict buildings. Roadblocks were set up to check cars and their drivers, and virtually every vehicle travelling along the main road to and from the Irish Republic was searched.

Twenty helicopters were in the air, criss-crossing the deceptively peaceful but rugged countryside and with spotters hanging out the doors with binoculars. Later they all recommenced the search at the point they had begun, in case the body had been moved or dumped in the meantime.

After twenty-four hours of non-stop speculation among the large media contingent, who were anxious for details, on Monday

16 May, the Provisional IRA issued a statement stating that Captain Nairac was dead: 'We arrested him on Saturday night and executed him after interrogation in which he admitted he was an SAS man. Our intelligence had a number of photographs of him and he was recognized from them.'

But the Army's intelligence corps and the SAS were still not completely convinced that Nairac was dead. No one could remember another case where a British soldier had been killed where his body or remains had not been discovered – or indeed left where they lay at the time of death. They felt they could not rule out the possibility that he was still alive, and being tortured somewhere in the south to glean as much information from the man they called 'a walking encyclopedia' – although it was unlikely the IRA knew that. To them, he was a British soldier, probably SAS.

Two days later, the Irish police, to whom the RUC had appealed for help, brought in some vital information which led them to believe that Nairac had indeed been taken across the border. It did not prove he was dead, but showed that he had been involved in a terrific struggle and must have been badly wounded. Two men who had been fishing just a few hundred yards inside the border on the southern side, near Dundalk, stopped a Gardai patrol. They gave them two bullet cases and said there was blood at the point where they found them, by a bridge over the River Flurry in Ravensdale Forest.

The Irish police made an immediate search of the area suggested by the men and discovered heavy bloodstains close to the bridge parapet at Ravensdale. There were also bloodstains on the grass, a number of coins and signs of a struggle and perhaps someone being dragged along.

Three days later, the Provisional IRA twisted the knife. Its mouthpiece newspaper, *Republican News*, headlined its front page with a story of Robert Nairac's 'execution', accompanied by a photograph of him in his Guards uniform. The story read as follows:

> The elimination of Nairac is an obvious breakthrough in the war against the Special Air Service. Sources close to the IRA refuse to say how much detailed knowledge they now have of the SAS but they are obviously highly pleased with what Nairac has either given them or confirmed. IRA sources have revealed that Capt. Nairac was a high-ranking SAS officer. When arrested he had in his possession a Browning automatic with two magazines. He pretended he had been in Canada and brought the gun home with him. When arrested, he gave as his identity that of a Republican Clubs' Member; this Stick identity was broken almost immediately by an IRA officer. SAS morale must now be shattered as one of their most high-ranking officers has been arrested, interrogated and executed, and has disappeared without a trace.

The IRA was demonstrating that it was equally capable of psychological games as the British Army. Its ploy was to attempt to fool the Army into believing that Nairac had revealed under torture the details of particular SAS and Army operations, which would now have to be abandoned. Few who knew him well believed he would have broken, especially as he had received intensive training in anti-interrogation techniques.

There was now little doubt, however, that although, as the article said tauntingly, he had vanished without trace, Nairac had in fact been murdered. The newspaper statement by the IRA confirmed intelligence reports that the Army had been receiving during those first few days after Nairac's abduction. The continuing massive search by the Irish police, the RUC and the British Army failed to discover any clue as the whereabouts of his body.

It was a traumatic week for all concerned, not least Robert Nairac's distraught family in Gloucestershire. The former abbot at Ampleforth, Cardinal Basil Hume, had appealed to the IRA: 'I beseech those who have kidnapped him to release him as soon as possible for the sake of his family.' His mother Barbara clung to the hope that he was still alive, a hope born out of past experience when her own brother was 'lost' for weeks after the evacuation of the British Expeditionary Force from Dunkirk in June 1940 but eventually turned up alive and well. Later, she said in one of the family's few statements to the media: 'From the time of his first tour of duty in Northern Ireland all he ever wanted was to help bring peace to that troubled land. Of course, we all knew of the dangers. My son never talked of it but I knew that was the reason why he would not contemplate marriage.'

This was borne out at the time in an interview given to the *Daily Mail* by one of his former girlfriends, Mary Price, whom he had met at a cocktail party in Oxford in 1971. They came from similar backgrounds: she too was a Roman Catholic and her brother served with the Guards. According to the *Daily Mail*, Mary said:

> He immediately struck one as a very strong-minded person. He had a detached manner that was different … enigmatic and charming. I was swept off my feet. He was a tremendous romantic but he had an element in him that although he always seemed as if one day he intended to fall in love with a girl and settle down, first there was something he wanted to do. I suppose from the beginning there was no real future for him and me because he was so dedicated to the Army, which I knew. But I always hoped that he might come back and everything would click into shape.

Mary, who has married and lives in Surrey, wrote to me after the publication of the hardback edition of this book. Her letter was fascinating and throws additional light on the character of Robert Nairac, a man clearly driven by inner turmoil. Her words speak for themselves:

I was intrigued by your extremely well-written book ... it was extraordinarily revealing to me ... and confirms what I have discovered since [Robert's] death, that he lived very much in a world of fantasy whilst at the same time grappling with the grimmest of reality. He was always, in the short time that I knew him, a complete enigma to me and, for a man who described me (I discovered later), to friends who knew him much better, as the girl he was going to marry, extraordinarily cold (he never even tried to kiss me!) and ruthless.

Fortunately, my instincts told me to be wary of him and I was not unduly upset by his strange behaviour, but I can imagine that he must have broken many a girl's heart as he did have a certain charm. The only time, though, that I ever saw him express feeling was when I first met him at a Pimm's party at Oxford after he had just taken his finals – and when a group of us later went out to supper. He sang a strange mixture of Welsh and Irish rebel songs and became quite morose – and that was before he had even embarked on his curious mission.

The *Daily Mail*, in their excitement to try to find a girlfriend when doing a series on him just after he died, went over the top with their reported interview, much to my mortification. But really, of course, I should have known better. Only the urge to talk about someone you knew who had died in such a horrid way inclined me to agree to the interview. At the time of the interview, I had neither seen nor heard of him for two years plus – not surprisingly, since I was going out with a different Robert to whom I am still married, 21 years on!

It is true that I went to a ball in Chelsea with him. I found him very altered and furtive. He kept looking over his shoulder, thinking someone was spying on him, and, although he had supposedly completed his first mission in Ireland, he was determined that he would plead to be sent back for a second one. This in my opinion was a grave mistake. He was like a man obsessed; he told me that evening that because he was a Catholic and because he was in the Army, he felt he could personally bring the two sides together.

In that sense, I think he was living out a fantasy and in his personal life quite definitely did. It was said in accounts of his friends that I was the girl he intended to marry (the first I knew of it) and that he often talked about me (but never wrote to me). He would only telephone me, completely out of the blue and even then only on about four occasions in three years to ask me to some function or other, expecting me to drop everything and go as the phone call was always at very short notice.

The last time I saw him – at this Army ball in Chelsea in 1976 – the atmosphere was very strained and I had told him before he invited me that I had a serious boyfriend. He did not see me home but told me to get a taxi. I got a message a day or two later from his sister Rosamunde (of whom I was very fond) that he had tried to telephone, and in order to try to reciprocate and effect a kind of healing I invited him and his sister to supper at my flat a few weeks later. On the evening in question, his sister arrived punctually and, when an hour or so later he still hadn't turned up, I rang his barracks and got put through to two very nice young army officers, also Grenadier guardsmen, who had been given his dog to look after while he supposedly went to see one of his men. They ended up coming to supper instead – with the dog! He never did tell why he hadn't come.

He had a lovely family but never communicated with them and I think the tragedy of his brother's death had a very bad effect on him. From then onwards, he felt he had to make up for it and threw himself in a maniacal fashion into rugger and boxing, despite having a bad accident in the latter and being told to give it up. This maniacal energy led, I believe, to his quite unnecessary death in Ireland and I think it was a costly sacrifice that must have been so hard for his family to bear.

Final confirmation of his death came soon after the IRA statement. Clive Fairweather remembers:

Later that week it was established that he had been taken south of the border and shot. There had been a number of pieces of low-level information that the IRA had killed him. [After] information came in from the Gardai that they had found a site where there were bloodstains and teeth and hair, there was information coming in identifying which IRA unit had killed him.

There were reports that he had been dumped down a well or put in water, and other stories that his body had been buried; there was even a story that his body had been brought back over the border and buried near Belfast. All sorts of rumours were doing the rounds. I don't know where the information came from. Some of it came from the Gardai.

The mood in the SAS at the time was that we had made a fool of ourselves in front of the RUC. Back in Hereford the SAS feeling was akin to 'Christ, we really have blown it here and someone who is not part of the regiment has let the side down.' There were feelings amongst the commanders that we had lost a brave officer – he had been out on other operations, he had done other things and he was doing well in other areas. It was a mixture.

There was puzzlement, and there was horror among people like myself that it had happened and if we had seen the overall picture we probably could have stopped Robert doing this sort of thing, but we hadn't seen the complete picture until too late. I think that in the end he was out of control. He had bitten off far more than he could chew.

There was, however, another side to these events that the Army did not appreciate at the time, which suggested that all was not what it seemed with the IRA statement. Nairac had not been 'arrested'; nor had he been properly interrogated. In fact, he had told them nothing. The IRA were bluffing to cover the true facts and were attempting to at least salvage some propaganda out of what had been, according to one source:

> [It was] a total fuck-up by the gang of amateurs who snatched Nairac. Half of them were pissed out of their skulls. They hadn't got a clue who they'd got, except that he was probably Army, and when they took him over the other side and beat the living daylights out of him, they still couldn't get him to talk. It wasn't an IRA active service unit as such – just three fairly low-level IRA people and a few helpers whom they needed because Nairac was obviously going to be a tough bugger to deal with. They called in a more senior IRA man who actually killed him, but it was still a fuck-up from start to finish.
>
> They committed the cardinal sin of not letting the Army Council or the top brass in the Provisionals' command know what they were up to or even that they'd kidnapped a guy who was probably a British soldier. If they had, rest assured Nairac would have been taken in for interrogation at some safe house south of the border and kept there until he talked, however long it took, just as they had in the past with informers they had captured. The 'hooded men' syndrome would have had nothing on

what they would have done to Nairac – believe me. IRA intelligence had heard about Nairac in Crossmaglen. They'd been hearing about 'Danny Boy' from Belfast for some time and they said they had a photograph of him, but I don't believe it. The only photo I know of was one taken of him by a newspaper about three months before his death, when he was in Army uniform talking to some kids in Belfast. They weren't sure what he was up to and just let him go ahead and prod around. They were watching, although they had not tracked him to Drumintee, which is a pretty remote place. Who in their right minds would ever go to Drumintee? But as luck would have it, it was there that these wankers had to go and snatch him and kill him before he'd even told them his bloody name!

The Provisional area command and IRA intelligence went absolutely spare when they learned who they'd got. They would just have loved to have got their hands on him, and you can be sure that the propaganda they got out of it would have been far greater than the two piddling statements they put in *Republican News*. Anyhow, they were very, very pissed off by what had happened and even more angry when the RUC, the SAS, the British Army, the Gardai and Uncle Tom Cobley and all blitzed South Armagh over the next two weeks so that nobody could move a muscle. There were helicopters swarming all over the place. The word was that the people who snatched Nairac were carted by their own side, partly as punishment and partly to get the Army and the RUC off their backs.

Arrests were certainly made in double-quick time. Intelligence filtering to the British side of the border, to the RUC Special Branch, led the Gardai to arrest Liam Patrick Townson, a 24-year-old 'unemployed joiner' from Meigh outside Newry, on 28 May, just two weeks after Nairac vanished. Townson – ironically the son of an English civil servant who married an Irish girl – was living in Dundalk and known to be a Provisional. He was already on the list of terrorist suspects in Northern Ireland compiled by both Army intelligence and the RUC. He was arrested at a Gardai roadblock near the border and four days later was charged with Nairac's murder, even though no body had been found.

During the investigation, Townson drew a map for Irish detectives showing where he had hidden a package containing two guns, one the modified Browning belonging to Nairac and the other a weapon belonging to himself. These were recovered and at another spot he marked out, detectives found a plastic bag containing clothing, which he said belonged to those who were present that night and had been dumped because of the bloodstains. Among the clothing was a pullover owned by Townson and under an armpit forensic experts found strands of hair which matched hairs on a brush belonging to Nairac.

Townson was brought before a special criminal court in Dublin in June, and remanded in custody until his trial, which would not take place until 7 November. Meanwhile, in the north the RUC had been equally busy, in pursuit of the remainder of the gang. They arrested five men from South Armagh in connection with Nairac's death. Two others the police wished to interview fled to America and were never heard of again. The case would make legal history because it was the first time ever that anyone had been arrested and subsequently tried within the United Kingdom for an offence committed in the Republic of Ireland.

Three of the men, Gerard Fearon, twenty, Thomas Morgan, eighteen, and Daniel O'Rourke, thirty-two, were jointly charged with murder. Michael McCoy, nineteen, was charged with kidnapping and Owen Rocks, thirty-three, was accused of withholding information about the kidnapping of Nairac. Much of what later transpired in their eventual trials focused on the statements of Liam Townson. He made seven statements in all, although he retracted them later, claiming they had been made verbally under duress, and, as we shall see, only two were allowed as admissible in evidence to the court. They were made to Irish detectives at the time of or soon after his arrest. They more or less confirmed that Nairac's abduction had not been a high-level IRA operation. Townson's first statement to detectives was:

> I shot the British captain. He never told us anything. He was a great soldier … I had been drinking in a pub. Danny O'Rourke came in. He told me to get a bit of hardware, that there was a job to be done. We went down the road in Kevin Crilly's car. I got my gun, a .32 revolver. I went to the bridge near the road at Ravensdale. I fired a shot from the gun on the way to test it. They were all there when I got there … I had a lot of drink taken. I asked the captain who he was and he said he was a Sticky. I asked him who knew him and he said Seamus Murphy. I told him I didn't believe him, and that he was a British soldier and I had to kill him. I hit him on the head with my gun.
>
> He said, 'If you're going to kill me, can I have a priest?' He was in a bad state. I aimed at his head. I only put one shot in him. The gun misfired a few times. I left the body there and went home across the fields. I have no idea where the body is and that's the truth.

The second statement was made at Dundalk police station after Townson had consulted his solicitor. He became distressed and hysterical. His doctor was called to give him an injection to calm him. Later, he himself called for a priest to make a 'proper confession'. He screamed: 'I'll swing for nobody. They will never put a rope around my neck. They can shoot me if they like. I will kill myself tonight. I will tear my heart out. Nobody's going to hang me for a British soldier.' Superintendent Andrew Murphy, in charge of the investigation, calmed him down: 'There's no danger of hanging and even if there were now's not the time to worry about it. Have a cup of tea!'

Neither statement threw much light on the terrible circumstances surrounding Nairac's abduction and death, and even if they had been known to the media at the time, they would not have sated the media's desire for more graphic descriptions. In the days and weeks after the disappearance of Robert Nairac journalists were clamouring to discover who he was, exactly, and what he had been up to during his time in Northern Ireland.

His murder provided one of the few occasions for journalists to push open the window on the secret war a little further and extract information that had until now remained obscured by the Official Secrets Act, but little light was thrown on that area of SAS operations.

The Army was naturally protective of its position and put out statements that included the basic facts but were as devoid of detail as it was possible to be, disclaiming Nairac's membership of the SAS, which was true. The Army's spokesman Brigadier David Woodford went only so far as to admit: 'On occasions he would have been working actively with the SAS.' He added that Nairac's role at the Three Steps Inn was 'not normal and we are looking into the circumstances of the affair ... Captain Nairac was an outstanding and courageous officer who was not the sort to take unnecessary risks ... something went wrong on this occasion and we are trying to find out what it was.'

The Army's reticence over the detail was to be expected, given the nature of the work Nairac was involved in and the fact that there were others still actively engaged in it, not to mention the host of questions the Army needed answering internally, which were certainly not for public dissemination at the time. The fact that the IRA claimed to have knowledge of SAS and intelligence operations, drawn from Nairac's interrogations, was most likely untrue, but no one could be 100 per cent certain. There could be no possibility of revealing more details to the media that might prove useful to IRA intelligence.

The issue of press comment in relation to this specific incident was shut down by June, however, following the arrest of Townson, and the others soon after, which made all discussion of the matter *sub judice*. There were still, however, many questions to be asked and answered, and not all of them would come out at the trials.

# 17

## The Full Story

The Special Criminal Court in Dublin was to be the scene of the first of the trials that would throw additional light – but not a lot – on the activities and death of Captain Robert Laurence Nairac. The smallish pillared courthouse is set in a maze of grey streets close to the city's fruit market, on the north of the River Liffey. The 'special' courts were originally created to deal with cases of subversive activity, which included the IRA and now the Provisionals, and possibly northern loyalists arrested within the Republic of Ireland. Just as Britain had instituted trials without jury in the north, justice in the special criminal courts was administered by a panel of three judges. Irish juries in the south had always been reluctant to convict members of the IRA, especially if they came from the north.

Here, Liam Townson was brought to trial for the murder of Nairac. For almost three weeks, the tiny court was packed with British journalists, Irish detectives, SAS and British government observers, whose mostly huge forms were pushed together like so many sacks of potatoes in two rows of pew-like seats. There as much of the story that was going to be revealed unfolded, with evidence from arresting detectives and from Captain David Collett, the SAS officer who was on duty the night Nairac disappeared, as well as the forensic evidence, such as the blood at the murder scene and the strands of hair found on Townson's pullover matching those found on the hairbrush found in Nairac's room.

The evidence revolved around the statements made by Townson to the Irish police and other somewhat circumstantial detail that enabled the prosecution to present its case alleging that it was Townson, along with others, who shot Nairac after he had been abducted from the Three Steps Inn. The atmosphere was to say the least emotive, surrounded as the case was by issues that encompassed a whole gamut of controversial elements: that the accused was a Catholic whose father was an Englishman, a resident of Northern Ireland, a member of the IRA, being tried in an Irish court without a jury for the alleged murder of an English captain, who came from an old Catholic family and had been drinking at the time of his disappearance in a notoriously Republican district that was teeming with a tough urban guerrilla force of the Provisional IRA.

There were other overtones, too, promoted by the defence, whose lawyers alleged they had been denied access to certain documents and SAS statements, and that the accused's statements were made under duress. Further, there were allegations that Townson had made his statements after being threatened by the Irish police that he would be handed over to the SAS in the north unless he cooperated.

In a submission to the judges, counsel for the defence, Patrick MacEntee, a leading Dublin advocate, made some other remarkable counter-claims that, outside the confines of the court, set a whole new batch of rumours flying – to the effect that Nairac may possibly be still alive and had been given a totally new identity, like the supergrasses.

MacEntee claimed there were two other possible hypotheses beyond that of his client being involved in a murder. The first was that Captain Nairac had been abducted and Townson was involved in some fracas that may have ended in death, but there was no compelling evidence linking the two incidents; it was inconceivable that the prosecution had proved beyond doubt that he was. The other 'real possibility', he said, was that:

Captain Nairac is not dead. There was only the evidence of Captain Collett that he had not seen him again. They [the judges] should look at what Captain Nairac was involved in … elaborate undercover work in a specially equipped car in civilian clothes or, not to put too fine a tooth in it, in espionage or special activities. Was he going to pay informers, to assassinate some person, to gather information? Whatever happened that night they [the Army] knew that Captain Nairac's cover was broken. Could it be that after the fracas Captain Nairac lay doggo and then made his way back, to be spirited away to safety? There was the case of an author of a well-known book on illegal organizations this side of the border who had disappeared off the face of the earth with the help of Her Majesty's Government. Captain Collett was careful in saying that he never saw Nairac again, nor did Nairac ever return to Bessbrook. But there is no evidence that he had not turned up elsewhere.

Dramatic or ridiculous though the idea was, depending upon one's penchant for conspiracy theories, the judges paid no heed to the notion. They did, however, ponder upon long legal arguments by the defence about the admissibility of certain evidence, including the alleged statements of confession by Townson, none of them signed. They went into secret session to listen to legal arguments about the statements made by Townson at various times to police officers and upon which rested the main thrust of the prosecution's case against him. After a lengthy recess, the presiding judge, Mr Justice D'Arcy, returned to read an hour-long statement of the court's ruling on the pleas of the defence that the statements were inadmissible. The length of the adjudication demonstrated the knife-edge on which the trial was balanced.

The first statement that was allowed in evidence was a verbal confession allegedly made by Townson to the two police officers, Inspector Courtney and Sergeant Canavan. It came soon after Townson's arrest. Townson himself had said in evidence that he had denied all knowledge of the killing and gave the police an account of his movements. He said they then threatened to put him across the border, where he was 'wanted for three murders'. Judge D'Arcy said the court did not accept this claim.

The two officers stated in evidence that Townson later changed his story, which was when he admitted to them that he had killed Captain Nairac, with the words – 'I shot the British captain. He never told us anything. He was a great soldier …'

The second statement was made, again verbally, when Townson became distressed and hysterical. This was recorded by three police officers, Detective Lane, Inspector McCabe and Superintendent Murphy. They took notes of the moment when Townson said to them: 'I will swing for nobody.'

Five other statements which the prosecution sought to have admitted in evidence against Townson were made by the accused man at various times and noted by accompanying police officers at the time. One of them was said to have been dictated by Townson as he sat handcuffed to Detective Lane while they sat in the back of a police patrol car. There was, as the judge pointed out, no corroboration other than that provided by the police officers themselves.

Mr Justice D'Arcy concluded that the court recognized that, as argued by the defence, some of the defendant's constitutional rights had indeed been breached – those in relation to access to a lawyer. It was for that reason therefore that the court discarded five of the statements as inadmissible and relied on the remaining two statements as sufficient to indicate a confession; and the court was satisfied these statements were made without duress and voluntarily.

Until that moment, in the concluding hours of the trial, journalists were betting amongst themselves that Townson would be freed on a technicality because most of the evidence had been provided by Townson himself – albeit 'as told' to Irish detectives. In spite of these unsatisfactory elements in the prosecution's case, which may well have affected its outcome before a jury, either in Ireland or England, the trial was brought to a swift conclusion. The defence submissions on whether Nairac was alive or dead provided one more element of mystery in a trial that left many questions unresolved, especially in view of the sensitive nature of the work in which he was involved. The judges, well aware of these limitations, pushed on towards a conclusion, leaving a number of stones unturned, though clearly at the end of the day they were satisfied as to Townson's guilt. He was given a mandatory sentence of penal servitude for life.

There remained one other restricting aspect that affected immediate journalistic investigations of Nairac's death – the fact that five other men were still awaiting trial in Northern Ireland, facing charges connected with his abduction and murder. Their trial was put off for a further twelve months, until November 1978 – seventeen months after Nairac was killed. The trial, with more defendants and charges to be considered, ran until 15 December 1978. It was the first ever murder case in Northern Ireland in which the victim's body had not been discovered.

At the end of it, Gerard Patrick Fearon was given a life sentence for murder and twenty-two years for causing grievous bodily harm. Thomas Patrick Morgan was ordered to be detained at Her Majesty's pleasure for murder and twenty-two years for possession of a gun and kidnap. Daniel Joseph O'Rourke was given ten years for manslaughter and membership of the IRA. Michael Joseph McCoy was sentenced to five years for kidnap. Owen Francis Rocks was given two three-year sentences for withholding and failing to give information, to run concurrently. Not one of the five – nor Liam Townson – served more than the minimum possible term inside.

After accounting for their term in prison while on remand, Owen Rocks was freed one month after the trial, in January 1979, and later became a Sinn Fein activist and election worker. McCoy was released in December 1979. O'Rourke was released in March

1982 and also became an election worker for Sinn Fein, as well as president of Drumintee Gaelic Football Club and a 'well known and respected' member of the local community. Fearon was freed in 1985 and Morgan the following year, having served nine years. Morgan would have been safer inside: eleven months after his release he was dead, killed in an accident with a concrete mixer. No attempts were ever made to extradite the two others who had been named in statements by the accused, Kevin Crilly and Pat Maguire and were known to have fled to America.

Liam Townson served twelve years of his life sentence and was released from prison in 1990. He moved back to the hamlet of Meigh, near Drumintee, not far from Owen Rocks, there to resume his place in society.

It was in many respects an unsatisfactory conclusion to a tragic event. Journalistic investigations, after two delayed trials, were few and inconclusive, with the notable exception of that by David Blundy of the *Sunday Times*, who came closest to describing the full story and, much later, Martin Dillon's chapter on Nairac in his book *The Dirty War*. Dillon remained convinced that Nairac was 'following orders, and any criticism of the events which led to his capture and death must be directed towards the intelligence hierarchy'.

Rumours to this effect have abounded ever since Nairac's death. Some have suggested that he was even being used as a decoy, to flush out the IRA for some much wider intelligence operation. Down the years various writers pointed out that too many questions remained unanswered.

There was never any public inquiry on either side of the border. No formal explanations were ever offered by the Army; nor are they likely to be. Even in the early summer of 1998, when references to Nairac were made again during the reporting of the Good Friday Peace Agreement and its consequences, Nairac's story was being recounted with difficulty because of the lack of precise detail.

Most of the missing pages in the story of his undercover years have, I hope, been supplied by this narrative thus far. The events on the night he died are further illuminated by the recollections of Major Clive Fairweather, who, it will be recalled, was G2 Int, Northern Ireland at the time Nairac was there. He subsequently wrote a private report, much of the contents of which he described during a long, taped interview for me.

Going back to the events of that night which I got from the RUC and listening to the people who killed him at their trials. I have a picture of what happened. I actually sat down and wrote a report on everything that had happened so the Army, Special Forces and everyone else could learn the lessons of what had gone wrong. That night Robert Nairac had it in his mind to go to the Three Steps Inn to see who was meeting with whom, and who was associating with whom, and from that he would have a better picture of what the IRA might be doing next in South Armagh. He didn't want back-up because I think he thought that another car sitting in the area might have blown his cover. He obviously felt he had sufficiently good cover to allow him to get away with what he was intending to do. He drove down there probably just as the light was changing, about nine or ten o'clock at night. It gets dark later over there than it does in London.

It would appear that when he got there, having locked his car in the car park, he didn't walk in wearing his pistol. It would appear he left his pistol either in the glove box or under the car seat. You would normally wear it in your waistband, but he deliberately left it behind because I think he knew he was going to be up on the stage singing. He had it in his mind that if he was going to stand up on the stage and sing and put his arms out, then a waistband holster or shoulder holster was

237

going to show. Leaving his gun behind in his car was his first mistake. It would appear he was in the bar drinking with people he knew from before.

He was chatting away in an Irish accent pretending to be drunk, I gather. There was a band playing that night and he got up on the stage and he sang probably not once, but several rebel songs. There are suggestions he went back up several times ... but people were asking, 'Who's this? What's going on here?' And others were saying, 'That's Danny McAlevey who's some guy from Ardoyne, who's working in the area.' He obviously had some cover story which he told people.

I think a group of people, very low level connected to the IRA, thought: Right, we'll have to deal with this guy.

Probably two things happened – they made a phone call south of the border to the local IRA commander saying what was going on and then they decided to get Robert outside. Again this is speculation, but the evening was coming to a close, people were going, I think the band even had packed up their instruments and were leaving and even said to Robert, 'Do you want to come with us'? I think Robert said no. I can't prove this, but I think he was challenged by these people. They might not even have been IRA.

The same thing can happen in a pub in Glasgow at the end of the night when somebody says to a stranger: 'Ootside, pal.' I think Robert knew he was going to go outside with them. I think he had it in his mind that as there were only a couple of them he was going to go outside and, as an ex-boxer, he was going to enjoy giving them a good hiding. Now his pistol was in the car fully cocked and he had the car keys on his person.

When he got outside I think there was another group waiting for him and there was a fairly big punch-up with

Robert handing back as much as he was given. I think at one point he even got to the car – he might even have unlocked it; I think he even got his hands into the car to get the pistol. That's why there was damage to the car. At what stage they got the pistol off him I don't know.

I have often wondered about that, but I was told that at one stage they got a scarf, threw it round his neck and pulled him back, and that stopped him. He was a very strong guy, a good boxer. Something that has always puzzled me was what the hell anyone was doing with a scarf on a May night. I had seen Robert wearing a scarf a couple of times, but whether he was wearing one that night I don't know. They had a car or two cars waiting, and they managed to bundle Robert towards a car. At that point they clubbed him with a pistol and they then drove off. I don't know if they had a plan, or how long they had to put this together. I don't know whether they intended to beat the shit out of him and leave him, or whether they intended to beat the shit out him and put him in a car and take him away, but the way he reacted and fought with them and all the rest began to determine events and he was bundled into one of the cars and driven off.

I would imagine it would only take them about ten minutes to cross the border, where they would obviously have much more time and freedom to deal with him – not that they didn't have a deal of freedom in that part of the north at that time. Another puzzle is the fact that although Robert should have had an ID card, as far as I know we never recovered his ID card and again, as far as I know, the terrorists didn't have it. They didn't find anything on him which definitely said he was Army. Whether they managed to get that out of him I don't know, but he was conscious as he was driven south. He

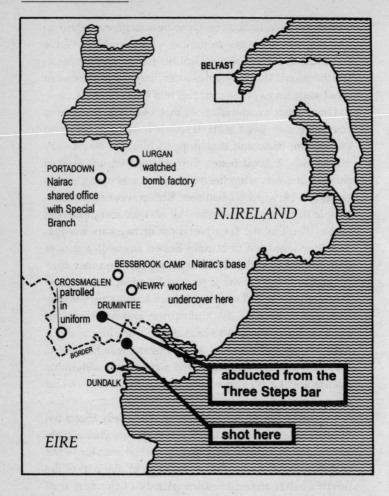

BELFAST

LURGAN
watched
bomb factory

PORTADOWN
Nairac
shared office
with Special
Branch

N.IRELAND

BESSBROOK CAMP  Nairac's base

CROSSMAGLEN
patrolled
in
uniform

NEWRY  worked
undercover here

DRUMINTEE

BORDER

abducted from the
Three Steps bar

DUNDALK

shot here

EIRE

*Captain Robert Nairac's last hours were spent drinking in plainclothes
in an Irish border bar. But how could he have hoped to be unspotted
when as the map shows he had worked locally, and was well known as a
soldier in Crossmaglen eight miles away? Or was he a decoy, who
wanted to be seen?*

was driven to a field near a stream and there was a bridge – I have never been there because it is in the south – and that is where they got him out of the car. Thereafter he took a fairly heavy beating, with various individuals taking chances to punch and kick him. I don't know how long that went on. As far as I am aware he managed to grab his pistol back at one point and managed to get a shot off, hitting one of them in the leg.

Meanwhile Liam Townson, who was a local IRA commander and an Englishman to boot, who had gone to Ireland and, like all Englishmen, had to show how much more Irish he was, had got the call to come and deal with Robert. This must have been about half one or two in the morning. I imagine they hatched their plan in the pub after seeing Robert going backwards and forwards to the stage. On his way to the scene Townson had had to go to get his pistol. He didn't keep it at home. He kept it under a stone wall somewhere. He had had to fetch that and then turn up at the scene.

By then I think they had also got some wooden stakes out and were laying into Robert with these, he having shot one of them. I think Townson turned up to chaos. There were eight or nine of them with Robert, and I think they didn't know what the hell to do with him and he was still insisting he was Danny McAlevey, a Sticky from Ardoyne who was working locally and could they leave him alone?

When Townson turned up, there was a further session of beating Robert and further questioning, and then at one point Townson didn't really know what to do with him, but took him away from the group with another guy and marched him up the field, and as they went up the field Robert, from what I am led to believe, managed to grab the pistol Townson had brought with him. He managed to turn it on Townson and he managed to pull the trigger but it misfired. So he very nearly got away again. He fought very hard for his life. He had almost certainly nearly got away in the car park; he nearly got away when he managed to shoot one of them in the field; and he nearly got away by turning on Townson. He had gone through an enormous amount of punishment, but his wits were still there and he was still speaking in an Irish accent and sticking to his cover story, his own established cover story.

He was asked how he managed to have a 9mm Browning pistol, which was what the Army carried, and he even had a story for that. He said he had worked in Canada and at that time most British Army 9mm Brownings had 'made in Canada' on them. He was questioned about Ardoyne at length and he did quite well because he had been there with his own Guards battalion, but I think he did say things that led people to be suspicious. They weren't absolutely sure whether he was a Sticky, whether he was a British Army guy or what. I don't think any of them quite knew who he was.

By this time Robert had had an awful beating. Townson and the others left him for a while lying face down in the field, whimpering and crying. They then came back and one pretended to be a priest. Robert was a Catholic and the 'priest' said he had come to take his confession and pretended to administer the last rites. Even at that point Robert continued to say he was Danny McAlevey from Ardoyne.

Townson still didn't know what to do, but nearly having been shot himself by Robert and having to show that he was the local commander I think they had no option but to shoot him. However, I don't think that was ever the plan at the outset. As I understand it the gun then misfired two or three times because it had been lying in a wall – until finally they managed to put a round in his head. I don't know whether they hit him with more than one round, but it must have been coming up to first light at that point, and he must have gone through two or three hours being severely beaten, probably tortured and kicked, and throughout he resolutely stuck to his cover story and denied he had anything to do with the Army. He very nearly, I think, succeeded in convincing them that he was who he said he was. They had a feeling he was SAS but they didn't quite know.

At that point, having shot him, they then had the major problem of disposing of his body. All the information that kept coming back said he had been put in water or down a well or whatever else.

The trial was held in Dublin in the autumn of that year and two of us from the British Army were required to attend: myself and Captain David Collett, who was the duty ops officer when Robert disappeared. It wasn't clear what evidence we were going to be required to give other than to establish that Capt. Nairac had existed and that now he no longer existed. There were a number of things we had to take with us like dental records. We were there essentially to give evidence of when he had last been seen.

We flew from London, having been briefed in London about it at a fairly high level at the Ministry of Defence, mainly by the Crown lawyers about what the trial was likely to involve and how we were to conduct ourselves. The difficulty, which was never resolved, was that we were going to a trial which was in a country outside Britain's jurisdiction. By law we couldn't be compelled to go there; it was up to us what evidence we gave, and we would have to answer truthfully or risk being in contempt of the Irish court. But if we were questioned on sensitive operations and answered truthfully, would we then be prosecuted under the British Official Secrets Act on our return for giving away information and methods of operation? No one was able to assure us; they just said: 'You're on your own on that. You will have to make your own judgement if you are asked something sensitive.' As it so happened I cannot recall anything that either Capt. Collett or I were asked that put us in that position. We sat through the whole trial and listened while the people were dealt with.

We flew to Dublin on a scheduled civil aircraft and the Gardai kept a discreet watch over us. They looked after us. I remember sitting in the court ... I remember listening to the evidence with a mixture of horror and the realization that all the way through his ordeal Robert had been extremely brave, even though he had set himself up.

There was an awful lot of feeling of 'If, only...' I did manage very briefly to talk to the man who killed him after he was taken down to the cells. We were taken in and out via an entrance below the court which passed the cells and that was when I got my chance to snatch a few words with him. I just wanted to see him, to try to find out what sort of individual he was and to try to find out a little bit more. He was in a very agitated state and didn't want to say too much in case it prejudiced an appeal. He didn't know who I was or my background.

From what I remember, he himself was quite horrified at what had happened. I don't know that he set out that night to kill Robert but, in the end, he had no option. I don't think that any of the low-level people involved thought it would end in murder; I don't even think they knew what they were setting out to do. It wasn't some cold premeditated act. He was a murderer and part of a really vicious gang who gave a really vicious beating to a man, but in a way he found himself in a situation which was way beyond what he expected that night, and I think that Robert ended up in a similar situation that night. I don't think Robert ever thought of ever being captured like that. He said that Robert had been one of the bravest people he had ever met.

# 18

## AFTERMATH

As Cardinal Basil Hume and other prominent figures supported the call for IRA information as to the whereabouts of Robert Nairac's body, so that he could be laid to rest by his family with a proper burial service, his faith seemed to count for naught among those who had produced his killers. There was even apparent dissension within the hierarchy of the Roman Catholic Church, which became apparent when the new leader of Ireland's 3.5 million Roman Catholics, Monsignor Tomas O Fiaich, took office a few weeks after Nairac's death.

Shortly after his appointment as Archbishop of Armagh and Primate of All Ireland was announced by the Pope, he called a press conference in which he repeated his well-known and strongly held views in support of a united Ireland. But he went further, pointedly condemning press coverage, mostly arising during reports of Nairac's death, in which the area of South Armagh close to the border had been described as 'bandit country'. He himself was born in the village of Anamar, near Crossmaglen, and he said that the region had been much maligned by the media. 'I have no hesitation in going there at any time of the day or night and never felt in danger there,' he said, in a somewhat naïve appraisal which rankled with those still investigating Nairac's murder. He went on to state categorically he had never had any association with the Provisional IRA and abhorred the acts committed by them and other paramilitary organizations, but added that he condemned all violence, including that by the British security forces.

The Primate, whose brother was a doctor in Crossmaglen, went on to say: 'I have seen patients carried in with the effects of beatings and other tortures I do not care to mention. A very good friend of mine who was interned had his skin burned by cigarette butts and so on. All this sort of thing – it doesn't matter what side it comes from – has to be condemned.'

While it was easy to take issue with him on some of his comments, it remained an indisputable fact that events surrounding the Troubles as they existed in South Armagh, where the SAS had been designated to concentrate its efforts recently, focused generally on the IRA, which also figured predominantly in both public condemnation of terrorism and the military planning to combat it. Yet terrorism in Northern Ireland remained a multi-handed affair, with the loyalist groups like the UVF still exceedingly active throughout the Six Counties even though they had been depleted by a large number of arrests for murder and terrorist activities. During the mid-1970s, the loyalist gangs had in fact killed more people than the IRA, but they did not generally attack the security forces.

While the Catholic communities in the southern regions of Ulster took the brunt of rancour for succouring the Provisionals, and the Republic of Eire was lambasted for not confronting the issue of harbouring IRA suspects, the loyalist terrorist groups achieved much less of a media profile as they pursued their own ambitions against Republicans and Catholics. Only Protestant hard-liners, like Dr Ian Paisley, took the headlines.

Another fact about the Troubles was that successive British governments, with the Army as its blunt instrument, had managed in the eight years since the Troubles began to alienate all sides in the struggle and with one ill-conceived policy after another had attempted to rule without the support of either side. The resultant and on-going crisis that existed in the province was no better summed up than by R. P. H. O'Neill, a former serving officer who arrived in Belfast with the first British troops in 1969. In an article in *The Times* on 15 August 1977, he wrote:

In this to date disastrous policy in which soldiers have

died to no discernible effect, the Army has been an all-
too-compliant instrument ... the main practical effect of
the Army's presence in Ulster, operating under the
present policies that it has, has been to protect the IRA
from the retribution that would long since have
overtaken it, whether at the hands of Ulstermen or
Irishmen.

The approach was set to change, once again. Northern Ireland
Secretary Roy Mason had already recognized some of these
failings and had taken up some of the points raised by Kenneth
Newman, then Chief Constable of the RUC, in a confidential
document which he circulated in March 1977, a month before
Nairac was killed. Entitled *The Way Ahead*, it set out proposals for
a stepping-up of the intelligence war, in which the IRA
commanders, the quartermasters and officers would be
specifically targeted. The top men needed to be identified, located
and arrested; once they had been taken out, the theory was, the
organization would fall apart. The document was already in
circulation when Nairac began his deeper, solo incursions into
what the Primate did not like being described as 'bandit country'.
At that time there were already major discussions going on at the
intelligence briefings he attended with Mike Rose, projecting the
need for more localized intelligence. It is possible that he saw a
copy of it.

A review of undercover activity was already in progress in
Westminster and there were plans for a fresh onslaught and a
new approach in the struggle against terrorists, with the
Provisionals singled out as Public Enemy Number One. Within a
month of Nairac's death, Roy Mason announced that more
specialist troops trained in anti-terrorist activity would be
dispatched as soon as possible to join the SAS in their secret
operations against the Provisional IRA. It would be overstating
the situation to suggest that Nairac or his death had anything to

do with these moves; they were already on the drawing board and he himself had read the signs that the war was moving underground.

As has already been identified, he was trying to spot some of the helpers the IRA had established throughout the province – the watchers, the couriers, the signalmen and the triggermen – and it was at the hands of these very people, albeit relative nonentities in the terrorist chain of command, that he lost his life.

By the autumn of 1977, there were 300 covert troops operating in the province, compared with the 60 who had made up the SAS contingent for most of 1976. The targets and the goals were specific. The 14,500 troops in the province at that time remained, for mass deployment on the streets of the Six Counties, but privately Mason was hoping to decrease their numbers by at least two battalions, bringing their numbers down to 13,000 in the short term with a target figure of half its peak of 22,000 in 1972 within the foreseeable future. The theory was less but more: i.e. fewer major troop deployments, more small undercover groups. The covert troops had their own specialists, spotters, agent handlers, surveillance operaters and even 'muggers', who spent their time studying photographs of crowds and those taken clandestinely.

What the Secretary of State was saying was, in effect, that the use of the Army had to change. 'The battle against the IRA is not being won fast enough,' Mason declared. 'The Army must concentrate more on the collection of intelligence and much more is being done in the field of SAS-type activities than the public realize; we intend to intensify these activities.'

The announcement about the 'type' of the SAS's activities was a veiled reference to the still highly secret operations of 14 Int, the undercover unit based in Belfast, to which Nairac had been attached as a liaison man in its earliest days. Mason was emphatic, if over-optimistic in his view:

Specialization is the key to successful Army operations

nowadays ... and you have my solemn pledge that for
me there is no acceptable level of violence; there is no
lack of will to bring this province back to peace and
normality and to prove to the Provisional IRA who are
the principal enemies of society that our will to defeat
them is unshakeable.

This was clearly no knee-jerk reaction to recent events in
Northern Ireland but the result of considerable and intense study
by the Army, with input from MI5, into the very aspect of the
struggle that had engaged Robert Nairac so intently in his own
quest – that of ground-level intelligence to identify, track and
capture IRA commanders, the top men.

The study had shown that the Army could no longer rely on
the RUC Special Branch as its prime source; indeed Lord Carver,
the former Chief of General Staff, said in his autobiography that
the Special Branch had lost the will to carry out rigorous
interrogation – something of a turning point in the Army's
intelligence operations.

The Army's frustration ... led to gradual and increasing
pressure that it should rely less on Special Branch and do
more to obtain its own intelligence, a tendency I was
initially reluctant to accept, all experience in colonial
fields having been ... in favour of total integration of
police and military intelligence. However, the inefficiency
of the RUC Special Branch, its reluctance to burn fingers
and the suspicion, more than once proved, that some of
its members had close links with Protestant extremists led
me finally to the conclusion there was no alternative.

It was partly because of this new and concerted intelligence effort,
linked to the period immediately before and soon after Nairac's
death, that allegations of his association with MI5 were so readily

acceptable to writers, propagandists and others campaigning for their own particular causes. As we have seen, in time, he became the link and the target as accusations flourished about the Dirty War, and all that it had involved. Most of those allegations have been covered in earlier pages and the fullest evidence that is ever likely to be given is now available for the reader to judge. As for the issue of whether he was a tool of MI5, the truth will never be known. There are still those who are convinced that at the time of his death, Nairac was working under orders – not those of the SAS, but those of MI5 – and that it was MI5 who asked him specifically to get underneath the general run of intelligence, go out into the heartlands of PIRA people and take in as much as he could. What is known, and the information is drawn from those in service in Northern Ireland at the time, is that from the mid-1970s onwards MI5, having gained ascendancy over MI6 in all Ulster operations, was desperate to expand its own agent-running operations. MI6 was supposed to be concerned with intelligence interests outside Ulster. It was an almost impossible division, because the activities of the IRA emanated from within the province and in the Republic. Intelligence from source could only be achieved by recruiting their own agents, and this need intensified as MI5 operations expanded.

Unlike the RUC or the Army – who were themselves rivals in the same business – MI5 had no direct access to potential recruits to intelligence, who were most likely to turn during arrest and questioning. MI5, which was not generally involved at that stage of proceedings, either had to poach informers from other agencies or go out and find their own. They were especially concerned about the lack of information coming out of the Republican areas, close to the border, where Nairac was a specialist.

The pressures upon MI5 operatives were such that they led to the breakdown of one of their officers named Michael Bettaney, who between 1977 and 1980 worked from the MI5 office in Stormont. He spent much of his time as an agent handler and claimed to have had several narrow escapes himself. He converted to Catholicism, he claimed, and began drinking heavily. He had a personal collapse, which he blamed on his experiences in the province, which he said also led him to a change in his political views. On his return to London, where he gave training lectures on counter-espionage and Northern Ireland, he made a bungled attempt to pass information to the Soviet Embassy. In 1984, he was sentenced to twenty-three years in prison and was released in 1998.

The pressures that Bettaney faced were well known. Many officers in both the Army and the security services had similar problems and had to be removed. One committed suicide; another regimental commander had a nervous breakown; Fred Holroyd – discussed earlier – was clearly under strain when he was moved out. Nairac himself was tired at the time of his death and had been under pressure because of the restrictions which had been imposed upon him.

It was not an impossibility that Nairac was serving two masters. SAS officers above him have noted that there was a portion of his working time that they could not necessarily account for. MI5, of course, will not comment, either to confirm or deny. Others, though, have been more forthcoming in sharing their views and experiences during my research for this book. Clive Fairweather remains adamant that Nairac was not working for MI5 at the time he was abducted. Colonel G, similarly a man of substantial background in Army intelligence and the SAS, was of the same view. Since they were both frank in their responses to my questions, there is no reason to doubt that this is what they truly believe.

It is possible to explain away Nairac's expeditions into bandit territory as a personal quest. Perhaps they were. Having listened to the comments of all those who contributed to this book, I would prefer to use the Scottish legal term 'not proven' to allegations that Nairac was working for MI5.

If nothing else, the tightening up of procedures in the aftermath of his death saved others from a similar fate as thereafter the SAS and 14 Int insisted that the operations manual for undercover specialists should be followed to the letter.

In retrospect, it can now be seen that Nairac had in fact set out to put into effect some of the recommendations that were being discussed on high at the time about getting closer to the source of intelligence and to IRA operatives, especially in Republican areas.

Intelligence work moved towards that very aim of scouting in the midst of the 'bandits'. With Roy Mason's unrevealed expansion of 14 Int's operations, the military had an extension of its own intelligence base that would provide for greater cover. When originally formed in 1974 in the wake of the demise of Frank Kitson's Military Reconnaissance Force, 14 Int had three detachments. This number was eventually to be increased to nine, with the whole operation commanded by a colonel, usually from the Special Forces, who reported directly to the General Officer Commanding Northern Ireland. Members of 14 Int continued to be drawn from all three services and, over the years, included many women operatives. Training became far more intensive, lasting at least six months, and the members became the élite of the Army's Ulster counter-terrorist effort.

Some of their training was done at SAS headquarters in Hereford, although they were extensively tutored in other military establishments in the use of techniques that were unique to Northern Ireland. It was not unusual for only a dozen of so out of a hundred who started the course to pass the rigorous tests of stamina and psychological strength. Like the SAS, 14 Int's main target was the IRA, although in later years loyalist terrorists increasingly found themselves in their sights.

Even by the autumn of 1977, there were some interesting statistics on Mason's desk, reflecting work in the early part of the year when Nairac was operating. An Army intelligence assessment showed that if there was sufficient evidence to arrest and convict 100 'untouchables' – known but elusive IRA leaders – the organization would be brought to its knees. In the first six months of 1977, seventy-five IRA officers had been picked up and charged with various offences. The credits for these arrests, and the many underlings who were netted, were shared between the RUC, the SAS and 14 Int. The future, then, was greater intelligence and attrition against the IRA 'godfathers', as they were once described.

Roy Mason also stated that he wanted the SAS to go province-wide with a unit attached to every serving regiment in Northern Ireland. The SAS did not like that idea greatly, but obliged. They would head the statistics chart in what thereafter became more or less a head-to-head with the IRA: in the decade following Nairac's death, the SAS shot and killed twenty-three Republican terrorists, in addition to the two (Peter Cleary and Seamus Harvey) killed on operations involving Nairac. In the same timespan, the SAS lost two and 14 Int lost four undercover soldiers.

The SAS and 14 Int remained the two key Army elements in the undercover war and in the intervening years between then and now, 1998, the whole operation has been transformed into an exceedingly efficient and sophisticated counter-terrorist organization, backed up by MI5 who, as the Cold War melted, was able to devote a far greater proportion of its manpower to tracking the IRA. The presence of 14 Int remained relatively low-key, and only occasionally hit the headlines – once in 1989 when a woman member of the Group shot dead Brian Robinson, a UVF member, just after he murdered a Roman Catholic in the Ardoyne. In 1998, another woman officer seconded to 14 Int shot an RUC officer in the chest when an undercover mission in Belfast went wrong. In that case the RUC accepted that the soldier had acted with 'bravery and professionalism'. But it concluded that the main cause of the shooting was the failure of the joint RUC, MI5 and Army Tasking Coordination Group to ensure that police patrols were told that a 14 Int operation was taking place in the area.

In that regard, nothing had changed. The who-does-what rivalries that dogged all intelligence operations in the 1970s had clearly still not been eliminated.

As changes to intelligence operations were put into effect shortly after Nairac's death, his former regiment and the SAS began to prepare the wording for the all-important citation. Part of it had already been prepared by his regiment on the basis of earlier assignments in Northern Ireland, and he would have been decorated for that work later in the year had he not been killed. It was only when the full details of his career with the Guards and his subsequent service in the province were listed in chronological order that some of those whom he had worked with there realized the extent of his contribution to the struggle.

The citation had already been started by Nairac's brigade when it reached Clive Fairweather's desk and he did some more work on it. In a way, it was a revelation to him:

It began to dawn on us that not only had he done a lot of useful work in the area but that, having been captured, he conducted himself with enormous coolness comparable with some of the acts that happened in the war when people had been captured and had stuck to their story to the end. He had shown an enormous amount of courage. I think we can all imagine ourselves in that position. That courage was eventually to be recognized with the award of a posthumous George Cross. He was given the GC instead of a military-type decoration because in those days there were only two types of decoration which could be awarded posthumously, either the Victoria Cross or a mention in dispatches – rules that had been in place since the war. It all changed a couple of years later.

The only thing left to do after all this was to compile all the lessons learned. The main ones reinforced to the Army were that very close tabs had to be kept on individuals who were wearing civilian clothes and driving about on their own, and that the time-honoured rules of not setting patterns, of sticking to times and absolute attention to detail were required if you were not to stick your head in the tiger's mouth as happened in this case. I don't recall any major change in the way the Army operated. It was really a question of making sure that everyone stuck to the rules.

There was no panic as far as I can recall. The overall feeling afterwards was that people recognized how brave he had been once he had been captured, and they recognized that in other areas he had been very professional but that he had bitten off more than he could chew. They recognized that we should have all seen the signs and we didn't, and I think we all thought that in a way he had let himself down. Some individuals felt that if they had been more insistent on him sticking to the rules earlier that this might not have happened.

When one thinks of the countless operations which must have taken place in the twenty years since, that sort of thing has not occurred again. And when you think back you have to admit he almost got away with it. The fatal error was not having the back-up car, the second error was not having his weapon on him, the third was not getting out when the band gave him the hint and probably the fourth was that he had been late before, because if he had been absolutely meticulous about his timings earlier a search could have been mounted for him earlier and there is just the possibility a back-up could have reached him.

Even though Nairac was not a member of the SAS, Clive Fairweather later came to the conclusion that Nairac's name ought to be recorded on the clock tower at the Hereford base, which stands as a memorial to all deceased SAS personnel. He recalled:

> The reason his name did not go on the clock tower in Hereford is a simple one – he was not a member of the regiment. There was a debate about putting his name on the tower because he had been working for us and there was a member of the Dental Corps on there who had been killed in Oman, but the overall feeling was that those who went on the clock tower should be members of the regiment. In retrospect maybe we were being a bit parsimonious, because Robert died trying to do his best to provide information for the regiment.
>
> We might criticize the mistakes he made but he did die working for the SAS. I think it is splitting hairs a bit. I don't want to open a controversy, but actually his name should be on that clock tower, because if he had not have been the SAS liaison officer he would not have been in that position.

At Sandhurst, one of the study rooms was named after Nairac. The Grenadiers meanwhile staged their own tribute on the first anniversary of his death, a memorial service at the Guards Chapel in Birdcage Walk. It was attended by members of his family, and Father Corbould, Nairac's housemaster at Ampleforth, assisted the Army clergy. Colonel Greville Tufnell, Lieutenant-Colonel of the Grenadier Guards, who was also representing Prince Philip, led a large contingent of former colleagues and fellow officers.

Tears rolled down the cheeks of hardened soldiers as they sang a specially adapted version of 'The Londonderry Air'. The

plaintive Irish song that calls 'O, Danny boy' to the young man
who left his native land was rewritten to include the lines:

> I would be true for there are those who trust me ...
> I would be brave for there is much to bear
> I would be friend of all, the foe, the friendless.

# EPILOGUE

Twenty-one years later, there is still one outstanding question. The body of Robert Nairac has still not been found. He is one of the many of Northern Ireland's 'disappeared' – one of dozens of people in secret graves, whom grieving relatives have never been able to lay to rest and whose own lives virtually stopped still on the day they went missing. As in the cases of unfound places of burial of the Brady–Hindley victims, or the disappeared of Argentina, Vietnam or South Africa, relatives live with opened-ended grief, unable to finally put the past in the past.

In the summer of 1998, not long before the Omagh bombing, my inquiries in Belfast, Dublin and the border regions of South Armagh, the territory that was Nairac's destiny, still gave up no clues. The IRA continued to refuse to comment on the final place of his body and Sinn Fein, which runs a 'prisoners-of-war' office, was similarly unable to assist. Sinn Fein has recently promised to investigate and return the remains of the dozen or so 'disappeared'. Interestingly, they specifically included Robert Nairac among them, without political distinction.

In South Armagh, they remember the name of Robert Nairac and some will curse at the mention of it; they associate it still with the assassinated IRA captain John Francis Green and the murder of two members of the Miami Showband. Paddy Short, the owner of a pub in Crossmaglen, said sharply there were 'no regrets' thereabouts over Nairac's death because he was a Catholic turncoat who set up killings of Catholics by Protestants. There is no forgiveness, no forgetting.

The border regions of the county remain among the most volatile of all regions in Northern Ireland and it is to here that many of the released IRA men, coming home early under the terms of the 1998 Good Friday Peace Agreement, will return. Even so, visitors to that area or anyone making contact in an out-of-the-ordinary way, will sense apprehension among its people, regardless of their faith or political standing. Inquisitive writers are not welcome. When questions are asked about personalities from the past, previously friendly conversations are brought to a swift close, eyes narrow, backs are turned.

Even among the priesthood, there is a reluctance to discuss matters that have been, and still are, controversial, especially if you mention names like John Francis Green and Robert Nairac in the same breath. In the diocese where I sought an interview with Green's brother Gerry, I was passed from one official to another, and the answer was the same: 'I cannot help you – good day.' He is one of the few priests on the register for the whole of Ireland whose personal details and telephone number are not listed.

Not far away, on the very Saturday I sought answers there, a bomb exploded in the mainly Protestant market town of Banbridge, the very place where the Miami Showband had played on the night they were attacked by a loyalist gang. This time, the so-called Real IRA took responsibility for the bomb as they launched their attacks aimed at scuppering the 1998 Peace Agreement.

There have been many rumours about the outstanding issue of Nairac's body, and two that are recurring. One is that after being shot by Townson, the IRA sent in a two-man team to remove the body and take it far away, deliberately so that the Army would never find it. They did not want the police to discover the extent of the torturous beatings the gang had given him. One theory is that he was buried somewhere close to Belfast; another is that he is still in the south, in water or watery soil, perhaps peat bogs.

Another story, more gruesome still, emerged in 1998 when a former IRA intelligence officer turned supergrass, Eamon

Collins, produced an account in his autobiography *Killing Rage*. Collins claimed that Nairac's body was dumped temporarily in a pit before being destroyed in a meat-processing factory situated close to the field where he was killed.

Eamon Collins, who was one of the sources for this book, was found murdered in the very week of its original publication. The two events were, of course, unconnected and his death came as no surprise to anyone. He had a lot of enemies both within the republican movement on whom he had turned his back and among loyalists for involvement in killings. None the less, he had courageously moved back to his home near Newry and was philosophical about the prospect of being murdered. He told me he had come clean, admitted his past and spoke out against former IRA leaders. Only a short while before his death, he had given evidence against a former IRA commander at a libel trial in Dublin. He was murdered on 27 January, tortured and then run over to make it look like a hit and run.

Collins, who himself admitted involvement in five IRA murders, was not around at the time of Nairac's murder, but he later stayed at the house of an IRA member who carried out the disposal, although it was another IRA man in Dundalk who told him: 'He did the business on Nairac. That meat-processing factory was full of Provos, although the management didn't realize it. After the shooting they didn't know what to do with the body, so this guy suggested putting him through the meat mincer. They treated him just like any other carcass.'

Collins, supposedly horrified at what he was hearing, said: 'What do you mean, like any other carcass?' His friend said he had not been there himself but had heard it from a PIRA member who worked at the factory. They put the body through the machine during a slack period. Collins said that the man who disposed of the body is now in his late forties, no longer directly involved with the IRA and living in the Dundalk area. Major E, the former Military Intelligence Officer who had worked with

Nairac, heard a similar story quite soon after the event. 'I visited Newry SB a few months later and they were at the time quite certain that his body had been disposed of via the meat-processing plant.'

Police sources confirm that the story has been around for a number of years and they have failed to discover anything to support the claims. They took it sufficiently seriously, however, to organize the taking of blood samples at the factory. No evidence was found and the man who supposedly disposed of the body was never arrested. It is doubtful now that the truth will ever emerge.

There is, however, another, rather better connection with the past that is worthy of record. It is a legacy of Robert Nairac that was still being used by the Army in the 1990s in the hope of saving other lives – advice to incoming troops on dealing with the people of South Armagh and gaining information. While based at Bessbrook Mill, Nairac had been sufficiently well-versed in the local situation to produce a paper entitled 'Talking to People in South Armagh'. It was used as a guide to incoming undercover operatives and later circulated to Army officers. In 1998, it was still being handed out, this time to senior officers of 2nd Parachute Regiment who were based at Bessbrook Mill.

The essay highlighted a matter that was clearly uppermost in his mind at the time, the recruitment of agents and informers. He assessed that while it was reasonable to regard everyone with suspicion, it was also possible to regard any local as a possible source of information. But, he pointed out, aggression and brutality among the local populace was likely to be counter-productive. 'Most people (possible eighty per cent) are sick of the violence,' he wrote, 'and would like to see an end to the Troubles. Some would even go as far as doing something about it if approached in the right way. Among the fringe PIRA (or even active terrorists) there are those who might be turned by the right approach...'

Nairac went on to outline that approach in words that showed he was only too well aware of the dangers.

> South Armagh is traditionally a lawless and independently minded area. It is resentful of authority of any kind. Furthermore, certain things are taboo. It is said that if you raped your next-door neighbour it would soon be forgotten. If your grandfather had been an informer you would be an outcast ... Fear is the most important fact in keeping people's mouths shut ...To have been seen talking to soldiers may often mean a 'visit' and some sharp questioning. If this goes on, a beating or a knee or head job is the end result.
>
> It follows that there are certain deep-rooted traditions that will shut people up like a clam. Never ever use the words 'inform', 'information', 'witness' or 'intimidate'. Never write anything down; it smacks of police work. Never offer money for 'information'. (It may come to that after months of cultivation but to offer it is fatal.) There are ways round these taboos. 'May I call for a chat?' ... 'Can you help?' Avoid direct questions. Hint, suggest and work round the subject. If you wish to say 'It is high time the bad men were locked up', try to get them to say it for you. Ask their advice and opinion in very general terms.

Nairac offered advice on how to engage young people – those aged between fourteen and twenty-five – in conversation. 'The best line is to try to share their convictions. Some of them have a conscience and if so they will have some doubts. One good line from you could shake them out of their attitudes.' At the same time, he did not underestimate the support for the IRA in the area. At heart, he said, all Catholic men and women had some sympathy for the Provisionals and in the end it was a waste of time to pour scorn or heap abuse upon the PIRA.

With the benefit of hindsight, Nairac's guide to 'Talking to People in South Armagh' was perhaps a little naïve, except in one important observation – his belief that while the IRA might be contained by military action, they would not be defeated. He concluded: 'If approached the right way, the fence sitter will come down on our side ... when that happens we've won.'

It was, perhaps, the recognition by both sides that continued violence, murder and bombing were getting them nowhere that most influenced the development of the Peace Agreement in 1998. Indeed, events came to such a pitch that each new explosion or atrocity only served to underscore this fact: it was an abomination to continue in the same old way – a fact that the IRA demonstrated it had finally confronted when it appealed to the splinter group, the Real IRA, to give up the armed fight in the wake of the Omagh bombing, although it ominously added that its own aims remained the establishment of a United Ireland, which is around the point at which we came in.

Robert Nairac was in the eye of the storm when similar discussions were being thrashed out first time round, when the Official IRA was attempting to persuade the Provisional IRA to hold back. Nairac recognized and wrote down then many of the elements that eventually formed part of the peace discussions in 1998, which required the courage and determination of those who were attempting to establish the peace to see them through.

His own attempts to make some sort of contribution to peace took him along a desperately risky path prodded by those seeking greater insight. His motivation was more personal, driven by a coming-together of experiences and opinions formed from his adolescent years through to early adulthood – years which seemed to pass with such speed that he barely had time to stop, think and consider. In the end, he was travelling so fast he overreached himself, became involved in dangerous alliances on both sides of the divide – and like so many others, he eventually became a statistic in the roll call of death.

A hero? His former colleague Major Richard Bethell compared Nairac's situation to that of Falklands hero Colonel 'H.' Jones. Many people later questioned whether Jones was a hero, asking what a commanding officer was doing storming a machine-gun post. 'His actions were extremely sensible and noble and he did change the course of events in the Falklands war,' said Bethell. 'In doing what he did, he was prepared to put his neck on the line ... and that, I suppose in the end is exactly the same analysis you can draw with Robert Nairac.'

Nairac was prepared to put his neck on the line.

# SELECT BIBLIOGRAPHY

Adams, James, *New Spies: Exploring the Frontiers of Espionage* (Hutchinson, London, 1994).

Benn, Tony, *The Benn Diaries* (single volume edition, Hutchinson, London, 1995).

Cavendish, Anthony, *Inside Intelligence* (Collins, London, 1990).

Collins, Eamon, *Killing Rage* (Granta Books, London, 1997).

Coogan, Tim Pat, *The Troubles: Ireland Ordeal 1966–96 and the Search for Peace* (Arrow Books, London, 1996).

Dillon, Martin, *25 Years of Terror* (previously published as *The Enemy Within*) (Bantam, London, 1996).

— *The Dirty War* (Arrow, London, 1990).

Foot, Paul, *Who Framed Colin Wallace?* (Macmillan, London, 1989).

Geraghty, Tony, *Who Dares Wins: the Story of the Special Air Service* (Arms and Armour Press, London, 1980).

Harclerode, Peter, *Para: Fifty Years of the Parachute Regiment* (Orion, London, 1992).

Lindsay, Oliver, *Once a Grenadier: the Grenadier Guards 1945–1995* (Leo Cooper, London, 1996).

Murray, Raymond, *SAS in Northern Ireland* (The Mercier Press, Dublin, 1990).

Pimlott, Ben, *Harold Wilson* (HarperCollins, London, 1993).

Stalker, John, *Stalker* (Harrap, London, 1988).

Urban, Mark, *Big Boys' Rules: the Secret Struggles Against the IRA* (Faber and Faber, London, 1992).

White, Terry, *The Fighting Skills of the SAS and the Special Forces* (Century Random House, London, 1993).

Weale, Adrian, *Secret Warfare* (Hodder and Stoughton, London, 1997).

Ziegler, Philip, *Wilson: the Authorised Life* (Weidenfeld and Nicolson, London, 1993).

# INDEX